S0-BRY-009

Literature as Exploration

FOURTH EDITION

LOUISE M. ROSENBLATT

The Modern Language Association of America
New York

Copyright © 1976, 1968 by Louise M. Rosenblatt
Copyright © 1938 by D. Appleton-Century Co., Inc.
Copyright Renewed © 1965 by Louise M. Rosenblatt

Fourth edition, 1983. Published by the Modern Language Association,
10 Astor Place, New York, NY 10003-6981.

Fifth printing

ISBN 0-87352-103-X
(previously published by Noble & Noble, ISBN 0-8107-6027-4)

Foreword

THE NEARLY FORTY YEARS since the first publication of *Literature as Exploration* have seen a number of shifts in literary theory and the practice of teaching literature in schools and colleges in the United States. Through these permutations, Louise Rosenblatt's magnificent discussion of the relationship between reader and literary work has remained the major document on that subject. Critical and pedagogical theory being two fields noticeably subject to vicissitude, one might be surprised that a book that bridges the two would have so long a life. When one reads the book, however, one can understand why.

First of all, the book is far from narrowly conceived; there is not the polemical bias that mars so many books dealing with literature and its teaching. In treating the literary work, Louise Rosenblatt does not argue for an emphasis on form or content, but recognizes the organic nature of a story, novel, or poem. In discussing teaching, she again asserts the dominance of neither teacher nor student, but envisions a classroom in which teacher and student share honestly. Most importantly, she sets forth one of the clearest descriptions of the literary experience that has been portrayed.

Many have dealt with the literary experience since the time of Aristotle's discussion of catharsis; most of Louise Rosenblatt's predecessors dealt with it as a social experience, as a psychological experience, or as an esthetic experience. *Literature as Exploration* treats each of these aspects of the reader—the individual psyche, the individual as a member of society, and the individual as seeker of form and order—and sees them all as aspects of the essential humanity of the reader, as part of the conceptual baggage that the reader brings to the text and that is modified during and long after the reading of the text. The literary experience —what others have since called response to literature—is, as the "Coda" to this volume indicates, a performance, a transaction between reader and text in which both are modified in many of their aspects.

Literature as Exploration first abetted changes in the teaching of literature in the schools; later it provided the theoretical basis for research in the teaching and study of literature, much of which either explicitly followed from the theory or tended to support it from an empirical standpoint. The research has shown that readers project their world into what they read; that readers tend to ask critical questions directed in part by the text and in part by their culture; that readers gain diverse insights and satisfactions from their reading; and that readers change as they grow. Each act of reading becomes a unique encounter between an individual and a text. Obviously there are some constraints set by the text and some set by the common bonds of humanity, but *Gulliver's Travels* read by a ten-year-old child is not the same experience as *Gulliver's Travels* read by that same person twenty years later.

Most recently, the ideas of Louise Rosenblatt have become an accepted part of literary theory. When *Literature as Exploration* was written, many critics advanced theories based on a "correct" reading of a text, even though that correct reading might never be achieved by any one critic. In the past decade, a number of critics have come to realize that critical truth is illusory and that even the most synoptic of critics cannot give a complete reading of a poem; there is always another performer.

Literature as Exploration deserves republication now for several reasons: it is a classic; it is a superbly reasoned exploration of the reader; and it is a timely warning. The danger that the teaching of literature will slip back into a phase where the individuality and creativity of the reader will be stifled, where the emotions will be neglected, where detachment will replace commitment, always lurks and threatens to produce a generation of people who will spurn literature because the schools have deadened it for them. *Literature as Exploration* speaks against this possibility, and its importance is like that of Milton's *Areopagitica* and Shelley's *Defense of Poetry*: for this time and for a long time to come, it is the major defense of the reader.

ALAN C. PURVES

University of Illinois
July 1976

iv

Preface to the Third Edition

"THE MAXIM that a book once published leads a life of its own was confirmed for me when the initiative for this edition came from others. I have therefore been diffident about making substantial changes in its general pattern, despite considerable revision in presentation. . . ."* The preceding opening words from the Preface to the second edition apply also to the present one; again the initiative has come from others,** and the changes consist mainly in the prefatory materials, and the bibliography. I am gratified that teachers of literature in both schools and colleges, as well as those concerned with the education of teachers of literature, have again affirmed the continuing usefulness of this book.

"Since the varied powers of literature cannot be confined within a single phrase, the title of this book should be understood as a metaphor, not as a limiting definition. The word *exploration* is designed to suggest primarily that the experience of literature, far from being for the reader a passive process of absorption, is a form of intense personal activity. The reader counts for at least as much as the book or poem itself; he responds to some of its aspects and not others; he finds it refreshing and stimulating, or barren and unrewarding. Literature is thus for him a medium of exploration. Through books, the reader may explore his own nature, become aware of potentialities for thought and feeling within himself, acquire clearer perspective, develop aims and a sense of direction. He may explore the outer world, other personalities, other ways of life. Liberated from the insularity of time and space, he may range through the wide gamut of social and temperamental alternatives that men have created or imagined. Part of my task will be to outline some of the realms into which the reader may thus penetrate, and to sketch some of the personal and social benefits that may flow from such literary discovery."[1]

As I think back over the years since this book first appeared, I find confirmation of one of my basic points: i.e., what readers make of a work will vary with different situations and at different times, as they bring diverse preoccupations and interests to the text. In their reception to this book, readers have stressed varying implications at different times. I cannot here attempt to give an historical explanation—after all, in these decades we have lived through wars, cold and hot, affluence and recession, times of optimism and times of anxiety. But it has occurred to me that some of these different emphases might be of interest to those coming to this book for the first time, or who knew it in earlier editions. As one advocating change and reforms, I was often a minority voice, yet I am grateful that I was so often listened to, and that I was involved in so many of the important educational developments, even at times when in the colleges and universities very alien theories predominated.

The first edition was given a surprisingly warm reception. (For instance, soon after it appeared I found myself addressing the general session of the National Council of Teachers of English meeting in the Manhattan Opera House in New York. And leaders of the Modern Language Association asked me to join with them in writing a statement on literature.) The book struck a chord most con-

* In this discussion, I shall from time to time draw on the first and second prefaces, indicating the source of a "1" or a "2" following the quotation.
** For reasons of space, the acknowledgments listed in the prefaces to the preceding editions have regretfully been omitted. Of the various people involved in launching the present edition, two *must* be mentioned: Richard Adler, of the University of Montana, and especially Paul O'Dea, Director of Publications of the National Council of Teachers of English.

genial to those who were actively seeking to loosen the bonds of the traditional cut-and-dried English curriculum —the standard book lists of so-called classics, the emphasis on generalized interpretations and paraphrases, the organization by historical periods and genres, the barrage of questions to be answered about each work.

My emphasis on the relationship between the individual reader and the text was cited by those concerned with introducing the study of literary works closer to student interests. (I recall a meeting at Harvard in those early days, in which I was invited to defend my call for the introduction of contemporary literature into school curricula.) As the years passed, book lists and anthologies provided an increasingly diversified fare, and the advent of the paperback enabled enterprising teachers to institute individualized reading programs supplementing the group work.

Some especially welcomed the reminder that readers, and especially young readers, respond most readily to literature as an embodiment of human personalities, human situations, human conflicts and achievements. The life situations and interests of students were more often seen as the bridge between them and books. Anthologies and courses organized around human-relations themes became increasingly widespread. (I recall, for example, journeying from Washington to New York, during World War II, to help plan the first edition of *Reading Ladders for Human Relations*, which was based on the idea that no matter what their reading level, young people want to read literary works that help them understand themselves and their world. The fifth edition of this work was published by the N.C.T.E. in 1972.)

Such themes and such provision for student differences continued to concern teachers and educators even during the period after World War II when Sputnik generated an emphasis on the intellectualistic and the scientific, and the New Criticism came to dominate many college and university English Departments. In Chapter 4, I cite I. A. Richards' pioneering study of readers' interpretations, *Practical Criticism* (1929). The formalist New Critics drew on Richards also, but, true to my point about readers taking what they want, they took over mainly his close reading and concentrated on the technique of the work. By 1938 I had already absorbed from Dewey, Coleridge and the German philosophers a sense of the subjectivity of all perception, so that Richards mainly reinforced my interest in the reader's response. Like the New Critics, "I was reacting against the predominance of literary history. Like others, too, I rejected the oversimplified social approach of the thirties. But having written a critique of the art-for-art's-sake theorists, I was also disillusioned with the engrossment in technique and so-called purely literary matters. Focusing on the nature of literary experience enabled me to see the mutual interdependence of all facets. Today's readers will recognize that although the discussion opens with the social aspect, emphasis throughout is on the literary experience in its totality. If there is much talk about the social sciences, the purpose is to relegate them to their place as less powerful propagators of social attitudes than the arts, especially literature."[2] Even at the height of the intellectualism and formalism of the early sixties, many in the elementary and secondary schools maintained a lively interest in the personal nature of reading. This approach was supported by work in adolescent and developmental psychology and by the growing preoccupation with the quest for individual identity.

In this retrospective glance at responses to this book, I must not forget the many elementary schoolteachers and librarians who throughout were quick to see the implications for their work with younger children. Perhaps they were less hampered by the baggage of literary history and critical terminology. If it had been possible, I would have liked to deal with the literary experience from the very beginning, before the child learns to read. Although my illustrations tend to be drawn from high school and college years, everything I say about the nature of literary experience and the teaching process applies as well to the youngest readers.

In the late sixties, a strong reaction against the over-intellectualized, pseudo-scientific and analytic educational emphases in the colleges, including the New Criticism, led young people and many of their teachers to be especially receptive to the sensuous and emotional aspects of literary experience. This found special reverberations in the demand for literary works "relevant" to students' interest in the contemporary world, and adapted to their psychological needs. In many ways it seemed to me that the college and university faculties were discovering what the schools had known all along—a responsibility to the students as well as to the discipline. Thus by the time of the second edition, attention was focused particularly on my making the students' response the starting point for all growth in understanding and critical powers. Moreover, I had been saying all along that sound teaching requires a sound underlying theory of the nature of literary experience—and now the dynamics of literary response, rather than the author's technique or the theme or "content" of the work, came into the limelight. The interest in inductive methods of teaching at that time also led me to differentiate between the old method, whereby leading questions were aimed at preordained conclusions, and my view, that "the most fruitful inductive learning arises out of the involvement of the student—in this instance involvement in a literary experience—which leads him to raise personally meaningful questions . . . [and] to seek in the text the basis for valid answers and the impetus to further inquiry."[2]

At the present moment, contradictory forces seem to be at work in the educational arena. On the one hand—a legacy from the social and moral upheavals of the last decade—some are calling for the nurturing of greater spiritual and artistic strengths and personal creativity. The efforts to take over such British methods as the open classroom and creative dramatics reflect this trend. On the other hand, the economic recession has fostered in some quarters narrowly utilitarian demands for eliminating "frills" such as the arts, and concentrating on "basic skills." Only if we possess a philosophy of literature teaching can we justify the importance of literary experience, and make clear the criteria on which we base our classroom methods or curricular patterns. When literature is rescued from its diminished status as a body of subject matter and is offered as a mode of personal life-experience, all other kinds of relevant knowledge and skills can be added to it. Then we can explain that the "basic skills"—whether of beginning reading or sophisticated interpretation—will be learned within a meaningful context: the only reliable mode of learning.

Our courts, in prescribing the education of all the children in our democracy to their fullest capacity, are forcing us to face reality. The need for programs that start with what the student brings to the printed page is surely an idea "whose time has come." This must be the rationale for "efforts to make literature accessible to all in our schools and colleges—including those born outside the mainstream of American culture, those whose tempo of growth is fast or slow, those emerging from the narrow life of the urban ghetto or the affluent suburb, and those who are alienated or seeking new goals."[2] Literature can be an important medium, as various chapters show, for enhancing a pride in ethnic roots while at the same time fostering a sense of community with other Americans of different ethnic heritages—an orchestration of diversities in our pluralistic society.

Research in reading, no matter what else it has demonstrated, has found the teacher to be a most important—perhaps *the* most important—factor in the educational process. Theoretical movements come and go, but change comes slowly. In the classroom, teachers often fall back on the ways of their own teachers, because of lack of practical implementation of new theories or because of fear of failure in trying new methods. Or administrators fail to understand that imposition of change by fiat, without the active understanding of the participating teachers, is doomed. In this book, accounts of classroom discussions and teaching processes are interspersed as illustrations of theoretical points. For those prospective or practicing teachers who might find it hard to make the transition from more traditional methods, I have added to the bibliography, "For Further Reading," a section on teaching methods. This and the "Coda," supplemented by use of the Index, will serve, I hope, as a springboard for returning to those parts of the book that deal directly with teaching methods.

At present, the reaction from the aridity and sterility of much of the formalist analysis of literature has in some quarters become so extreme that I find myself, after years of attacking the New Critics, seeking to redress the balance. The New Critics did make a contribution in rescuing the literary work from being studied mainly as an historical or biographical document. While rejecting the New Critical view of the work as a closed system apart from author and reader, we can broaden the concept of close reading to encompass the reader's close attention to his responses to the text. Some critics and teachers today, in rejecting formalist impersonality, have swung to the opposite pole, insisting on the reader's response as a kind of absolute, a position even more extreme than the old impressionism. Others—especially those who espouse psychoanalysis—use the reader's responses as a basis for analysis of the reader's personality and obsessions. Still others, rejecting the estheticism of the New Critics, nevertheless retain their neglect of the student-reader and use literature simply to indoctrinate political and social ideologies. I believe that mine is a voice warning against all such extremist pendulum swings.

My book has much to say about the impact of the reader's personality and experience on what he makes of the text. But I do not reject responsibility to the text. Similarly, I have much to say about the reader's growth in self-critical insight into his own identity through his intercourse with literature. But I warn also against teachers' assuming the role of psychologists or psychoanalysts. I stress the social as well as personal nature of literature. But I am concerned with the social and cultural role of literature above all in a democracy. Chapters are devoted to the processes through which teachers can foster the growth of more self-aware and self-critical readers, able independently to do greater justice to the text, and able to relate their experience more perceptibly to other literary works and to their own lives.

In our present-day world of rapid social transitions, of changes in the roles of men and women and in family life, in this world beset by the evils of poverty, pollution, and war, no ready-made answers or decisions seem possible. It is imperative that we reflect on the values implicit in the potential long-term human consequences of one or another alternative solution. We need to understand our own priorities so that we may be guided to humane choices. Wrongdoing in high places and the spread of violence and crime have intensified the sense of crisis. This situation has led teachers, parents, and administrators to propose the introduction of a concern for values into school programs. An educational movement has emerged, mainly sponsored by social scientists, setting forth strategies to achieve what they call "values clarification." Studies are also in progress to ascertain stages in moral development that parallel Piaget's findings in cognitive development. Like Molière's M. Jourdain, who discovered that he had been talking prose all his life, teachers of literature find here a new name for something that is inherent, it has been my thesis, in any sound teaching of literature.

A large part of the present book involves students' clarification of the choices they participate in through literary works, the values affirmed and denied, and the light that reflection on the work and their response to it throws upon their own value systems. Without disparaging the approaches used in other disciplines, I try to show how the literature classroom offers something unique—the opportunity to participate directly and imaginatively in value choices, and to reflect on them within an emotionally colored context. In short, we can be helped to think clearly about issues that engage our emotions. Also, I suggest the context within which values are acquired and the processes by which they may be tested and revised.

It happens that these words are being written on the day that our democracy moves into the beginning of its third century. Joy in its survival and achievements is mingled with sadness at failures to achieve fuller economic and social democracy—yet also with hopeful aspirations for the future. Our democratic institutions have resiliently weathered recent threats from within and challenges from without, and there is being rekindled among us that vigilance which from the beginning we were told would be the eternal price of liberty. More than ever, we need to foster the growth of people who will have the inner strength and the humane values needed to face constructively these times of crucial decisions and awesome yet wonderful possibilities. This book is testimony to my belief that teachers of literature can contribute in vital ways to those goals.

L.M.R.

Princeton, New Jersey
July 4, 1976

As the fourth edition goes to press, the concerns of the book are more urgent than ever. Since reader-response criticism has acquired the dimensions of a literary movement, *Literature as Exploration* is being cited as the first empirically based theoretical statement of the importance of the reader's contribution. Hence, some circles are stressing the theoretical aspect of the book—without neglecting, I trust, its insistence on the essentiality of both reader and text and its theory of the teaching of literature.

Literature as Exploration and my 1978 book *The Reader, the Text, the Poem* both present the transactional theory of the literary work. The more recent book elaborates the theory, differentiating aesthetic from nonaesthetic reading processes and dealing with such topics as validity of interpretation and evaluation. *Literature as Exploration* considers more fully the personal, social, and cultural contexts of the reading act. In opposition to signs that some critical groups are reviving formalist and elitist doctrines, both books affirm the dignity of the common reader and of literary experience as a potential source for understanding the self and the world.

Princeton, New Jersey   L.M.R.
March 15, 1983

Contents

The Province of Literature

The Challenge of Literature

In a turbulent age, our schools and colleges must prepare the student to meet unprecedented and unpredictable problems. He needs to understand himself; he needs to work out harmonious relationships with other people. He must achieve a philosophy, an inner center from which to view in perspective the shifting society about him; he will influence for good or ill its future development. Any knowledge about man and society that schools can give him should be assimilated into the stream of his actual life.

Nor is it only for some future way of life that he needs to be prepared. During his school years, he is already part of the larger world, meeting the impact of its domestic and international tensions, adjusting to adults who bear the marks of its successes and failures, discovering the possibilities it holds open to him. As he plays his youthful role, he is creating the personality and ideals that

3

will shape his role as an adult. Young people everywhere are asking, "What do the things that we are offered in school and college mean for the life that we are now living or are going to live?"

Teachers of literature have been too modest about their possible contribution to these demands. Their task, they have felt, is to make their students more sensitive to the art of words, to induct them into our literary heritage. Leaving to others more mundane preoccupations, they had enough to do, it seemed, in busying themselves with purely literary matters.

The demand that the teaching of literature have some relation to the pupil's immediate human concerns has usually been countered by pointing to the horrors of the didactic, moralistic approach to literature. Wise teachers have opposed any tendency to make of literature a mere handmaiden of the social studies or a body of documents illustrating moral points. The Victorians, the argument runs, demonstrated the sterility of seeking in literature only social or moral lessons; those who see literature in such terms reveal their blindness to the special nature and primary value of literature.

Yet when the literary experience is fully understood, it becomes apparent that teachers of literature have indeed been somewhat shortsighted. They have not always realized that, willy-nilly, they affect the student's sense of human personality and human society. More directly than most teachers they foster general ideas or theories about human nature and conduct, definite moral attitudes, and habitual responses to people and situations. Preoccupied with the special aims of their field, they are often not conscious of dealing, in the liveliest terms, with subjects and problems usually thought of as the province of the sociologist, psychologist, philosopher, or historian. Moreover, these attitudes and theories are proffered in their most easily assimilable form, as they emerge from personal and intimate experience of specific human situations, presented with all the sharpness and intensity of art.

The teacher of literature will be the first to admit that he inevitably deals with the experiences of human beings in their diverse personal and social relations. The very nature of literature, he will point out, enforces this. Is not the substance of literature everything that man has thought or felt or created? The lyric poet utters all that the human heart can feel, from joy in "the cherry hung with snow" to the poignant sense of this world "where youth grows pale, and spectre-thin, and dies." The novelist displays the intricate web of human relationships with their hidden patterns of motive and emotion. He may paint the vast panorama of a society in a *War and Peace* or a *Human Comedy*. He may follow the fate of an entire family in a *Buddenbrooks*. He may show us a young man coming to understand himself and life, grappling with his own nature and the society about him, as in *A Portrait of the Artist as a Young Man* and *The Way of All Flesh*, or he may lead us to share in the subtle moods and insights of men and women, as in *The Ambassadors* and *Remembrance of Things Past*. The writer of stories catches some significant moment, some mood, some clarifying clash of wills in the life of an individual or a group. He may give us the humorous tale of *Rip Van Winkle* or the revelation of character in Chekov's *The Darling* or the harsh image of frustration in *Ethan Frome*. The dramatist builds a dynamic structure out of the tensions and conflicts of intermingled human lives. He may use the comic incongruities of social conventions and human affectation, as in *The Rivals*, or he may create a somber symphony out of man's inhumanity to man and the inscrutable whims of fate, as in *King Lear*. The joys of adventure, the delight in the beauty of the world, the intensities of triumph and defeat, the self-questionings and self-realizations, the pangs of love and hate—indeed, as Henry James has said, "all life, all feeling, all observation, all vision"—these are the province of literature.

Whatever the form—poem, novel, drama, biography, essay—literature makes comprehensible the myriad ways in which human beings meet the infinite possibilities that life offers. And always we seek some close contact with a mind uttering its sense of life. Always too, in greater or lesser degree, the author has written out of a scheme of values, a sense of a social framework or even, perhaps, of a cosmic pattern.

No matter how much else art may offer, no matter how much the writer may be absorbed in solving the technical problems of his craft, in creating with words new forms of esthetic experience, the human element cannot be banished. Thus, a writer such as Gertrude Stein, who was preoccupied with technical innovation, will have lasting value only as her work suggests to other writers new means of conveying emotions and a sense of the flow of life. The most sophisticated reader, extremely sensitive to the subtly articulated qualities of the poem or play or novel, cannot judge its technical worth except as he also assimilates the substance which embodies these qualities. Even the literary work that seems most remote, an imagist poem or a fantasy, reveals new notes in the gamut of human experience or derives its quality of escape from its implicit contrast to real life.

Santayana has summed up this basic appeal of literature:[1]

> The wonder of an artist's performance grows with the range of his penetration, with the instinctive sympathy that makes him, in his mortal isolation, considerate of other men's fate and a great diviner of their secret, so that his work speaks to them kindly, with a deeper assurance than they could have spoken with to themselves. And the joy of his great sanity, the power of his adequate vision, is not the less intense because he can lend it to others and has borrowed it from a faithful study of the world.

Certainly to the great majority of readers, the human experience that literature presents is primary. For them the formal elements of the work—style and structure, rhythmic flow—function only as a part of the total literary experience. The reader seeks to participate in another's vision—to reap knowledge of the world, to fathom the resources of the human spirit, to gain insights that will make his own life more comprehensible. Teachers of adolescents, in high school or in college, know to what a heightened degree they share this personal approach to literature.

In contrast to the analytic approach of the social sciences, the literary experience has immediacy and emotional persuasiveness. Will President Madison or Rip Van

[1] George Santayana, *Reason in Art* (New York, Charles Scribner's Sons, 1924), pp. 228–229.

Winkle live more vividly for the student? Will the history of the Depression impress him as much as will Steinbeck's *The Grapes of Wrath*? Will the theoretical definitions of the psychology textbook be as illuminating as *Oedipus* or *Sons and Lovers*? Obviously, the analytic approach needs no defense. But may not literary materials contribute powerfully to the student's images of the world, himself, and the human condition?

The English teacher will urge that his aim is to help students understand what they read, to acquaint them with the history of literature, to give them some insight into literary forms, and to lead them toward a measure of critical discrimination; this seems to have nothing to do with teaching them psychological or sociological theories. The answer is that when he most sincerely seeks to fulfill these aims, he inevitably finds himself dealing with materials that at least imply specific psychological theories and social attitudes. Since literature involves the whole range of human concerns, it is impossible to avoid assuming some attitude toward them. Moreover, because the implied moral attitudes and unvoiced systems of social values are reinforced by the persuasiveness of art, the teacher should bring them out into the open for careful scrutiny.

English teachers are trained to be scrupulous concerning the scholarly accuracy of their statements about literary history. But how often do they stop to scrutinize the scientific bases of the views concerning human personality and society that insinuate themselves into their work? How often have they critically considered the ethical criteria implicit in their judgments on literature, and incidentally, on life? How often is there even an awareness of the ever-present implied generalizations concerning man and society? While attention has been lavished on the historical and technical aspects of literature, these assumptions have been accepted as a by-product requiring no preparation.

WHAT, THEN, ARE SOME OF THE WAYS in which the teaching of literature does impinge on problems usually associated with the concerns of, for example, the psychologist or sociologist? A review of the accepted practice in literature classes—indeed, of much literary criticism as well—would reveal an amazing amount of attention given to topics which could be classified under the heading of psychological theorizing. The creation of vivid characters constitutes a large part of the novelist's, the dramatist's, the biographer's art. How can we read *Hamlet* or *Crime and Punishment* or *The Great Gatsby* without preoccupation with the psychology of the characters?

The student, therefore, is often asked to define the nature of the particular characters in the work he has been reading. He is also encouraged to see some relationship between motive and action: To what influences did Macbeth respond? What can explain Lady Macbeth's early determination and later breakdown? What was the influence of the characters upon one another in *A Separate Peace?* We do not need the abundant evidence of textbook and teacher's manual to know that such questions will arise. After reading *Hamlet*, the high school student, like the Shakespearean authority, often turns to theorizing about the rational and irrational elements in human behavior. Conrad's *Lord Jim* imposes reflection on the effect of a sense of guilt and failure upon personality. Moreover, the teacher is usually careful to develop the student's sensitivity to the evidence of changes in character set forth in such works as *Ethan Frome, Great Expectations, Huckleberry Finn,* or the plays of Shakespeare.[2]

Once we embark on anything approaching a discussion of characters, it is impossible for us to avoid committing ourselves to some definite assumptions. Many different views of human motivation may lend themselves to the attempt to understand Othello's rapidly aroused jealousy, to square that with his nature as it is displayed at the opening of the drama, and to see why his jealousy should have led so unswervingly to murder. Of course, these problems may be evaded by maintaining that the psychological consistency of Othello's character is merely a theatrical illusion. Professor E. E. Stoll contended that any psychological interpretation is merely superimposed upon a series of incidents, actions, and speeches that were dictated by dramatic conventions and theatrical needs for the sole purpose of creating a convincing and exciting play, without concern for subtle psychological consistency. However, it would still be necessary to explain why Othello seems a living, integrated personality and not a mere series of theatrical effects. In thinking back over our experience of the tragedy, we find that we have fitted what the dramatist offers us into some preconceived notions about human behavior, about the extent of human

[2] Since the discussion applies to the whole literature program, illustrations will be drawn from both high school and college levels. Chapters 4 and 7 consider the adequacy of the usual reading lists.

credulousness or the effects of jealousy. We judge whether Othello is a credible character in the light of our own assumptions about human nature.

For instance, when high school students make the relationship between Hamlet and his mother the core of their interpretation of his actions, whether or not they even know the name Freud, they have absorbed, somehow, somewhere, certain of the psychoanalytic concepts. Similarly, in interpreting *Othello* students may reveal an extraordinary diversity of theoretical frameworks. One student may emphasize the details offered by the dramatist concerning Desdemona's and Othello's sense of racial difference and may base on that his explanation of Othello's readiness to believe in his wife's infidelity. Another student may see Othello as a man fundamentally insecure, unsure of his ability to hold Desdemona, and thus ready to believe himself betrayed. Still another student may phrase Othello's problem in moral terms as the struggle between the nobler and the baser elements in his nature. There will also be the student who accepts the characters' statements about their acts, assumes that everything they do is consciously willed, and passes judgment accordingly. Each has found the play intelligible in terms of his own understanding of human motivation.

Students (and teachers) often assume that they are merely making explicit the author's particular view of human psychology. The process of interpretation is more complex than that, however. The reader must remain faithful to the text. He must be alert to the clues concerning character and motive present in the text. But he does more than that: he seeks to organize or interpret such clues. His own assumptions will provide the tentative framework for such an interpretation. He may discover that this causes him to ignore elements in the work, or he may realize that he is imputing to the author views unjustified by the text. He will then be led to revise or broaden his initial tentative assumptions.

Such a process surely would have been generated by an interchange among students holding the opinions about Othello sketched above. The challenge would be twofold: to determine whether their interpretations were supported by the text, and at the same time to test the adequacy of the psychological assumptions guiding their responses to the text. The body of critical writings on *Othello* demonstrates that the text permits a wide range of interpretations which bring to bear a variety of psychological hypotheses. The student reader will be less likely to impose irrelevant or unjustified interpretations if he has been led to scrutinize his psychological assumptions and to become aware of alternative possibilities.

When the text provides an unambiguous view of characters and reflects a particular psychological theory, as in the plays of Ben Jonson or in many recent works based on Freudianism, the task of the classroom might seem to be restricted to simple explication. If it were possible not to intrude any direct or indirect comment, the effect would still be implicit approval of each author's view of human motivation. This could result only in the student's being subjected to a series of discrete, inconsistent notions. But such complete neutrality would be impossible. Something of approval or disapproval would be conveyed through tone of voice, kinds of questions raised, length of time devoted to the work, or emphasis on one or another aspect. Hence the necessity remains for the teacher to recognize his responsibility toward the handling of psychological concepts. The students need to be helped both to understand the author's presentation of his characters and to acquire some means of critically relating it to other views of human nature and conduct.

Works of the past—the *Odyssey*, the Arthurian legends, *Beowulf*, Elizabethan drama, Victorian novels—engender a major psychological question: What are the basic human traits that persist despite social and cultural changes? To what extent are the resemblances of one age to another, as well as the differences, due to environmental influences? Indeed, this question of persisting or "universal" human traits is one that arises constantly in discussions of literature. The phrase *human nature* recurs again and again in the discussion of books, and the manner of its use conveys a great many unformulated implications.

Questions such as the following about *David Copperfield* are often encountered:

> One passage in this chapter shows David beginning to read human nature correctly. Where is it?
> What baseness of human nature is revealed by different persons in this chapter? What goodness of human nature?

Or consider a very recent instance, a third grade unit on the fable which suggests to the teacher such psychologically oriented questions as these:

> Why did each of the animals leave home?
> Was the story the bandit told his friends really what he thought he saw?

Did he make it up to shield his cowardice?

How would each of these animals act if they were people?

Or in a sixth grade unit on Chaucer's *Chantecleer and the Fox*:

How do these animals form particularly appropriate pictures of the human follies, evils, or incongruities which they exhibit?

The term *human nature* is itself a controversial one. Nevertheless, some set of notions dominates our sense of human behavior, and discussion of particular characters or works builds up in the student's mind a predisposition toward such a set of ideas. "These are the significant elements in human personality; these are the kinds of forces that dominate men's lives and lead them to act in certain ways," are the generalizations constantly implied in discussion of specific characters. Even if the teacher desired to, he could not evade transmitting certain generalized concepts concerning character and the ways in which it is molded and motivated.

IN RECENT YEARS, great strides have been made in the fields of psychology, sociology, and anthropology toward a clarification of the fundamental problems of human behavior. The layman's tendency to speak of human nature as though it were constant and unchanging has been searchingly questioned; the plasticity of the human creature has been discovered to be almost endless. Anthropologists have revealed to us societies in which human beings have suppressed or rigidly regulated some of the drives, such as sex or the desire for self-preservation, that we tend to consider most fundamental and ineradicable.

Our primary impulse is to equate human nature with the particular motivations, modes of behavior, and types of choice that we have from childhood observed in the society about us. The inescapable molding influence of the culture into which we are born is an extremely important concept. The teacher should have this clearly in mind before discussing questions concerning character and motivation or even before introducing the student to the images of human behavior presented in our own and other literatures.

The danger is in the unquestioning adoption of the general attitudes toward human nature and conduct that permeate the very atmosphere we live in. Unfortunately, the ideas that are taken most for granted are often the ones that merit the most skeptical scrutiny. For instance, the notion that the conscious motives of the individual determine action is implied in most casual discussions of behavior: If man transgresses, it is because he has willed it. The problem of praise and blame is thus a simple one. Yet present-day psychology stresses the importance of unconscious factors that motivate behavior. A classroom discussion of essays, letters, journals, autobiographies, or any of the other literary forms that deal with individual conduct automatically creates the necessity for advancing one or another view. Whether he wishes to or not, the teacher will either reinforce or counteract these assumptions. He will increase the hold of the voluntaristic view of human motivation or replace it with a keener sense of the complexities in the many environmental, physiological, and involuntary psychological factors that influence behavior. Even writers, like Shakespeare, who may not have consciously held this broader view have nevertheless often indicated significant environmental and physiological factors that may explain their characters' personalities and actions. The teacher may or may not make the student aware of the possible relationships between such things. In either case he is helping to determine the student's sense of these questions.

Despite the desire to leave these issues to the specialists in psychology, teachers of literature must resign themselves to the fact that they cannot avoid encroaching upon these extremely important and interesting questions concerning human behavior. The problem is that the average teacher or college instructor in literature is not necessarily equipped to handle these topics in a scientific spirit. Hence the discussion of characters and motivation tends to follow the superficial lines of ordinary everyday conversations about people. The students may thus very easily conclude that merely on the basis of one's own meager experience and casually acquired assumptions, one may make valid judgments on human motives and conduct. To provide a critical framework, the instructor needs some knowledge of the dominant conceptions in psychology.

THE TEACHING OF LITERATURE inevitably involves the conscious or unconscious reinforcement of ethical attitudes. It is practically impossible to treat any novel or drama, or indeed any literary work of art, in a vital manner without confronting some problem of ethics and without speaking out of the context of some social philosophy. A framework of values is essential to any discussion of human life. In most cases the concern with specific episodes or characters may veil the fact that these generalized attitudes are being conveyed. Yet any specific discussion implies the existence of these underlying attitudes.

When the student has been moved by a work of literature, he will be led to ponder on questions of right or wrong, of admirable or antisocial qualities, of justifiable or unjustifiable actions. The average student spontaneously tends to pass judgment on the actions of characters encountered in fiction. Sometimes this tendency is furthered by the type of analysis and discussion of literature carried on in the classroom. Although the practice of many teachers is superior to the level represented by the suggested questions in textbooks and prepared unit materials, and although there has been a reaction—too extreme in some quarters—against "moral" interpretations, questions that ask the student to pass judgment still tend to be common teaching practice. For example, in the third grade unit on the animal fable mentioned earlier, the children are asked to build a "repertory of words and phrases" suggested by the antithesis of the "wise" beast and the "foolish" beast. This would elicit and perhaps crystallize attitudes toward different types of behavior. Or consider the implications of questions such as these concerning *The Scarlet Letter:*

> Which in your opinion is the guiltiest of the three: Hester Prynne, Arthur Dimmesdale, or Roger Chillingworth? Which suffered most?
> What characters do you consider admirable? Why?

There is little in the first question to suggest to the student that perhaps he should seek not to pass judgment but to understand how the whole tragic complication grew out of the way of life in that Puritan community. The question also rules out an interpretation of this novel as a study in the effect of a sense of sin on character.

The teacher would do neither literature nor students a service if he tried to evade ethical issues. He will be exerting some kind of influence, positive or negative, through his success or failure in helping the student to develop habits of thoughtful ethical judgment. The teacher should scrutinize his own ethical criteria, which must color anything that he says or does in the classroom. He should not foist his own bias on students, but objectivity should not create the impression that value judgments are unimportant. The literature classroom can stimulate the students themselves to develop a thoughtful approach to human behavior.

Thus far, only those ethical and psychological assumptions have been mentioned that seem to deal with the more personal elements in the field of human relations. The nature of literature also embraces matters that are special to the historian, the economist, and the sociologist. Such concerns are implied even by the traditional phrasing of the aims and content of the literature program. For example, the object might be to acquaint the student with tales of adventure in exotic settings. Suggested readings might be *The Count of Monte Cristo, Kon Tiki, The Time Machine, Mutiny on the Bounty,* or the *Odyssey.* In these books, the student's attention will be focused on the vigorous action and the foreign scenes. Yet various considerations that might be classified as historical or sociological will creep in. Some novels, for instance, will involve an understanding of the historical periods treated. Such works as the *Iliad* or Elizabethan dramas invite reflection on the idea that in different ages and in different parts of the world man has created extraordinarily dissimilar social, economic, and political structures which pattern the life of the individual in ways very different from our own. Perhaps in some genres, such as science fiction, this is even a too glibly presented cliché.

Social and historical considerations enter even more obviously into the study of any period of literature or the chronological treatment of any form such as poetry or the drama. In presenting these materials, the teacher consciously, and probably even to a greater extent unconsciously, will be stressing various notions concerning historical problems; he will be transmitting various positive or negative assumptions concerning the influence of social and political circumstances upon other phases of man's life. The process of social change (of which literary change is but one aspect), the influence of technological conditions upon the social and intellectual life of a society, the factors that lead men in one age to be obsessed by aspirations very different from those of another age—such problems are necessarily implied by any survey of the history of literature. Even by ignoring them the teacher is affecting, though in a negative way, the student's ability to understand these problems.

And what about attitudes toward personal relationships? Here the role of the teacher of literature is most clear. Think, for instance, of such works as *Ah Wilderness!*, *Romeo and Juliet*, *All My Sons*, or *The Scarlet Letter*: they evoke attitudes toward the relationship between husband and wife, patterns of family life, and the concept of romantic love. Or consider the attitudes toward the child and questions of relationships between parents and children implied in the reading of *Tom Sawyer, David Copperfield, The Ordeal of Richard Feverel, Sons and Lovers,* and many of Wordsworth's poems.

The young people who encounter such works of literature are building up their sense of the socially favored types of adjustment in our culture. In books they are meeting extremely compelling images of life that will undoubtedly influence the crystallization of their ultimate attitudes, either of acceptance or of rejection. Here again the teacher will exert an influence through the whole framework of ideas and attitudes that he builds up around the experience of the particular sense of social relationships presented by any particular work.

Literature treats the whole range of choices and aspirations and values out of which the individual must weave his own personal philosophy. The literary works that students are urged to read offer not only "literary" values, to use a currently favored abstraction, but also some approach to life, some image of people working out a common fate, or some assertion that certain kinds of experiences, certain modes of feeling, are valuable. The teacher who is aware of the potential absorption or rejection of social attitudes will be led to investigate his own role in this process.

How QUICK TEACHERS OF LITERATURE would be to condemn the teacher of history or zoology who interlarded his discussions with dogmatic statements about literature. How unscholarly they would think the biology instructor who felt that what he had absorbed about literature from newspapers, magazines, and perhaps a random course at college justified his passing on the merits of Milton's poetry, insinuating that free verse was a ridiculous innovation, or making casual judgments as to the authorship of the disputed passages in *Sir Thomas More.* Yet too often literature teachers feel that the social concepts and attitudes absorbed from everyday life, plus a scattered reading on a subject here and there or a rapid survey of the field in a college course, are ample preparation for using literature as the springboard for discussions of human nature and society. They are forced to the rejoinder that the very nature of literature necessitates such discussions; these matters cannot be evaded by judicious selection. But this should bring recognition of their responsibility to equip themselves to handle a vital and inevitable phase of their teaching.

Probably the comparative youth and lack of unanimity of the social sciences partly explain this casual encroachment upon their territory. A more respectful attitude developed long ago toward the natural sciences. The English teacher would be considered grievously lacking who propagated in his classroom the idea that the sun moves around the earth (cf. *Paradise Lost,* Book Eighth) or that incantation was the approved method of curing the sick. From a "purely esthetic" point of view, which ignores the fact that the person experiencing the work of literature comes to it out of a particular world and will return to it, this may not matter. One could appreciate many literary works just as well esthetically though holding these exploded beliefs. The fact is, nevertheless, that the student will return to the world of today. His literary experience will have been confusing rather than helpful if he brings from it ideas that are relics of an outgrown past.

A parallel scrupulousness is needed concerning psychological, social, and ethical concepts that the student may absorb from his reading. Just as the student will be able to enjoy Milton's *Paradise Lost* without necessarily accepting Milton's cosmology, so he must be able to absorb from the literature of the past and of the present what is sound and relevant to his own needs in this age. A zestful reading of, let us say, Walter Scott is compatible with a sense of the anachronism, particularly for an American, of an acceptance of Scott's feudalistic philosophy. The literature teacher may not be primarily concerned with giving scientific information; yet it is his responsibility to further the assimilation of habits of thought conducive to social understanding. He shares with all other teachers the task of providing the student with the proper equipment for making sound social and ethical judgments. Indeed, the English teacher can play an important part in this process, since the student's social adjustments may be more deeply influenced by what he absorbs through literature than by what he learns through the theoretical materials of the usual social science course.[3]

The already overburdened literary scholar, aware of the great mass of materials and information that he must absorb, will probably protest that he is now being called

[3] This argument cuts both ways, of course, and leads to the conclusion that literary materials have their place also in the social science curriculum. See Chapter 7.

upon to assimilate the great body of knowledge accumulated by the social sciences, too. This obviously is impossible. The prospective teacher of English cannot be given the training demanded of the social scientist. It is imperative, however, that undergraduate and graduate programs provide time for building up a sound acquaintance with at least the general aspects of current scientific thought on psychological and social problems. Many undergraduate programs now include some introductory work of this kind, but rather haphazardly. The practicing teacher must feel the necessity for constantly increasing such knowledge. Teachers of literature cannot neglect to establish a rational basis for this inevitable and highly important phase of their work.

THIS CHAPTER HAS SOUGHT to suggest how intimately the concepts of the social sciences enter into the study of literature. Many problems remain to be clarified concerning the relation between this much neglected aspect and the more widely recognized concerns of English teaching. The emphasis thus far may seem to resemble "the social approach" to literature. Unfortunately, the champions of this view, in a pendulum-swing reaction against extreme estheticism, have sometimes been led to neglect the fact that literature is a form of art. The defenders of "esthetic" or "literary" values, on the contrary, have often felt it necessary to reject all social concerns. The thesis of this book is that no contradiction should exist between these two phases of art—that, in fact, they are inextricably interrelated. Those who see in literature only social documents and those who admit only so-called pure esthetic values offer equally limited insights. The increase of literary sensitivity, no less than the fostering of social awareness, requires a concern for the issues raised in this chapter. A philosophy of teaching based on a balanced recognition of the many complex elements that make up the literary experience can foster the development of more fruitful understanding and appreciation of literature.

To view literature in its living context is to reject any limiting approach, social or esthetic. Although the social and esthetic elements in literature may be theoretically *distinguishable,* they are actually *inseparable.* Much of the confused thinking about the esthetic and the social aspects of art would be eliminated if the debaters realized that an object can have more than one value: It can yield the kind of fulfillment which we call *esthetic*—it can be enjoyed in itself—and at the same time have a social origin and social effects. The task of the coming chapters will be to make this point clear and to elaborate its implications for the reader and the teacher.

The Literary Experience

TERMS SUCH AS *the reader, the student, the literary work,* have appeared in the preceding pages. Actually, these terms are somewhat misleading, though convenient, fictions. There is no such thing as a generic reader or a generic literary work; there are only the potential millions of individual readers of the potential millions of individual literary works. A novel or poem or play remains merely inkspots on paper until a reader transforms them into a set of meaningful symbols. The literary work exists in the live circuit set up between reader and text: the reader infuses intellectual and emotional meanings into the pattern of verbal symbols, and those symbols channel his thoughts and feelings. Out of this complex process emerges a more or less organized imaginative experience. When the reader refers to a poem, say, *Byzantium,* he is designating such an experience in relation to a text.

Teachers at all levels should have the opportunity to

observe the child's entrance into the world of the printed page. The child must have attained the physical and intellectual capacity to perform this highly complex operation, the act of reading. He should be emotionally ready to meet this challenge. Essential, too, is a sufficiently rich experience, so that words are signs for things and ideas. A set of marks on a page—CAT—becomes linked to a certain crisp sound in the ear, but is read as a word only when that sound points to a certain class of furry, four-footed creatures.

It is easy to observe how the beginning reader draws on past experience of life and language to elicit meaning from the printed words, and it is possible to see how through these words he reorganizes past experience to attain new understanding. Those who work with older students in school and college do not always recognize that they are faced with a similar situation. Like the beginning reader, the adolescent needs to encounter literature for which he possesses the intellectual, emotional, and experiential equipment. He, too, must draw on his past experience with life and language as the raw materials out of which to shape the new experience symbolized on the page.

The teacher of literature, then, seeks to help specific human beings discover the satisfactions of literature. Teaching becomes a matter of improving the individual's capacity to evoke meaning from the text by leading him to reflect self-critically on this process. The starting point for growth must be each individual's efforts to marshal his resources and organize a response relevant to the stimulus of the printed page. The teacher's task is to foster fruitful interactions—or, more precisely, transactions—between individual readers and individual literary works.[1]

Literature lends little comfort to the teacher who seeks the security of a clearly defined body of information. He does have "knowledge," of course. There are even those reassuring things called facts—facts about the social, economic, and intellectual history of the age in which literary works were written; facts about the responses of contemporary readers; facts about the author and his life; facts about the literary traditions he inherited; facts, even, about the form, structure, and method of the work. Yet all such facts are expendable unless they demonstrably help to clarify or enrich individual experiences of specific novels, poems, or plays. The notion of "background information" often masks much that is irrelevant and distracting.

The uniqueness of the transaction between reader and text is not inconsistent with the fact that both elements in this relationship have social origins and social effects. If each author were completely different from every other human being, and if each reader were totally unique,

[1] The usual terminology—e.g., "the reaction of the reader to the literary work," "the interaction between the reader and the work," or references to "the poem itself"—tends to obscure the view of the literary experience presented here. Hence at times the need to differentiate between *the text*, the sequence of printed or voiced symbols, and *the literary work* (*the poem*, *the novel*, etc.), which results from the conjunction of a reader and a text.

In various disciplines *transaction* is replacing *interaction*, which suggests the impact of distinct and fixed entities. *Transaction* is used above in the way that one might refer to the interrelationship between the *knower* and what is *known. The poem* is the transaction that goes on between reader and text. Cf. John Dewey and Arthur F. Bentley, *Knowing and the Known* (Boston, Beacon Press, 1949).

there could, of course, be no communication. There are many experiences that we all have in common—birth, growth, love, death. We can communicate because of a common core of experience, even though there may be infinite personal variations. Human beings participate in particular social systems and fall into groups such as age, sex, occupation, nation. These, too, offer general patterns upon which individual variations can be played. The forces of social conditioning are also pervasive in the formation of specific emotional drives and intellectual concepts.

Just as the personality and concerns of the reader are largely socially patterned, so the literary work, like language itself, is a social product. The genesis of literary techniques occurs in a social matrix. Both the creation and reception of literary works are influenced by literary tradition. Yet ultimately, any literary work gains its significance from the way in which the minds and emotions of particular readers respond to the verbal stimuli offered by the text.

In the past the danger has been that one aspect or the other of the literary experience has been emphasized. On the one hand, literature deals with and ministers to human life and human needs. On the other hand, this is accomplished by means of artistic form, through the exercise of literary craftsmanship creating works of high esthetic appeal. To treat literature merely as a collection of moralistic pamphlets, a series of disquisitions on man and society, is to ignore that the artist is concerned not with indirect commentary on life but with the addition of a new experience in life, namely, the work of art.

When concern with the human elements in literature has become confused with the purely practical approach to those elements in life itself, distortion and critical confusion have followed. Literary works have then been judged solely in terms of their conformity to conventional aims and standards. Such an approach made possible the elevation of the novels of the now unread Miss Yonge over those of George Eliot or Charlotte Brontë. This approach is possible only when the nature of literature as an art is forgotten.

When, usually in reaction against the practical point of view, only the formal and technical elements of the work have been considered important, an equally disastrous distortion has resulted. An excessive preoccupation with the externals of form and technical brilliance, such as Oscar Wilde exemplifies, has led to a breakdown of sound critical standards. The very remoteness of a work from the living core of human preoccupations comes to be considered a merit. The literary craftsman is elevated above the true artist.

In recent decades the influence of the "New Criticism" and other critical approaches has also tended to diminish the concern with the human meaningfulness of the literary work. The stress on "close reading" was unfortunately associated with the notion of the "impersonality" of the poet and the parallel impersonality of the critic. "The work itself" was said to be the critic's prime concern, as though it existed apart from any reader.[2] Analysis of the technique of the work, concern with tone, metaphor, sym-

[2] See Louise M. Rosenblatt, "The Poem as Event," *College English*, Vol. 26, No. 2 (November 1964), pp. 123–128.

bol, and myth, has therefore tended to crowd out the ultimate questions concerning relevance or value to the reader in his ongoing life.[3]

Since to lead the student to ignore either the esthetic or the social elements of his experience is to cripple him for a fruitful understanding of what literature offers, the teacher of literature needs much insight into the complex nature of the literary experience.

WHAT, THEN, HAPPENS IN the reading of a literary work? Through the medium of words, the text brings into the reader's consciousness certain concepts, certain sensuous experiences, certain images of things, people, actions, scenes. The special meanings and, more particularly, the submerged associations that these words and images have for the individual reader will largely determine what the work communicates to *him*. The reader brings to the work personality traits, memories of past events, present needs and preoccupations, a particular mood of the moment, and a particular physical condition. These and many other elements in a never-to-be-duplicated combina-

[3] "The pernicious practice of converting every literary work into a moral homily is perhaps the abuse most frequently committed. But the Commission believes that no discussion, no study, no reading of any work is complete without some consideration of possible extrinsic meaning, meaning that brings that work directly against the reader's own philosophical convictions and experience. It may be ironic that, after so many years of complaint about teachers who taught the moral instead of the work, warning should now be given against the incompleteness of any study of literature that avoids this consideration. But the Commission believes that 'close reading' may as readily sterilize the study of literature as moralizing once stultified it." *Freedom and Discipline in English*, Report of the Commission on English, College Entrance Examination Board (Princeton, New Jersey, 1965), pp. 72–73.

tion determine his response to the peculiar contribution of the text. For the adolescent reader, the experience of the work is further specialized by the fact that he has probably not yet arrived at a consistent view of life or achieved a fully integrated personality.

Another factor which adds to the variability of the teaching situation is the great diversity in the nature of the literary works themselves. There is a decided difference between the emotional satisfactions to be derived from a lyric by Sir Philip Sidney and a lyric by Browning; an even greater diversity of appeal is made by works of different literary types and moods, such as *The Brothers Karamazov* and *As You Like It*. Obviously, very different kinds of sensitivity and knowledge are required for the fullest appreciation of each of these works. The infinite diversity of literature plus the complexity of human personality and background justify insistence on the special nature of the literary experience and on the need to prepare the student to engage in the highly personal process of evoking the literary work from the text.

Those who associate psychological or social interests with a narrow didacticism or instrumentalism tend to misinterpret the thesis of Chapter 1—hence the need to reiterate that we are concerned with social and psychological insights as they flower from the actual esthetic experience. Grammar and syntax are involved in any literary work, yet no one would mistake a novel for a treatise on grammar. One should be just as careful to avoid the confusion of seeming to discuss literary works as though they were treatises on sociology or psychology. The crux of the matter is that the text embodies verbal stimuli toward a special kind of intense and ordered experience—sensuous, intellectual, emotional—out of which social insights may arise. The following discussion will seek to dispel the confusion that so often results from a fixation *either* on something called pure art *or* on the social implications of literature, cut off from their roots in personal esthetic experience.

Philosophers, to be sure, have defined the esthetic experience in a great many ways. Often they have been concerned with fitting art into previously developed metaphysical systems, or they have emphasized one out of the many springs of esthetic enjoyment. The play impulse, the instinct for imitation, the urge for self-expression, the desire to communicate, the religious or the mythic impulse, are some of the many suggested sources of man's drive to create and enjoy art. This is merely further documentation that art satisfies a great many different human needs and impinges upon the broad range of man's personal and social concerns.

In our everyday lives, preoccupied as we are with accomplishing some task or attaining some goal, we must often ignore the quality of the moment as it passes. Life presents a confused mass of details from which we select for attention only those related to our practical concerns. Even then our attention is focused not on the details themselves but on their practical bearing. We usually cannot stop to savor their quality. In our approach to a work of art, interest is centered precisely on the nature and quality of what is offered us.

This illuminates the difference between reading a literary work of art and ordinary reading. When we read for some practical purpose, our attention is focused on the information or ideas or directions for action that will remain when the reading is over. Hence a paraphrase or a summary of a biology text or a rephrasing of the technical language of a law may be quite as useful as the original. Someone else can read the newspaper or a scientific work for us and summarize it acceptably. But no one can read a poem for us. The reader of the poem must have the experience himself. It may later have repercussions in actual life, but as he sees the play or reads the novel or poem, he is intent on the pattern of sensations, emotions, and concepts it evokes. Because the text is organized and self-contained, it concentrates the reader's attention and regulates what will enter into his consciousness. His business for the moment is to apprehend as fully as possible these images and concepts in relation to one another. Out of this arises a sense of an organized structure of perceptions and feelings which constitutes for him the esthetic experience.

Definitions of the esthetic experience often postulate that art provides a more complete fulfillment of human impulses and needs than does ordinary life with its frustrations and irrelevancies. Undoubtedly, such a sense of fulfillment and emotional equilibrium is largely due to the intense, structured, and coherent nature of what is apprehended under the guidance of the text. Yet those engaged in the task of developing sensitivity to a particular art form will not need to be reminded that any such complete experience depends not only on the work itself, but also on the reader's capacities and readiness. Sound literary insight and esthetic judgment will never be taught by imposing from above notions of what works should ideally mean. Awareness of some of the things that actually affect the student's reactions will allow the teacher to help the student in handling his responses and achieving increasingly balanced literary experiences.

WHEN IN THE COURSE OF OUR DAILY AFFAIRS we exclaim "How funny!" or "How tragic!" we have engaged in an embryonic artistic process. We have seen a pattern in human life; we have juxtaposed certain events in our minds, have perceived their relationships, and have thus disengaged their humor or tragedy. The author does this in a more completely creative form, since he enables us to share his vision. No one would question that in the creation of the literary work the writer does more than passively reflect experiences as through a photographic lens. There has been a selective force at work. From the welter of impressions with which life bombards us, the writer chooses those particular elements that have significant relevance to his insight. He leads us to perceive selected images, personalities, and events in special relation to one another. Thus, out of the matrix of elements with common meaning for him and his readers, he builds up a new sequence, a new structure, that enables him to evoke in the reader's mind a special emotion, a new or deeper understanding—that enables him, in short, to communicate with his reader.

The reader, too, is creative. The text may produce that moment of balanced perception, a complete esthetic experience. But it will not be the result of passivity on the reader's part; the literary experience must be phrased as a *transaction* between the reader and the text. Moreover, as in the creative activity of the artist, there will be selective factors molding the reader's response. He comes to the book from life. He turns for a moment from his direct concern with the various problems and satisfactions of his own life. He will resume his concern with them when the book is closed. Even while he is reading, these things are present as probably the most important guiding factors in his experience.

The same text will have a very different meaning and value to us at different times or under different circumstances. Some state of mind, a worry, a temperamental bias, or a contemporary social crisis may make us either especially receptive or especially impervious to what the work offers. Without an understanding of the reader, one cannot predict what particular text may be significant to him, or what may be the special quality of his experience. Hence it is important to consider some of the selective factors that may mold the reader's response to literature.

The reader seeks in literature a great variety of satisfactions. These sometimes quite conscious demands are in themselves important factors affecting the interrelation between book and reader. A freshman class at a New England women's college was unexpectedly asked, "Why do you read novels, anyway?" Here are some of the spontaneous answers:

> I like to read a novel for relaxation after I have been studying hard all day.
> I like to read anything that is well written, in which the author gives you interesting descriptions and exciting adventures.

I like to find out about the things that happen to people, and how they solve their problems.

I had an interesting experience with a novel a few weeks ago. I discovered that one of the characters was in the same fix that I was in. I got a great deal from seeing how the character in the book managed.

I like to read about as many different kinds of situations as possible—just in case I, myself, might be in such a situation some day.

These students summarized, in simplified form perhaps, a number of the personal satisfactions that adolescent and adult alike seek from literature. Their remarks are akin to de Maupassant's comment:

The public as a whole is composed of various groups, whose cry to us writers is:
"Comfort me."
"Amuse me."
"Touch me."
"Make me dream."
"Make me laugh."
"Make me shudder."
"Make me weep."
"Make me think."
And only a few chosen spirits say to the artist:
"Give me something fine in any form which may suit you best, according to your own temperament."

In its simplest terms, literature may offer us an emotional outlet. It may enable us to exercise our senses more intensely and more fully than we otherwise have time or opportunity to. Through literature we may enjoy the beauty or the grandeur of nature and the exotic splendor of scenes in far distant lands. Furthermore, it may provide experiences that it would not be either possible or wise to introduce into our own lives. The love of action and adventure, the interest in kinds of people and ways of life alien to our own, the delight in scenes of strong emotion, in pictures of physical violence, even in images of hatred and evil, may be due to the release they provide for drives repressed by our culture. Nor does literature afford an outlet only for antisocial emotions. A great work of art may provide us the opportunity to feel more profoundly and more generously, to perceive more fully the implications of experience, than the constricted and fragmentary conditions of life permit.

The college students, bearing out the contention of the preceding chapter, placed greatest emphasis on literature as a means of broadening one's knowledge of people and society. This reflected their curiosity about life, a curiosity shared with younger adolescent and preadolescent students. For the average adult reader as well, literature contributes to the enlargement of experience. We participate in imaginary situations, we look on at characters living through crises, we explore ourselves and the world about us, through the medium of literature.

The capacity to sympathize or to identify with the experiences of others is a most precious human attribute. Scientific studies of reactions to works of art have revealed how pervasive is our tendency to identify with something outside ourselves. This has been found to be true even of nonhuman subjects. We tend to "feel ourselves into," to empathize with, the painting of the tree that is swaying in the wind, until the successful artist will have somehow made us that very tree itself. Even the delicate poise of an architectural column or the symmetry of a Greek vase will be felt in the pull and balance of our own muscles, though we may not be conscious of the source of our pleasure. How much more directly and completely is this tendency to project ourselves into the object of our contemplation fulfilled when we are concerned with the personalities and joys and sorrows, with the failures and the achievements, of characters in literature!

This tendency toward identification will certainly be guided by our preoccupations at the time we read. Our own problems and needs may lead us to focus on those characters and situations through which we may achieve the satisfactions, the balanced vision, or perhaps merely the unequivocal motives unattained in our own lives.

The students valued literature as a means of enlarging their knowledge of the world, because through literature they acquire not so much additional *information* as additional *experience*. New understanding is conveyed to them dynamically and personally. Literature provides a *living-through*, not simply *knowledge about*: not the fact that lovers have died young and fair, but a living-through of *Romeo and Juliet*; not theories about Rome, but a living-through of the conflicts in *Julius Caesar* or the paradoxes of *Caesar and Cleopatra*. In contrast to the historian's generalized and impersonal account of the hardships of the pioneer's life, they share these hardships with Per Hansa and Beret in Rölvaag's *Giants in the Earth*. The sociologist analyzes for them the problems of the Negro in our society; in Wright's *Native Son*, Baldwin's *The Fire Next Time*, Ellison's *The Invisible Man*, they themselves suffer these problems in their human dimensions. The anthropologist can teach them the ethnology of the Eskimo and the social patterns in the Philippines or India;

in Peter Freuchen's novel *Eskimo,* in Bulosan's *The Laughter of My Father,* and in Markandaya's *Nectar in a Sieve,* they themselves become part of these cultures. They may read encomiums on the devotion and disinterestedness of the scientist; in *Madame Curie* or *Arrowsmith* they share his single-minded zeal, his frustrations, and the intellectual and emotional rewards of his success.

The college girls were equally frank about the escape value of literature. They were especially ready to speak of release from the circumstances and pressures of their everyday lives. This term *escape* has perhaps been used too often in an indiscriminately derogatory sense; there are useful and harmful forms of escape. Anything that offers refreshment and a lessening of tension may have its value in helping us to resume our practical lives with renewed vigor. The unfavorable overtones of the term are due to the failure of much of the so-called literature of escape to accomplish this.[4] The greatest literary works may have for a particular reader the value of an "escape." Our lives may be so monotonous, so limited in scope, so concentrated on practical survival, that the experience of profound and varied emotions, the contact with warm, subtle personalities, the understanding of the wide range of human capacities and human problems, may be denied us except through the medium of literature. Or a great work may give even to the person living a full and happy life a moment of change, of "escape" from the demands of "reality." The capacity of a particular book to offer such values will be directly related to the emotional needs of the reader and his particular situation and preoccupations.

[4] See Chapter 7, pp. 209–214.

Another important potential satisfaction from literature, which the students only implied, is the possibility of compensating for lacks or failures through identification with a character who possesses qualities other than our own or who makes fuller use of capacities similar to our own. The young girl may in this way identify with Juliet or with Elizabeth Bennet; the boy, chafing at his childish status, may identify with an epic hero. This compensatory mechanism may in part explain our vivid identification with characters very different from ourselves. Here again, the force of the reader's emotional reactions will be channeled in ways dictated by his sense of his own lacks. This process is usually considered in terms far too crude, since literature may provide very subtle kinds of compensation. The human being has latent capacities for many modes of life and action that he would not elect, but whose exercise through literature will nevertheless give him satisfaction.

The ability to understand and sympathize with others reflects the multiple nature of the human being, his potentialities for many more selves and kinds of experience than any one being could express. This may be one of the things that enables us to seek through literature an enlargement of our experience. Although we may see some characters as outside ourselves—that is, we may not identify with them as completely as we do with more congenial temperaments—we are nevertheless able to enter into their behavior and their emotions. Thus it is that the youth may identify with the aged, one sex with the other, a reader of a particular limited social background with members of a different class or a different period.

One student made rather surprisingly articulate another personal value of literature: its objective presentation of our own problems. It places them outside ourselves, enables us to see them with a certain detachment and to understand our own situation and motivation more objectively. The young girl irked by the limitations of the small-town environment may derive such objectivity from Anderson's *Winesburg, Ohio*. The boy unconsciously rejecting an overpossessive mother may gain insight from Howard's *The Silver Cord*. This process of objectification may also go on in a disguised form. Without conscious admission of the relevance of the literary experience to our own practical situation, our attitudes may be clarified either by a violent reaction against what we have read or by assimilation of it.

To have impact, a work need not treat circumstances overtly similar to the reader's situation. The power of the work may reside in its underlying emotional structure, its configuration of human drives. Thus, an adolescent boy may resent restraints imposed by accepted authority —family, school, or employer. At this moment of his life, he might find in *Mutiny on the Bounty* satisfying expression of his rebellion; he might react with extraordinary intensity to *The Devil's Disciple* or *The Loneliness of the Long Distance Runner*. College freshmen have been known, very disconcertingly, to sympathize inordinately with Lear's unfilial daughters. Similarly, the youth who has just experienced disillusionment with friends might find the relationship between Othello and Iago the most significant part of the entire play. When *Hamlet* is a moving experience for the adolescent today, may it not be because the play gives form to a prevalent mood of uncertainty and disillusionment, of reluctance to undertake aggressive action in a world gone awry?

An intense response to a work will have its roots in capacities and experiences already present in the personality and mind of the reader. This principle is an important one to remember in the selection of literary materials to be presented to students. It is not enough merely to think of what the student *ought* to read. Choices must reflect a sense of the possible links between these materials and the student's past experience and present level of emotional maturity.

There is an even broader need that literature fulfills, particularly for the adolescent reader. Much that in life itself might seem disorganized and meaningless takes on order and significance when it comes under the organizing and vitalizing influence of the artist. The youth senses in himself new and unsuspected emotional impulsions. He sees the adults about him acting in inexplicable ways. In literature he meets emotions, situations, people, presented in significant patterns. He is shown a causal relationship between actions, he finds approval given to certain kinds of personalities and behavior rather than to others, he finds molds into which to pour his own nebulous emotions. In short, he often finds meaning attached to what otherwise would be for him merely brute facts.

SUBSTANTIATING DE MAUPASSANT's complaint, none of the students made articulate a sense of that emotional equilibrium which is a mark of a complete esthetic experience. This omission is undoubtedly explained in part by the difficulty of describing such moments of mental and emotional poise or illumination. It is probably even more largely explained by the fact that the adolescent's attention is to an extraordinary degree focused on the personal import of what he reads. We have glanced at several of the factors that produce this preoccupation with the human contribution of literature.

Yet for the adolescent, too, these human concerns are embodied in the esthetic experience. The student who has lived through the experience of *Othello* will have been carried along on the wave of feeling and insight to the moment of ultimate resolution. His sense of the gamut of human experience and emotion will have been broadened. He will have entered, for the time, into a world of strange moral values and responsibilities. But this participation in human affairs will have been possible only because *Othello* is above all a work of art. The resonant blank verse, the opulent imagery, the swiftly paced structure of the play, are an integral part of this reliving of Othello's and Desdemona's tragedy. The entire experience has a structure and an inner logic, a completeness that only the great work of art can offer. The student would tend not to speak of this phase of the matter, precisely because these formal and stylistic elements of the drama were an aspect of his apprehension of its human import.

It is possible to do justice to this problem of form and style without being false to the psychological process involved in the relationship between book and reader. Note that we have been discussing those social insights and the human understandings that may arise specifically from the experience of literature. *The enhancement of these human values will therefore depend upon the intensification and enrichment of the individual's esthetic experience.*

Any theory about art that tends to break up the response to literature into distinct segments, whether under the headings "social" versus "esthetic" or "form" versus "content," is misleading. Of course, the teacher must himself have a zestful appreciation of the sensuous and formal aspects of literature if he is to be of any help to his students. Yet if he does not in addition see these aspects of literature in their organic relation to those broader human aspects that we have been discussing, he will merely tend to impoverish his students' sense of both literature and life.

More than merely the intellectual "content" of literature was involved in the discussion in Chapter 1, and in the preceding consideration of factors molding the reader's response. Those factors influence the reader's sensitivities to all aspects of the work of art as an integral whole. Indeed, although one may talk about qualities of form and style or about content, this theoretic division has little to do with the actual psychological situation when we are responding to a given literary work. Each of these aspects of the work exists by virtue of the other aspects.

We may, for example, talk about something called the sonnet form, but such a form can be apprehended only as it is embodied in a particular sonnet made up of particular words. We cannot dissociate from the total effect of the poem the meaning of the words—the images, concepts, and emotions that they denote, the nuances of feeling and the associations that cluster about them. It is equally impossible to distill from the total effect the sound of the words or the beat of the verse. We can tap out the rhythmic pattern of a poem, but will anyone contend that our sense of that tapping is the same as our experience of the rhythmic pattern when it is embodied in a sequence of sonorous and meaningful words? Obviously, the effect of a sonnet on a person who does not know the language can offer few clues to the impression that would be produced by the sound and rhythm upon a person who understood the meaning of the words as well. The complete effect of a particular sonnet results from the fact that different elements act on us simultaneously, reinforce and, one might almost say, create one another. Similarly, in music we may define a particular form such as the fugue, but we can never experience the form abstracted from the complex texture of some specific musical work.

It is equally impossible to experience "content" apart from some kind of form. It is a cliché to say that a paraphrase of a poem does not represent the actual content of the poem. Certain of its concepts and implications have merely been abstracted and rephrased. One might, for example, state the various ideas and name the various emotions encountered in "The Rime of the Ancient Mariner," but this would, in a sense, be offering not only a different form but also a different "content." The various concepts and images take on significance and emotional and intellectual overtones from precisely the form in which they are experienced in the poem. Even a transposition of the different stanzas would have given them a different significance. To encounter an idea after our emotions have been aroused through various images and rhythms gives that idea a very different significance from what it would have if presented in another rhythmic pattern or in another sequence. Hence the term *content of the literary work* is confusing when used to indicate abstract intellectual import.

If we think in terms of the total experience of the reader, we shall not be thus misled. We shall see that the formal relationships in the literary work—the verse form, rhyme scheme, sentence structure, plot structure—or the other sensuous elements, such as the imagery, do not have a separable or even a clearly distinguishable effect. How can we legitimately dissociate anything called the content of a poem from the interplay of sensations and concepts and emotional overtones produced by the particular words in the particular relations to one another in which they are found in the text itself? Only as we become sensitive to the influence of subtle variations in rhythm and in the sound and emotional overtones of words, only as we become more refined instruments upon which the poet can play, will we be able to experience the full import of the poem.

Similarly, it is essential to hold firmly to the totality of the reader's experience of the literary work whenever we are tempted to speak as though the structure of a play or novel were distinct from the specific sensations, emotions, personalities, events, presented in the work. The sense of the form or structure of the play or novel results from the fact that these particular elements and no others are *experienced* in particular relations to one another. Just as in a melody a particular note takes on color and character from its context, so in a play or novel, the signi-

ficance of any particular scene or personality is the result
of the context in which it is encountered.

To return to *Othello*: recall the scene in which Desdemona sings the "Willow Song." This has great poignancy;
we have lived through the mounting tension of the in-
trigue, and now the innocent Desdemona sings as Emilia
prepares her for the night. This episode would have little
pathos or even interest for anyone who knew only that
scene of the play or if that scene were placed at some
different point in the play. It would be hard to say
whether the transposition would be a change in form or
in content. The actual result would be to make the reader
or the audience see and feel fewer human implications in
the scene. Similarly, although we may speak of the structure of the play and even make diagrams that purport to
represent the rising tension and the climax, we must remember that the rising tension results from the reader's
identification with certain personalities presented to him
and from his vicarious experience of emotions and ideas.

Thus we find ourselves involved in a circular argument.
If we start with form or structure, we find that we are
merely talking about the particular relationships of certain
human sensations, concepts, and emotions. If we talk
about so-called content, we find that we are merely dealing with the significance that arises from a particular
series of relationships among certain sensations, concepts,
and emotions. Teaching practices and assignments should
be scrutinized to make sure that students are not given the
idea that the formal relationships in a literary work exist
apart from, and are merely superimposed upon, something
called the *content*. Much truer to the reality of both

literary creation and literary experience is the sense of how organically interfused are these two phases of the work of art.

Of course, students need to understand the nature of the diverse literary forms—the lyric, the epic, the novel, the essay, the drama—forms that our literary ancestors and contemporaries have developed through the cyclic process of "convention and revolt." We want to share with our students the pleasure to be derived from a discriminating response to the means that the author has employed and the variations or reversals he has based upon the traditional pattern. Knowledge of the problems of artistry, a recognition of the author's aims and of the technical difficulties involved in achieving these aims, often tend to increase enjoyment. Pleasure arises from discovering the kind of structure that the artist is creating, from seeing things fall into a pattern. Awareness of the function of various characters or episodes or images illuminates what the work as a whole "means." However, that perception of order or pattern is important to the average reader only in relation to the impact of the work as a whole. And these sensitivities to the author's technique are not necessarily best fostered or manifested through a labeling of devices or an analysis of forms.

One of the best ways of helping students to gain this appreciation of literary form and artistry is to encourage them to engage in such imaginative writing. In this way they will themselves be involved in wrestling with the materials offered them by life or by their reaction to it; they will discover that problems of form and artistry are not separable from the problems of clarifying the particular sense of life or the particular human mood that the work of art is destined to embody.

The reader's role, we recall, is an active, not a passive, one. The artist using the medium of words must, like other artists, make his appeal primarily to the senses if his desire is "to reach the secret spring of responsive emotions." Because he cannot tangibly represent what he offers, the writer must select significant images that will stimulate his reader to undertake the process of sensuous and intellectual recreation. The greater the reader's ability to respond to the stimulus of the word, and the greater his capacity to savor all that words can signify of rhythm, sound, and image, the more fully will he be emotionally and intellectually able to participate in the literary work as a whole. In return, literature will help the reader to sharpen further his alertness to the sensuous quality of experience. Such training is extremely necessary in our society, geared as it is toward a neglect of the quality of the means in an obsession with practical ends.

Here again, even a discussion of the writer's artistic medium necessarily leads to emphasis on the kinds of human experience toward which words point. Words themselves, it is true, not only refer to something else but also possess a sensuous quality of their own. The child, long before he understands the meaning of the words, will derive pleasure from the sound, the rhythmic movement, and subtle inflection of a lyric by Blake. But this represents only the thinnest and most fragmentary response to words. Those pleasant sounds can evoke for him extraordinarily rich experiences as his mental and emotional capacities are enlarged and he comes to know what the words symbolize. We must foster the child's delight in the music of words, but we must also help him to link up definite experiences and concepts with those sounds as they occur in different contexts; he must come to understand more and more what a word implies in the external world. These aims apply, of course, throughout the whole process of the individual's acquisition of language. Perhaps adolescent students are often impervious to the appeal of literature because for them words do not represent keen sensuous, emotional, and intellectual perceptions. This indicates that throughout the entire course of their education, the element of personal insight and experience has been neglected for verbal abstractions.

The teacher who himself possesses a lively awareness of the world about him will seek to develop the student's sensuous endowment so that he may gain from life and literature the greatest measure of enjoyment of sound, color, and rhythm. As the student looks more closely at the world of sight and sound, he will also come to distinguish their effect upon his own moods. He will come to notice dominant impressions, to see certain patterns in events, to sense the clues to the states of mind of other people. Sensuous details will acquire significance as they lead him to glimpse the emotional undercurrents that flow so swiftly beneath the surface of everyday life. In the same way, greater receptivity to the sensuous stimuli offered by literature must be paralleled by enriched emotional associations with them.

On the one hand, emphasis on abstract verbalization, on intellectual concepts cut off from their roots in concrete sensuous experience, is destructive of responsiveness to literature. On the other hand, image, form, structure, the whole sensuous appeal of literature, can be fully apprehended only within the framework of a complex sense of life. Sensitivity to literary technique should be linked up with sensitivity to the array of human joys and sorrows, aspirations and defeats, fraternizings and conflicts.

THE TEACHER REALISTICALLY concerned with helping his students to develop a vital sense of literature cannot, then, keep his eyes focused only on the literary materials he is seeking to make available. He must also understand the personalities who are to experience this literature. He must be ready to face the fact that the student's reactions will inevitably be in terms of his own temperament and background. Undoubtedly these may often lead him to do injustice to the text. Nevertheless, the student's primary experience of the work will have had meaning for him in these personal terms and no others. No matter how imperfect or mistaken, this will constitute the present meaning of the work for him, rather than anything he docilely repeats about it. Only on the basis of such direct emotional elements, immature though they may sometimes be, can he be helped to build any sounder understanding of the work. The nature of the student's rudimentary response is, perforce, part of our teaching materials.

The individual reader brings the pressure of his personality and needs to bear on the inextricably interwoven "human" and "formal" elements of the work. If his own experience of life has been limited, if his moral code is rigid and narrow or slack and undiscriminating, the quality of his response to literature will necessarily suffer.

Conversely, any sensitivity to literature, any warm and enjoyable participation in the literary work, will necessarily involve the sensuous and emotional responsiveness, the human sympathies, of the reader. We shall not further the growth of literary discrimination by a training that concentrates on the so-called purely literary aspect. We go through empty motions if our primary concern is to enable the student to recognize various literary forms, to identify various verse patterns, to note the earmarks of the style of a particular author, to detect recurrent symbols, or to discriminate the kinds of irony or satire. Acquaintance with the formal aspects of literature will not in itself insure esthetic sensitivity. One can demonstrate familiarity with a wide range of literary works, be a judge of craftsmanship, and still remain, from the point of view of a rounded understanding of art, esthetically immature. The history of criticism is peopled with writers who possess refined taste but who remain minor critics precisely because they are minor personalities, limited in their understanding of life. Knowledge of literary forms is empty without an accompanying humanity.

When literary training is viewed as primarily the refinement of the student's power to enter into literary experiences and to interpret them, there will be little danger of excessive emphasis on one or another approach. We shall be aware of the need to sharpen the student's responses to the sensuous, technical, and formal aspects of the literary work. But we shall see these as merged with—reinforcing and reinforced by—responses to those elements in the work that meet the reader's need for psychological satisfactions and social insights. Particularly for the adolescent reader, the desire for self-understanding and for knowledge about people provides an important avenue into literature. The young reader's personal involvement in a work will generate greater sensitivity to its imagery, style, and structure; this in turn will enhance his understanding of its human implications. A reciprocal process emerges, in which growth in human understanding and literary sophistication sustain and nourish one another. Both kinds of growth are essential if the student is to develop the insight and the skill needed for participation in increasingly complex and significant literary works.

THIS VIEW OF THE literary experience raises a number of questions. What does it signify for actual teaching aims and methods? How can students develop sensitivity to all the organically related facets of the literary work? What adolescent needs and interests should the teacher be aware of? How can the study of literature enable students to understand themselves better and to see human beings and society in a broader context of emotions and ideas? In short, how can students be helped to achieve literary experiences of higher and higher quality? Parts Two and Three will consider such questions.

PART II

The Human Basis
of Literary Sensitivity

The Setting for
Spontaneity

DURING A REORGANIZATION of education on the Indian reservations some years ago, it was discovered that in some classes the Indian boys and girls were being required to read Restoration comedies. It seems ridiculous that these children, whose past experience had been only the conditions of the reservation village and the vestiges of their native culture, should be plunged into reading the sophisticated products of a highly complex foreign country remote in space and time. Can it be doubted that the children could "make nothing of it"? Any show of "understanding" a Restoration play would undoubtedly be only a parroting of empty words and phrases to satisfy a teacher's demand.

The plight of these Indian children probably differs only in degree from the average American child's relation to much of the literature he reads in his classroom. The relevance of literary materials has too often been measured in terms of purely verbal operations. To demonstrate "understanding" of a work has been primarily a matter of paraphrasing, defining, applying the proper rubrics. This can be accomplished even when the work presents nothing that awakens an intimate personal response. Too often, the average student might utter Coleridge's lament in "Dejection" when he gazed at the sky and the stars, and could only "see, not feel, how beautiful they are!" The teacher is concerned with making the student "see" what in the work of literature has made *others* deem it significant. Whether the student himself "feels" this is an entirely different question, and one that is rarely considered.

Undoubtedly in many English classes today the student functions on two separate and distinct planes. On one plane, he learns the ideas about literature that his teacher or the literary critic presents to him as traditional and accepted by educated people. On the other plane, he reads the literature and reacts to it personally, perhaps never expressing that reaction or even paying much attention to it. Only occasionally will there be a correlation of these two planes of activity. Teachers frequently approach a book or a poem as though it were a neatly labeled bundle of literary values to be pointed out to the student. If the consensus of critical opinion recognizes certain virtues in a given work, the critics' direct experience of it has led them to perceive those values. The student's repetition of that critical opinion would have validity only when he himself had lived through an experience similar to the critics'. When the images and ideas presented by the work have no relevance to the past experiences or emotional needs of the reader, only a vague, feeble, or negative response will occur.

It is not at all surprising that so few of even our college graduates have formed the habit of turning to literature for pleasure and insight. The novel or play or poem has been made for them too much something to know "about," something to summarize or analyze or define, something to identify as one might identify the different constellations on a star map or define the qualities of a particular chemical element. For is there a great difference, after all, between the process of memorizing the properties of hydrogen or its peculiar reactions to changes in temperature, and the process of memorizing that the romantic movement was a reaction against eighteenth-century classicism, was concerned with the individual, and produced a great deal of "nature poetry"? How many students have reeled this off for an examination and yet never have felt the full impact of a romantic poem! Literary history has its values as have the various approaches developed by literary critics and scholars. But all the student's knowledge about literary history, about authors and periods and literary types, will be so much useless baggage if he has not been led primarily to seek in literature a vital personal experience.

Far from helping the student in this direction, much literature teaching has the effect of turning him away from it. He is to a certain degree insulated from the direct impact of the work. He comes to it with the idea that he should see in it first of all those generalized values or kinds of information that the "literature class" stresses—

summaries of plot and theme, identification of certain
characteristics that mark its period or genre, certain traits
of style and structure. Much of even the best literature
teaching is analogous to typical American "spectator
sports." The students sit on the sidelines watching the instructor or professor react to works of art. Though the
student may develop a certain discrimination in the
appreciation of professorial taste, this often tends to obscure the need for the student himself to develop a personal sense of literature.

The great value of the various scholarly and critical
approaches to literature *in their proper place* will be considered later.[1] But they can be very easily transformed
from useful aids into preoccupations that claim the center
of attention and crowd the student's personal experience
with literature into the dim outer fringe of vision. One
could, for instance, become quite proficient in the history
of Italian literature without knowing the language and
without having read any Italian work even in translation.
One would be able to sketch the sweeping lines of
literary change, to discourse glibly on the special characteristics of the different periods, to name the contributions of its great writers, and to recount their biographies.
It would be possible to learn summaries of the so-called
content of their works, as for example, the story and the
philosophy of *The Divine Comedy*. One might even hold
forth on its relations to the dying medieval culture and
the dawning Renaissance. Without acquaintance with the
works themselves, all this information would lack essential
substance. Much of the activity concerning literature with

[1] See Chapters 5, 7, and 8.

which the average student busies himself in school and college has something of this character. The frame is elaborately worked out, but there is a blank where the picture should be. Missing are the personal experience and understanding of the literary works which historical and biographical information should enhance.

The problem that the teacher faces first of all, then, is the creation of a situation favorable to a vital experience of literature. Unfortunately, many of the practices and much of the tone of literature teaching have precisely the opposite effect. They place a screen between the student and the book. The solution of this primary problem is therefore complicated by habitual attitudes and academic practices. The majority of English teachers still need to concentrate on this problem, for in many English classes today the instructor never even glimpses the student's personal sense of the work discussed. The teacher may be interested in, let us say, *Pride and Prejudice* from the point of view of the history of the novel form in England, or he may be eager to discuss the relation of style and theme. The student, however, may be impressed by the revelation that then, even as now, the business of finding a mate was no simple matter, and that then, even as now, personality clashes and the gap between generations were important. In many cases there is an unbridged gulf between anything that the student might actually feel about the book, and what the teacher, from the point of view of accepted critical attitudes and his adult sense of life, thinks the pupil should notice.

This often leads the student to consider literature something academic, remote from his own present con-

cerns and needs. He recognizes a traditional aura about
literature, but discards it when his school days are past.
(We all know the student who says, "but I have *had*
Shakespeare," as though it were something to suffer
through and forget, like the measles.) Thus he does not
learn to turn spontaneously to the literature of the past
or to the comparably good literature of the present; such
works, he feels, must be approached only in full dress
and with all the decorum of critical method handed down
by the teacher. He is cut off from the personal value they
might have for him. Instead he turns to the pseudo-litera-
ture of the "pulp" magazines, comic books, or lurid drugstore paperbooks.

For many students, the only thing approaching a personal literary experience is provided by such "trashy"
writings. This is certainly not because there is no good
literature that could arouse their interest and fulfill their
needs. Obviously, one reason for this situation must be the
frequently defensive attitude toward "good books" built
up in the mind of the student in school and in college. He
has been given to understand that there are proper ways
to react, there are certain things to look for—that he must
be ready to discuss the "characterization" or to analyze
"plot and subplot" or to talk about the author's "choice
of words." To some extent this is a reflection of that blight
on our educational system, its emphasis on the attainment
of good marks rather than on the value of the work or the
knowledge for its own sake. Instead of plunging into the
work and permitting its full impact, he is aware that he
must prepare for certain questions, that his remarks on

the work must satisfy the teacher's already crystallized ideas about it.

The teacher of college freshman literature courses is often perturbed to find this attitude affecting the work of even the most verbally proficient students. They read literary histories and biographies, criticism, introductions to editions, so-called study guides, and then, if there is time, they read the works. Their interest in the author's life is often on a par with the Hollywood gossip column; or they have learned at best to view the work as a document in the author's biography. Their quest is for the sophisticated interpretation and the accepted judgment. If they have learned techniques of close analysis, they tend to look upon the work as a means of displaying their analytic virtuosity. They seem shut off from the personal nourishment that literature can give. Hence they are often insecure and confused when given the opportunity and responsibility to express their own honest responses to the work.

I. A. Richards published the classic documentation of this point in 1929. He asked his class at Cambridge University to write comments on unidentified poems, giving no clues to title, authorship, period, school, or literary value. As he reports in *Practical Criticism*,[2] the students found it extremely difficult to make up their minds about the poems or even to work out possible opinions from which to choose. They set forth an extraordinary variety of views, and the "reckless, desperate" tone of many of their comments revealed their bewilderment. Instead of

[2] New York, Harcourt, Brace and Company, 1929.

being able to apply to the poems neatly ticketed interpretations and judgments appropriate to their authorship and their literary period, the students were forced to base their comments on their own intimate reactions. In most cases, their training in literary history and their fund of critical dicta on good poetry were of very little help in handling their unvarnished primary personal responses. They were thus at the mercy of personal obsessions, chance associations, and irrelevant conventional opinions about poetry. Hence they often failed to understand the poems or to discriminate differences in literary quality.

Evidently, in most cases an unprecedented demand was being made upon these students. Yet during the whole course of their literary training they should have again and again been given the opportunity to handle their primary responses to the text. A secure approach to poetry would have utilized the "background" they possessed; but it would have been a tool, not a crutch.

Surely the majority of American students, subjected to similar experiments, would not yield a different picture even today, after several decades in which "close reading" has been increasingly stressed in colleges and secondary schools. The average American student probably would not reveal as much "literary background," let alone the ability to utilize it. We insist that students should not consult histories of literature or works of criticism in order to find out what to think about an author, but we have usually not sought to discover why they are so lacking in self-reliance.

Few teachers of English today would deny that the individual's ability to read and enjoy literature is the primary aim of literary study. In practice, however, this tends to be overshadowed by preoccupation with whatever can be systematically taught and tested. Or the English program becomes what can be easily justified to parents and administrators, whose own past English training has produced skepticism about the value of the study of literature. The professional preparation of the English teacher, moreover, often has little relation to actual conditions in the classroom.

How THEN CAN STUDENTS be enabled to have such vital experiences with literature that they will indeed come intimately and lastingly into their literary heritage? This has always been the concern of the teacher who is also a lover of literature. He has known that without this all his conscientious lecturings and questionings, all his "techniques" are valueless. To attempt a comprehensive answer to this problem would, of course, be fatuous. The following discussion will naturally tend to emphasize those aspects that seem to have been most generally neglected. The purpose is not to set a pattern or formula for any one teacher or class to follow, but to underline general considerations that should influence practice.

Unless the teacher himself values literary experience, revision of his aims or his methods will be futile. By implication, any definition of the ideal relationship between the student and the literary work applies also to the teacher. As long as an artificial and pedantic notion of literary culture persists, students will continue in their indifference to the great works of the past and present.

The teacher's personal love of literature, however, has

not always been proof against the influence of routine, pedantic notions concerning teaching methods. He is dismayed at the results indicated by the low level of taste about him; he undergoes constant frustration, or he consoles himself by focusing on the rare student who seems to possess the divine spark. To develop many such students the teacher must liberate himself as well as his pupils from self-defeating practices. He should not relinquish his own zestful sense of literature as a living art.

The persistence of many of the routine procedures in literature teaching makes it necessary to phrase some primary duties in negative terms. First is the necessity not to impose a set of preconceived notions about the proper way to react to any work. The student must be free to grapple with his own reaction. This primary negative condition does not mean that the teacher abdicates his duty to attempt to instill sound habits of reading or sound critical attitudes. Nor does this imply that historical and biographical background material will be neglected. The difference is that instead of trying to superimpose routine patterns, the teacher will help the student develop these understandings in the context of his own emotions and his own curiosity about life and literature.

The youth needs to be given the opportunity and the courage to approach literature personally, to let it mean something to him directly. The classroom situation and the relationship with the teacher should create a feeling of security. He should be made to feel that his own response to books, even though it may not resemble the standard critical comments, is worth expressing. Such a liberating atmosphere will make it possible for him to have an un-self-conscious, spontaneous, and honest reaction.

When the student feels the validity of his own experience, he will cease to think of literature as something that only a few gifted spirits can enjoy and understand in an "original" way. How often, when urged to speak out for himself, a student will respond, "But I'm not literary, the way Jane or John is!" Nothing is more conducive to this than the attitude of the instructor that he is one initiated into the esoteric mysteries of art, suffering with amused tolerance the Philistine reactions of the class. His function is to help the student realize that the most important thing is what literature means to him and does for him.

Another negative means of furthering a spontaneous response is to avoid placing undue importance upon the particular form in which the expression of the student's reaction should be couched. He should be able to express himself freely. Nor should there be constant insistence on summaries or rehashes of the work. That may become as artificial and inhibiting as any of the other routine methods. The young reader should feel free to let his comment take the form dictated by what he has lived through in reading the book. To set up some stereotyped form will probably focus the student's attention on what is to be required of him after he has read the book, rather than on the work itself as he evokes it from the text.

The effect of such assignments is illustrated by a father's report of his twelve-year-old daughter's experience with *Great Expectations,* which she had selected for individual reading. Her reaction was intense. She said to him, "This is a very, very deep book. You're thinking about the story, the strange things that happen to Pip—and all of a sudden you see another meaning back of it." She groped toward a phrasing of those "deeper" symbolic meanings and offered an unusually mature interpretation of the book. Later, her father found her at her desk, in despair before a blank sheet of paper with only the title of the book written on it. To his remark that surely she had much to say, she replied that none of those ideas would serve; she had to write a book report—summarize the plot, sketch the setting, describe any two characters, write a brief opinion or blurb. The little formula provided by the teacher as a guide had instead divorced the youngster from her actual experience of the novel. The book report she finally ground out revealed none of this response. Fortunately, her involvement in this powerful work had made her temporarily forget the assignment. The next time, she would be on her guard, less likely to pay attention to much beyond what would be useful for the book report. Conscientious teachers often thus unwittingly defeat their long-term aims by classroom methods, day-to-day assignments, and devices for evaluation.

An experience reported by a teacher documents this point: "As I was leafing through a tenth-grade poetry text, I found myself drawn into rereading the old Scottish ballad 'Edward, Edward' with its step-by-step revelations of a crime and its fearful aftermath. In the dialogue with his mother, you recall, he reveals that the blood on his sword is that of his 'fadir deir.' He utters his desperate decision to do penance wandering over the seas, leaving his halls to fall into ruin, his wife and children to wander the world as beggars. And then there is that final stanza:

> 'And what wul ye leive to your ain mither deir,
> Edward, Edward?
> And what wul ye leive to your ain mither deir?
> My deir son, now tell me O.'
> 'The curse of hell frae me sall ye beir,
> Mither, mither,
> The curse of hell frae me sall ye beir,
> Sic counseils ye gave to me O.'

"As I finished the poem, it was as though I had been participating in a Greek tragedy in capsule. Associations with Oedipus and Orestes were a measure of my involvement. And then I turned the page—'What is the name of this kind of poem? What characteristics does it share with other poems of this type? What is the effect of the refrain?'

"The shock of these questions drew me away from all that I had undergone in reading the text—the structure of feeling called forth by the pattern of events, my darkening mood as I saw the destruction of the family by the son's desperate crime and desperate penance, the horror of the final interchange. For the moment, I was the student, rudely torn from all this by the textbook editor's questions."

Is this not typical of what often happens in the classroom? Out of misguided zeal, the student is hurried into thinking or writing that removes him abruptly and often definitively from what he himself has lived through in reading the work. It therefore becomes essential to scrutinize all practices to make sure that they provide the opportunity for an initial crystallization of a personal sense of the work.

Although all students should not be required to give the same sort of expression to their reaction, in most cases a personal experience will elicit a definite response; it will lead to some kind of reflection. It may also lead to the desire to communicate this to others whom the boy or girl trusts. An atmosphere of informal, friendly exchange should be created. The student should feel free to reveal emotions and to make judgments. The primary criterion should not be whether his reactions or his judgments measure up to critical traditions, but rather the genuineness of the ideas and reactions he expresses. The variety and unpredictability of life need not be alien to the class-- room. Teachers and pupils should be relaxed enough to face what indeed happened as they interpreted the printed page. Frank expression of boredom or even vigorous rejection is a more valid starting point for learning than are docile attempts to feel "what the teacher wants." When the young reader considers why he has responded in a certain way, he is learning both to read more adequately and to seek personal meaning in literature.

There is no formula for giving students the assurance to speak out. One experienced teacher has found that his students are encouraged by mention of comments made by other students in past discussions. Another finds that classes that are accustomed to the traditional recitation pattern may be reluctant to engage in spontaneous discussion but will welcome the chance to write brief anonymous comments on a work at the beginning of a meeting. Some of these comments selected at random will serve to elicit further frank reactions and interchange. This teacher sometimes analyzes the written comments and later reports on trends and contrasts as a way of focusing on problems of importance to the group. Sometimes a general "unstructured" question, to borrow a term from the psychologist, will be enough to open the discussion. The teacher needs to maintain the conviction that it is important to place the discussion of the text in this matrix of personal response. He will also need to develop the security to permit a rather free-flowing discussion to begin with, before the group can be helped to focus on problems and skills of interpretation relevant to them.

A situation conducive to free exchange of ideas by no means represents a passive or negative attitude on the part of the teacher. To create an atmosphere of self-confident interchange he must be ready to draw out the more timid students and to keep the more aggressive from monopolizing the conversation. He must be on the alert to show pleased interest in comments that have possibilities and to help the students clarify or elaborate their ideas. He must keep the discussion moving along consistent lines by eliciting the points of contact between different students' opinions. His own flexible command of the text and understanding of the reading skills it requires will be called into play throughout.

One of the most valuable things the students will acquire from this is the ability to listen with understanding to what others have to say and to respond in relevant terms. If they have thus far been subjected to the typical school routine, the tendency is at first for them to address themselves only to the teacher; the conversational ball is

72   LITERATURE AS EXPLORATION

constantly thrown to the teacher, who then throws it to
another student, who again returns it to the teacher, and
so on. In a more wholesome situation, the ball is passed
from student to student, with the teacher participating as
one of the group. This interchange among students must
be actively promoted.

BUT SHOULD NOT THE TEACHER or instructor enter more
positively into the picture? Should his function be only
to select a sufficiently wide range of good books, place
them upon the shelves of a library, turn the students loose
to seek their own mental and emotional nourishment, and
then listen to their spontaneous comments? Even the decision as to what should be placed on the shelves of this
library would make the teacher's task an influential one.
Ideally, general considerations such as have been suggested thus far would guide his choices: an understanding
of adolescent needs and conflicts, and a recognition of any
circumstances in their personal and social background
that would make certain books of the past or present
particularly interesting and illuminating.

This need to select from the body of literature those
works to which particular students will be most receptive
implies a knowledge not only of literature but also of the
students. If the language, the setting, the theme, the central situation, all are too alien, even a "great work" will
fail. All doors to it are shut. Books must be provided that
hold out some link with the young reader's past and
present preoccupations, anxieties, ambitions. Hence, a
standard literary diet prescribed for all has negated the

reality of the school situation. In our heterogeneous society, variations from group to group, and from individual to individual, require a wide range of literary materials that will serve as the bridge from the individual's experience to the broad realms of literature. Such factors as the students' general background, level of maturity, linguistic history, major difficulties and aspirations, would guide the teacher's selection of works to bring to their attention.[3]

There is much to be said for Newman's vision of a university as a place where young people have access to books. Until quite recently, after all, English literature was not a subject for organized study and teaching. Yet it was a vital and absorbing interest to many, perhaps because there was no superstructure of traditional teaching practice connected with it. If the student turned to English literature, it was because he felt its personal value. He read with a free spirit, not because the academic powers decreed a knowledge of it necessary, but perhaps precisely because it was outside the stultifying routines

[3] Much in the following chapters will relate to this matter of selection. Ultimately, of course, students should learn to select their own books. An account of how high school students developed increasing maturity and breadth of choice when permitted to choose the books to be added to the school library is to be found in Professor Lou L. LaBrant's *An Evaluation of the Free Reading in Grades Ten, Eleven, and Twelve* (Columbus, Ohio State University Press, 1936). See also *Were We Guinea Pigs?* (Holt, 1938), and the report on these students as adults, Margaret Willis, *The Guinea Pigs after Twenty Years* (Ohio State University Press, 1961). Under the restricted conditions of most public school systems, however, the pressing need is that teachers should be aware of what books students require and should exert pressure for their introduction into the school library.

of the curriculum. Unfortunately, it sometimes seems that it would be much better if students were turned loose in a library to work out a personal approach to literature for themselves.

Nevertheless, the teacher of literature may have a powerful and beneficial influence. The basic postulate is that such influence will be the elaboration of the vital influence inherent in literature itself. Important as it is, the selection of a humanly significant book list is only the first of the teacher's important functions. To reject the routine treatment of literature as a body of knowledge and to conceive of it rather as a series of possible experiences only clears the ground. Once the unobstructed impact between reader and text has been made possible, extraordinary opportunities for a real educational process are open to the teacher.

A situation in which students did nothing but give free rein to their reactions, their likes and dislikes, would undoubtedly have psychiatric value. The psychologists warn us about the neurotic effects of the driving nature of our whole culture. In the compulsive atmosphere of the average school and college today, there is a tremendous pressure on students to fulfill requirements and to meet standards. A literature class where the student could feel that everything that he thought or said was equally valuable might possibly have a therapeutic effect. But the development of literary understanding is a more positive goal. The study of literature should give the student the form of emotional release which all art offers and, at the same time, without strain or pressure, should help him gain ever more complex satisfactions from literature. A spontaneous response should be the first step toward increasingly mature primary reactions.

CERTAINLY, LIVELY, UNTRAMMELED discussion bespeaks an admirable educational setting. The fact that the student is articulate and eager to express himself is a wholesome sign. The teacher has given the student a feeling of adequacy, a sense that his experiences and ideas are worthy of consideration. Yet all of this, as great an achievement as it represents, only means that the obstacles to real education have been eliminated. The student still needs to acquire mental habits that will lead to literary insight, critical judgment, and ethical and social understanding. There still remains the necessity for positive aids to intellectual development. Though a free, uninhibited emotional reaction to a work of art or literature is an absolutely *necessary* condition of sound literary judgment, it is not, to use the logician's term, a *sufficient* condition. Without a real impact between the book and the mind of the reader, there can be no process of judgment at all, but honest recognition of one's own reaction is not in itself sufficient to insure sound critical opinion. Given this free response, all things shall be added unto us. The implication is that there are other things to be added. Teachers who have been pioneers in freeing themselves from the old routines will be especially aware of the importance of envisaging this constructive phase of the problem.

One occasionally meets a student who has been given unlimited scope and is refreshingly honest in expressing his reactions to literature. Often, nevertheless, although his attitude toward books may be unspoiled by false reverence for what is "correct," his is not an emotionally organized or reasoned approach to literature. He is still at the mercy of his raw reactions, still uncritically ready to proffer every judgment dictated by the chance circumstances of his own personal life. Undoubtedly he is much better off than students who have been deadened to any direct sense of literature, but he is still functioning at the lowest critical level. He needs to retain his spontaneity and yet to develop further, to make each literary experience the source of enhanced capacities for his next experience. For he can begin to achieve a sound approach to literature only when he reflects upon his response to it, when he attempts to understand what in the work and in himself produced that reaction, and when he thoughtfully goes on to modify, reject, or accept it.

THIS CHAPTER HAS UNDERLINED the importance of a relationship between teacher and students that will permit the student to respond intimately and spontaneously to literature. This aim, it was seen, has sweeping implications for classroom procedure and for the choice of works to be read and discussed. Yet enabling the student to approach the text without artificial restrictions and to respond in his own terms is only one aspect of the teacher's role. He has simply established the conditions for carrying out another equally important aspect of his task: to initiate a process through which the student can clarify and enlarge his response to the work. This entails complementary objec-

tives: on the one hand, a critical awareness of his own reactions, and on the other hand, a keener and more adequate perception of all that the text offers. Both kinds of
advance will go on simultaneously, each making the other
possible. The complementary character of these two
phases of the development of critical powers has hitherto
been insufficiently recognized. They will be the concern
of the next two chapters.

What the Student Brings to Literature

ONLY CERTAIN ASPECTS of the teaching process have thus far been considered; in any actual class the different phases will not be so sharply separate. The creation of a setting for personal response is basic, as is a situation in which students stimulate one another to organize their diffuse responses and formulate their views. But as the discussion proceeds, the teacher will become involved in the further task of leading the students toward a fuller participation in what the text offers. This requires that the student critically revaluate his own assumptions and preoccupations. The teacher can help in this process only if he understands some of the possible forces molding the student's response and can anticipate some of the major needs and concerns of adolescents in our society.

In the interchange of ideas the student will be led to compare his reactions with those of other students and of the teacher (later, if necessary, of established critics).

He will see that a particular work may give rise to attitudes and judgments different from his own. Some interpretations, he will discover, are more defensible than others in terms of the text as a whole. Yet he will also become aware of the fact that sometimes more than one reasonable interpretation is possible.[1] From this interplay of ideas questions will arise: Why was his reaction different from the other students'? Why did he choose one particular slant rather than another? Why did certain phases of the book or poem strike him more forcibly than others? Why did he misinterpret or ignore certain elements? The attainment of a sound vision of the work will require the disengagement of the passing or irrelevant from the fundamental and appropriate elements in his response to the text. What was there in his state of mind that led to a distorted or partial view of the work? What in his temperament and past experience helped him to understand it more adequately?

The reading of a particular work at a particular moment by a particular reader will be a highly complex process. Personal factors will inevitably affect the equation represented by book plus reader. His past experience and present preoccupations may actively condition his primary spontaneous response. In some cases, these things will conduce to a full and balanced reaction to the work. In other cases, they will limit or distort.

The experienced teacher will undoubtedly be able to recall many illustrations of responses to literature colored by some personal factor. A personal preoccupation or an automatic association with a minor phrase or an attitude

[1] See Chapter 5.

toward the general theme will lead to a strong reaction that has very little to do with the work. A word such as *home* or *mother* or a phrase such as *my country*, with its many conventional, sentimental associations, may set off a reaction that tends to blind the reader to the context of these words. The same thing happens on perhaps an even larger scale in connection with fiction and drama. A young college graduate, for example, expressed herself most forcibly concerning *Anna Karenina*. She had no sympathy, she said, for Anna, who was so preoccupied with her own affairs and who did not appreciate her husband; he was undoubtedly the kind of man who loves deeply but is unable to communicate his feeling to others. When asked to point out in the text itself the basis for her interpretation, she replied, "But there are people like that, with very warm hearts and intense affections, who are unable to let others know it. Why, my own father is like that!"

The personal sources of this reader's response were revealed here more clearly than is usually possible in a classroom or a school situation. Something accidental to the book had caused her to identify Karenin with her father. This is typical, however, of the less obvious ways in which we tend to project something out of our own experience which probably has been only vaguely suggested by the text. Some such projection of the student's own experience or preoccupation may also cause the reader to have a much more intense emotional experience than is appropriate. Rosamond Lehmann might have been astonished at hearing a seventeen-year-old girl pronounce *Invitation to the Waltz* "the greatest tragedy I ever read."

It is not difficult to deduce that this girl's own personal history and present preoccupations would explain her reaction to this wistful story of a young girl's first formal dance.[2]

It is easy to detect the influence of the reader's preoccupations and past experiences when, as in the preceding instances, they lead to an interpretation unsupported by the text. Richards labeled this kind of misreading "mnemonic irrelevance." Sometimes emphasis on the negative influence of the reader's personal concerns obscures their positive contribution. The reader's fund of relevant memories makes possible any reading at all. Without linkage with the past experiences and present interests of the reader, the work will not "come alive" for him, or rather, he will not be prepared to bring it to life. Past literary experiences make up an important part of this equipment which the reader brings to literature, but these have usually been emphasized to the exclusion of other elements derived from general life experience. In order to share the author's insight, the reader need not have had identical experiences, but he must have experienced some needs, emotions, concepts, some circumstances and relationships, from which he can construct the new situations, emotions, and understandings set forth in the literary work.

[2] A college teacher who read this chapter in manuscript was reminded of an example of such "overweighting" that occurred in one of his classes. "A young man of lax views, and, I fear, lax practice, suddenly discovered to his immense delight that he had Shakespeare's authority for what he was saying and doing. Quoting Sir Toby's 'Dost thou think, because thou art virtuous, there shall be no more cakes and ale?' he solemnly announced, 'That is the greatest sentence ever written!'"

Moreover, that work will have been a vital experience to the extent that these new elements can be assimilated into, and perhaps even modify, the original background of personality. The reader must possess not only the intellectual potentialities but also the emotional readiness to participate in just this vicarious experience. In a motion-picture theater a ten-year-old boy was heard to exclaim, just as the hero and heroine fell into the traditional closing embrace, "This is the part I always hate!" That feeling is evidently not shared by the millions of adults who view such pictures weekly. Another instance: The vocabulary of Hemingway's "The Killers" is probably within the range of fourth-graders, but they would be unable to organize the words into a meaningful story. They would not possess the awareness required to recreate it with all its implications. This quite obvious point concerning emotional readiness is often forgotten. In the molding of any specific literary experience, what the student brings to literature is as important as the literary text itself.

Under usual teaching conditions the opportunities for coming to know the individual student are unfortunately rare. All the more reason, therefore, for the teacher to acquire some general understanding of the possible experiences and preoccupations typical of the particular group of students with which he is dealing. This will aid him in his choice of appropriate literary works and in his handling of the students' spontaneous responses to literature. What, then, does the adolescent bring to literature?

One approach to this question would be to consider in detail the segment of the present adolescent generation self-consciously in revolt against the older generation and "the Establishment." Under the threat of global war, taking an existential stance in the face of the "human condition," rejecting the practical values of the society, distressed at the slow advance of civil and social rights for the Negro, eager to enter into adult sex life, seeking intensity of experience through music and drugs—surely, these young people reveal the seriousness of the problems of their whole generation. Yet basically they are manifesting in extreme form processes that have been inherent in the situation of the adolescent in our society for decades. The following pages will not attempt a detailed picture of the (by no means homogeneous) present adolescent generation, but will instead suggest some persistent underlying factors affecting the adolescent in our culture.

THE ADOLESCENT READER comes to the experience of literature out of a mass of absorbing and conflicting influences. It has become a cliché to describe as a time of storm and stress this period when the child is coming into possession of the physical and temperamental endowments with which he will function as an adult. The marked physical changes that occur at this time have probably been excessively blamed for the difficulties that beset the adolescent years. Anthropologists have pointed out societies such as Samoa where these physical changes occur without emotional upheaval. In other cultures the period of personal turmoil may fall at an entirely different age and without reference to physiological changes. Nevertheless, although not the sole reason for the problems of adolescence in our society, these changes do have certain emotional repercussions. The girl or boy recognizes transformations in his emotional drives and personality traits. A heightened self-consciousness and curiosity about the self usually follow. Obviously this will color his attitude toward the essentially human art of literature.

The self-consciousness of the adolescent often centers about a concern with normality. His size, his height, his weight, his speed in movement, his strength, are constantly measured against what is considered appropriate for his age and social group. Philip Carey's sensitivity about his deformed foot in *Of Human Bondage* or Piggy's self-consciousness in *Lord of the Flies* can symbolize the agonies of embarrassment that many boys and girls suffer because of much slighter and perhaps almost undetectable deviations from what they have come to consider normal. Temperamental traits are subjected to equally searching scrutiny: aggressiveness or shyness, physical courage or timidity, the capacity to make friends, will be measured against some kind of norm.

Even the subtler emotional traits, feelings of anger and envy, of loyalty and affection toward others, may trouble him if he is not sure that others have similar feelings. He seeks some standards against which to measure himself and derives his sense of them from a great many different sources, among which may be literature.[3] This preoccupation is at least a possible factor in students' responses to particular works.

The distress, insecurity, and bewilderment that often accompany these physical and social changes are probably in large part due to the lack of mental preparation for

[3] See Chapter 7, pp. 200–204.

them. Particularly is this true of attitudes toward sex. In some societies, sexual maturation brings with it no insecurity because from early childhood the youth has been prepared for it. The adolescent in our culture often must seek knowledge about sex from surreptitious and unwholesome sources. Even when he has been adequately informed, the nervousness, prudery, and even prurience about sex in the society about him will undoubtedly cause complications. These difficulties have been intensified in recent years by a paradoxically rapid change in legal and social attitudes toward frankness about sexual behavior in, for example, the mass media. Another complicating factor is that youth are seeking to adopt adult behavior at progressively younger levels. Many of the interests and problems formerly characteristic of the high school years are now encountered in the junior high school. In this context of fluctuating attitudes toward sex, the boy and girl must make an adjustment to this newly recognized phase of their nature.

Even teachers who are aware of this preoccupation of youth too often tend to evade or gloss over anything in literature that might have a direct bearing on this vital concern. They thus rule out one of the most unfailingly powerful factors in the student's experience with literature. There is, of course, the opposing danger: the adult excessively zealous to prove his emancipation may initiate a crude pendulum swing that will reinforce a self-conscious sexuality, already sufficiently exploited by advertisements, mass media, and recent fiction. The adult's responsibility is to free himself and the youth from the distortions of both prudery and exaggerated reactions against it. Then understanding of the potential beauty and dignity of this aspect of man's life can be honestly fostered.

The youth, like Maugham's Philip Carey, wishes to find out "man's relation to the world he lives in, man's relation with the men among whom he lives, and, finally, man's relation to himself." The adolescent becomes more conscious of himself as a member of a family and a community. He becomes eager to impress others, to gain their friendship, and to be admitted into special groups, particularly of his peers. This often leads to intense self-consciousness about his own personality and to a great interest in the ways in which people influence one another. Adolescents experiment with various ways of approaching people; they seem to "try on" different social personalities as one might "try on" new clothes. And, indeed, they are making clothing an important aspect of the "adolescent culture" that is emerging.

The initiated adult tends to forget the awakening curiosity of the adolescent eager to see behind the façade of appearances. During childhood he has accepted the bare framework of relationships as they have presented themselves to him, in his family, in his neighborhood, and in the larger world. Now as he nears adult years, he finds these relationships acquiring new and unsuspected meanings. Parents who had been taken for granted, their relation to one another summed up in their common parental role, are suddenly seen to have hitherto-unsuspected intense emotional ties. In many biographical novels the adolescent hero or heroine is shown suddenly discovering the complex, hidden emotional life of the parents.

Thus it is with much of the adult world. The boy and girl question: What are the emotional realities behind the world of appearances? What indeed does it mean to the individual—and potentially to me, the adolescent, about to "live"—to be a leader or a follower, to be a member of a community, to earn one's living, to create a family, a circle of friends, to meet the ups and downs of fate, to know love and birth and death? What does it "feel like," from within, to be this kind of person or that? To be angelic, cruel, dominating, passive? What are the satisfactions, what are the elements, of the many roles that may be played? No longer satisfied with a childlike acceptance of the mere external gestures and trappings, he wishes to experience these things from within. It is often to literature—and principally fiction—that he turns. Here he seeks emotional release for the impulses already strong within him but denied satisfaction in his life as a minor; he seeks also the insight he craves into the possibilities that life offers, the roles perhaps open to him, the situations in which he might find himself.

STILL IN THE DEPENDENT childhood relation to the family yet feeling himself practically an adult, the youth often begins to question its authority. Even in a fairly stable society the period of adolescence brings with it a heightened tension within the family group. The youth strives to assert his existence as an individual apart from it. He sets up the goal of psychological as well as economic independence. These attitudes frequently come into conflict with the desire of the family to continue its dominance, and with the psychic need of the parents to feel themselves still an essential force in the life of their offspring. In the present period of great social transformations such strains and stresses have been tremendously intensified, and emancipation from the family becomes of even greater concern to the adolescent. Moreover, many who are members of minority groups, in effect, subcultures, will have grown up in families structured differently from the dominant pattern. The adolescent needs to understand that different cultures or ethnic groups assign different functions to the family. He will profit also from comprehension of the role of both dependence and independence in the development of the individual.

In recent years increasing attention has been given to study of the individual in relation to the cultural environment. The theories of personality development represented by the various schools of psychology have also become quite generally known. They are often incorporated into the training of teachers and are discussed in books and newspaper columns for parents. Yet in the education given the adolescent in America there is still little to enlighten him along these lines. He will sense needs and curiosities, and here again, it will often be only from the reflection of life offered by literature that he will acquire such insights.

The difficulties of the present-day adolescent are tremendously complicated by the fact that he is living at a moment when our society is singularly lacking in consistency, when economic and social changes are going on with unprecedented speed, and when few of the traditional ideas remain unquestioned. The boy and girl are suddenly catapulted from the relatively stable environment of the family into a world of innumerable alternative patterns; the burden of many choices is placed upon them. They often find the ways of life, the ideas, and the activities valued within the family to be ill adapted to the conditions of a changing world.

More probably than any other generation, the adolescents of today have the opportunity—sometimes felt as an awesome task—to formulate their own ideal life patterns. It is no longer assumed that the families they establish will be organized on one pattern; an extraordinary range of possible relationships with their mates and with their children can be envisaged. Similarly, in their choice of work the settled values need no longer hold. The prestige of the successful businessman has dwindled; the social value of the scientist, the artist, or the technician is increasingly recognized. Similar breadth of choice and challenge to personal creativity meet the adolescent as he seeks to develop a social philosophy and a set of values. Formerly, political questions or possible alternative organizations of society often seemed remote and academic to the adolescent involved in plans for his own personal life. Today, even the least socially conscious individual is forced into some recognition of the influence of the surrounding society. As he turns to literature, he cannot ignore this welter of shifting and uncertain social conditions.

This jolt to habitual attitudes has probably increased awareness of the indirect ways in which these attitudes are usually assimilated. In a stable society, the image of the rights and the responsibilities appropriate to, for example, the various family roles would be absorbed from childhood experience in the family and the community. Although more of these aspects of behavior have been forced into consciousness in our changing age, the processes of social patterning must be recognized. Ready-made standards and attitudes are derived from the family background, from the actions of neighbors, from repeatedly encountered images of accepted behavior. The very emotions with which a situation is spontaneously met have, after all, been learned through the force of cultural suggestion. A woman is indignant at the thought of her husband taking a second mate because from childhood on she has constantly observed that situation coupled with that reaction. For the same reason, a woman in certain African tribes will automatically acquiesce when her husband proposes to take a second wife. Notions of right and wrong, of approved behavior and appropriate responses, are in largest measure the result of such unconscious assimilation.

The present-day youth must often mediate between conventional ideas of life roles and the unprecedented circumstances of contemporary life. Innumerable influences in his environment will have given him a definite image, for instance, of the ways of behavior and feeling, even of the kind of temperament, appropriate or possible for a man or a woman. His parents and his family, through their own example and through explicit statement of the accepted attitudes, will have done much at an early point to set this mold. These will have been reinforced not only by the men and women about him but also by the distinctions between the things proper for men and for women repeated endlessly in the newspapers and popular magazines, by the types presented with monotonous similarity on the screen. Literature, it should be recalled, is another of these image-forming media. The human complications that are recognized as important and valid enough to be given explicit attention in fiction, in the newspapers or other mass media, reflect overwhelmingly the stereotyped notions of masculine and feminine nature and behavior. The man, dominant, masterful, superior; the woman, emotional, dependent, clinging, are the images most often and most forcibly presented even in this supposed age of woman's emancipation. These stereotypes will affect in some way the actions, feelings, and choices of the individual.

The post-World War II generation that seems in such large measure to have broken away from these conceptions still feels the pressure of these older, more deeply rooted images. The redefinition of possible roles for man and woman has gone on constantly in terms of revolt or readjustment to the older attitudes which still permeate our environment. On the one hand, the traditional notions of the behavior of man and woman are being constantly reiterated; on the other hand, the adolescent meets with increasing frequency images of men and women behaving in ways alien to the traditional ideas. Women enter into activities thought appropriate only for men; children are given freedom that would formerly have been considered dangerous; grandmothers behave in ways formerly thought scandalous.

The adolescent's own assumption of adult roles cannot therefore be as automatic as in the case of the youth in a more stable society. Indeed, the adolescent group is increasingly self-conscious in its relation to the older generation, and many are seeking much earlier entrance into adult roles. The adolescent's choices, nevertheless, will probably in large part be made on an emotional basis. Against the weight and pressure of the traditionally accepted image, there will be exerted the dramatic appeal of the new and perhaps more practical image. Many today seem to have retreated into a "teenage culture" as a way of evading the effort to sort out what is sound in the adult world. The assumption of the new type of role will often be made under the compulsion of new economic and social conditions. The old attitudes and habits of response will be constantly intruding themselves, complicating the individual's life, creating insecurity and confusion.

Out of such preoccupations the adolescent comes to his experience of literature today. Anything that his reading may contribute must take its place in the complex web of influences acting upon him. His attention will be diverted to those phases of any work that apply most clearly to his own emotional tensions and perplexities. He may often conceal the reactions dictated by his particular obsessions, yet a teaching situation such as was outlined in the preceding chapter would encourage him to articulate his response.

Still another conditioning factor affects the student's sensitivity to literature. The individualistic emphasis of our society builds up a frequent reluctance to see the implications for others of our own actions or to understand the validity of the needs that motivate other people's actions. The fact that the success of the individual must so often be at the expense of others places a premium on this kind of blindness. Teachers of literature need to take this cultural pressure into account, since it is so directly opposed to the attitude of mind they are attempting to foster. For literature by its very nature invokes participation in the experiences of others and comprehension of their goals and aspirations.

Furthermore, much of what the student reads and sees will tend to coarsen his sensibilities and to make him less able to respond fully to the complex and subtle nature of good literature. It would be fatuous to ignore the crude, oversimplified, and false pictures of human behavior and motivation presented by the mass media and the drugstore paperbacks. Not even the school as a whole, let alone the teacher of literature with his much more limited scope, can hope fully to counterbalance the great weight of the influences met in the surrounding society and in such institutions as the newspaper or television. The mere reading of a play by Shakespeare or a novel by George Eliot or Henry James cannot in itself be expected to wipe out the effect of all the desensitizing influences met outside the school or college.

Yet this does not justify a defeatism that would despair of influencing any but the gifted or those with unusually favorable backgrounds. On the contrary, understanding of the function of the literature teacher must be revised and broadened. He must do more than merely expose the student to great art. Although the reading of a novel will not in itself counteract all the unfavorable pressures, it can be a means for helping the student to develop conscious resistance to those influences. And this requires constant alertness to the nature of the social forces acting upon the student.

WHEN A STUDENT reads a particular work, one of innumerable possible variations upon this general picture of adolescent concerns will come into play. The particular community background of the student will be a factor; whether he comes from the North or the South, from city or country, from a middle-class or underprivileged home, will affect the nature of the understanding and the prejudices that he brings to the book. Lillian Smith's *Strange Fruit* or Paton's *Cry the Beloved Country* will elicit a very different response from students of Northern and Southern (or Westchester and Harlem) background. *Main Street* and *Manhattan Transfer* will not mean the same thing to the city boy and the country boy. The daughters of a mill owner and of a factory worker will probably react differently to Norris' *The Octopus* or Anderson's *Poor White*. And similar differences appear in responses to the literature of the past and of England. The fact that the American people are becoming increasingly urban may explain the growing difficulty of keeping alive the love of English poetry, so permeated by country imagery.

THE STUDENT WILL BRING to his reading the moral and religious code and social philosophy assimilated primarily from his family and community background. His parents may stem from a Main Street setting, or they may have turned from a life such as Marquand pictured to assume the duties of parenthood. Or like James Baldwin, he may have survived a ghetto childhood. The adolescents of the mid-century especially reflect this diversity of social climate. The religious background of the student might also play an important part. In a class studying Milton's *Paradise Lost,* a devout Catholic responded very differently from the student who had been brought up in an agnostic milieu. Similarly, a discussion of *Romeo and Juliet* was given a rather unusual turn by one student's insistence that there was no tragedy since the lovers would be reunited after death. Such diversity of response arises also from varying social and economic views. The child of well-to-do, middle-class parents who, after reading Henry Roth's *Call It Sleep,* insists that "some people like to be dirty and ragged and just won't work" will have rather a special approach to Dickens' *Hard Times* or Hugo's *Les Misérables.* Students will necessarily differ in the sensitivity they bring to many aspects of literary works.

Nor is it only these broader and more easily detected differences of equipment that affect reading. The adolescent preoccupation with family relations may take a wide variety of forms. For example, the degree of adjustment or maladjustment between the student's parents may be reflected in the student's receptivities or rejections. An extreme instance is the woman who confessed that she had hated almost every story or play she had read in high school because they ended on the note "they lived happily ever after," so contradictory to her own parents' unhappy disagreements. Authors, she felt, must be in some vast conspiracy of untruth. Here, certainly, is an instance in which acquaintance with some of the novels dealing with marital maladjustments might have led her to realize that writers attempt to illuminate the whole range of human experience and that, therefore, their images of possible happiness might also be given some credence. As for this woman's daughter, growing up in the present era of explicitness about sexual relations, perhaps her literary fare is equally narrow but her need is to encounter some portrayals of fulfillment in marriage!

Anything, of course, that has entered into and shaped the development of the student's personality may be significant for his literary development. The teacher cannot hope to glimpse many of these factors, of whose import the student most of all will be unaware. Yet such general social attitudes will ultimately condition the whole texture of the student's experience of life as well as of literature. In the interplay between the book and the personality, failures in sensitivity, misinterpretations, and distorted reactions often have their roots in such influences. The effort to help the student arrive at a more balanced and lucid sense of the work thus involves the parallel effort to help him understand and evaluate his personal emphases.

THERE IS VERY LITTLE systematic information available concerning the specific ways in which the individual personality colors the responses to literature. The book by I. A. Richards cited earlier [4] offers some valuable illustra-

[4] See p. 63. This is a work that every teacher of literature should read. It has been a seminal book for two generations of critics and teachers. See also James R. Squire, *The Responses of Adolescents While Reading Four Short Stories* (Champaign, Illinois, NCTE Research Report No. 2, 1964), James R. Wilson, *Responses of College Freshmen to Three Novels* (Champaign, Illinois, NCTE Research Report No. 7, 1966), and Walter D. Loban, *Literature and Social Sensitivity* (Champaign, Illinois, National Council of Teachers of English, 1954).

tions of individual reactions to poetry. His elaborate and subtle analyses of his students' comments on poetry reveal some of the typical patterns of response, and his discussion of "Irrelevant Associations and Stock Responses" is especially pertinent here. Illustrations from his book as well as from the experience of other teachers will serve to place these findings in a social and psychological context.

The impact of the literary work is dulled when the reader brings to the text a fund of ready-made, sharply crystallized ideas and habits of response. These responses are so easily touched off that they sometimes interfere with interpretation. Richards gives an illustration of this in several students' comments on Edna Millay's sonnet, "What's this of death, from you who never will die?" The mention of death at once elicited ready-made responses concerning the question of immortality. These prevented the students from understanding either the idea or the effect that the poem was aiming at. The students made a number of irrelevant comments on death or responded to only those phrases in the poem that had some connection with their own preconceived ideas on the subject.

A similar instance occurred in a high school discussion of "The Eve of St. Agnes." One of the students announced that she thought the poem silly and sentimental. She defended this by adding that the poem was all about "romantic love twaddle." In her early adolescent rebellion against the seeming adult obsession with this subject, she had not been willing to respond and had completely misunderstood the tone of the poem.

Subjects such as "home," "mother," "childhood," "birth," "death," "my country," possess whole constellations of

fixed attitudes and automatic emotional reflexes. The
popularity of such authors as Edgar Guest, Ella Wheeler
Wilcox, and James Metcalfe depends in large part on the
emotion-arousing efficacy of such subjects, regardless of
what the poet may phrase about them. The discussions of
D. H. Lawrence's "Piano" by Richards' students offers
further examples of how ready-made responses and irrelevant associations may interfere with the reading of any
work that deals with a familiar subject (in this case childhood recollections of a mother playing the piano). The
Cambridge students were sufficiently sophisticated to be
on their guard against the automatic appeal of such elements in Lawrence's poem. For some of them, however,
this fear of sentimentality became a barrier to understanding the poem. They recognized the stereotyped nature of
the sentiments aroused by elements in the text and blamed
the poem for a conventionality inherent in their own feelings. They were so busy resisting the possible automatic
response to the idea of home and mother that they failed
to perceive how the text itself creates safeguards against
sentimentality.

When in wartime mediocre poetry on patriotic themes
elicits an intense response, the whole environment is creating the emotions which the text seems to arouse. An antipathy to war may similarly vitiate critical judgment. An
intelligent young man of pacifist beliefs picked up *A
Shropshire Lad* and glanced at "1887," written on the occasion of Queen Victoria's Jubilee. Shocked and indignant,
he did not wish even to finish this poem that, by the very
swing of its verse and the use of such traditional phrases
as "God has saved the Queen," "saviours," "the land they

perished for," seemed designed to arouse patriotic and warlike sentiments. Others have read the poem, especially its last stanza, as an ironic warning against blind patriotism. Whatever may have been the author's intention, the text permits either interpretation. At any rate, the reader's problem is to be aware of how much his own preconceptions enter into his interpretation of its tone, and to dissociate his attitude toward war from his judgment on the effectiveness of the poem.

Students will undoubtedly come to literature with increasingly strong attitudes toward political and social themes. Such subjects are being discussed frequently and heatedly in their homes, in the newspapers, over the radio and television. This suggests a whole complex of definite attitudes and automatic responses which may cause difficulties.

Richards reports such a stock response in the case of students whose antipathy to the glorification of royalty led them to object to a poem on George Meredith's eightieth birthday which referred to him as "king of our hearts today." (It must be recalled that the students did not have the benefit of the clue provided by the title.) At a performance of *King Richard the Second* in New York, one of the spectators revealed a similar blindness owing to antiroyalist sentiments. He was annoyed at the appeal that the play patently had for him. "Why should I care about whether Richard or Bolingbroke wins out? The whole idea of kingship is an anachronism for us today." This antipathy blinded him to the play's more universal interest, its subtly nuanced portrait of a man unable to wield the power thrust upon him, yet histrionically delighting in going through the motions of command, and as histrionically savoring the drama of his own downfall. If the protagonist had been a present-day dictator or the president of a great corporation or university, this irate spectator would have been able to grasp the revelation of human character that his automatic reaction to the idea "king" had obscured. We may sympathize with his political views and yet regret that he was not able to handle his primary response in such a way as to appreciate the basic values of the work before him. The controversial nature of much of the literature being written today often creates such obstacles to sound literary judgment. Students should be helped to handle their responses to the political and social tendencies of a work. These should not block attention to the sensuous, emotional, and intellectual elements actually embodied in the text. An attitude toward the work's social implication is by no means irrelevant, but it should be brought to bear upon the text itself, in its specific terms, and should not be a screen between the reader and his evocation of the work.

This type of predetermined response elicited by the general subject of the work is rather easily detected. The same kind of excessive reaction may be produced by a word or a phrase or an episode in a work whose general theme has nothing to do with this particular prejudice or emotional fixation of the reader. An instance of this is the Cambridge students' misreading of the poem on George Meredith merely because the word "king" set off an irrelevant automatic response. The young girl's reaction to the love element in "The Eve of St. Agnes" is another illustration.

The earlier discussion of some of the conditions affecting the adolescent today suggested various other factors that would encourage narrow or stereotyped preconceptions. For example, a rural or urban background or regional loyalty would tend to build up stock responses. The Southern girl who praised as "good books" all that offered a romanticized picture of the South and condemned such works as *To Kill a Mockingbird* obviously was not functioning on a literary level.

The fixed ideas and emotional associations that cluster about family and sex relations also may lead to irrelevant responses. An example is a Cambridge student's condemnation of D. H. Lawrence's poem "Piano" on the ground that no sensible person would want to give up his adult independence and return to the limitations of childhood. Resentment at restraints placed upon him in childhood may explain this reader's misunderstanding of the poem. His response was to something in his own mind and background, not the text. A group of college girls arguing about *Tom Jones* revealed the extent to which each girl's reactions were affected by her image of the ideal young man, an image, in some instances, sufficiently crystallized to hinder understanding of the various phases of Tom's character that Fielding presents.

IN ADDITION TO PREVENTING an understanding of what is read, rigid attitudes may seriously impair the reader's judgment even of what he has understood. Richards reports instances in which the reader had understood the fresh interpretation that the poem presented but condemned it because he was still dominated by stereotyped ideas and conventional feelings. Here the difficulties arise from the fact that a student will have absorbed from his environment cruder standards than are worthy of the literary experiences made available to him.

This was forcibly brought home to a teacher who in his course in short-story writing was perplexed by the superficial nature of the students' work. In his discussion of the problems presented by the short-story form, he had selected from such writers as Poe, Hawthorne, de Maupassant, Flaubert, and Mansfield those stories that seemed to handle in more subtle ways problems dimly suggested in the students' writings. However, he discovered that the usual literary diet of the students was not the work of writers of this caliber but the stereotyped products of third-rate magazines.

The students' justification of their reading was in psychological terms. These stories were easy to read, offered no difficulties to the understanding. They ended happily and gave one a sense that success was not too difficult of attainment. In some cases the explanation was merely that these cheap stories were more easily available. Obviously, the instructor's expression of disapproval would have accomplished little. He wisely started from the level at which he found his students. By getting them to discuss some of the stories they liked, he helped them to become aware of the stereotyped formulas and trick effects. The class then turned to other kinds of "escape" writing, such as Poe's stories, which require a more complex response and a more subtle perception of the writer's technique. The instructor's aim was gradually to lead the students to approach without resistance those stories he considered most significant.

At once the human element entered, for obviously the students were seeking in the cheap success stories a release from the sense of pressure and defeat that permeated the world in which they lived. They had to be willing to relinquish the easy relaxing drug that made up their reading diet and to welcome the challenge of those stories that attempted to present an honest and searching image of life.

The instructor had to dissipate any feeling that the stories he suggested were to be studied principally from the formal point of view. The concern with technique had to be subordinated to a concern with the state of mind, the attitude toward people and life situations revealed by great writers of the short story. Fundamentally, this also proved to be the sounder approach to the problems of technique. The subtle qualities of mood, the ironic contrasts between personality and situation, the nature of conflicts between characters as well as the solutions of the conflicts—all these things were involved in an understanding of the technical means that the writers had employed. The students had been unable to assimilate the examples of technical success in the short story because they had been unable or reluctant to understand and assimilate the insights that the writers of those stories had sought to give.

The teacher of literature should be on the alert for such possible "stock responses." In large part they represent the dogmatic, platitudinous ideas about people and life that one meets on all sides: in the newspapers and the mass media, or on the lips of the man on the street. Similarly, they show themselves in ways of feeling that have became so conventional as to have lost all individual quality or fine shades. Popular songs are repositories of such sentiments. Such responses are aroused with great ease in the commercialized appeal to stock sentiments represented by Mother's Day and Father's Day and by much of the advertising in the mass media.

Yet the very essence of literature is a rejection of such stereotyped, superficial, and unshaded reactions to the mere outlines of situations or to the appeal of vague and generalized concepts. A poem or a novel should provide fresh insight. The reader, therefore, must be helped to develop flexibility of mind, a freedom from rigid emotional habits, if he is to enter into the esthetic experiences the artist has made possible.

OBVIOUSLY, THE AIM should not be to create in the student such a state of flexibility and such a passivity to new kinds of experience that he will lose all the advantages of an integrated personality or a settled structure of ideas of his own. In one of his letters Keats describes the poet as possessing no character of his own because he could identify himself so completely with other forms of being and could adopt so readily new and untried forms of response. Precious as that capacity may be for a poet, in such an extreme form it is not a practical asset for the conduct of everyday affairs! A stock response, as Richards says, may often be a convenience. Just as it would be disastrous if at every occasion for walking we had to reason out the best way of putting one foot before the other, so in our intellectual and social life crystallized attitudes and ideas are useful. By automatically taking care of the major part of our lives, they leave us energy for meeting the new and unprepared-for situations.

Sufficient flexibility is needed to free oneself from the stock response when it prevents a response more appropriate to the situation. This is as true of the problems encountered in our daily lives as it is of our encounters with literature. Much of the mismanagement of personal relationships results from following a stereotyped and automatic reaction to the general outlines of a situation instead of responding to the special characteristics and changing qualities of that situation. The mother, accustomed to her children's dependence upon her for the management of their lives, continues to expect the same kind of dependence long after the children have grown beyond the need for it. The years of America's economic expansion promote the idea that the man without a job is shiftless and unenterprising; when the Depression makes it impossible for many of even the most enterprising to have jobs, this same attitude toward the unemployed persists in many quarters. The young man who has been accustomed to his mother's housewifely attention to his physical well-being becomes irritated when his wife, employed in business, overlooks these things.

In the experience of literature, free of the demands that practical life makes for speedy, economical response and action, this capacity for flexibility should surely be exercised and enlarged. Fundamentally, the goal is the development of individuals who will function less as automatic

bundles of habits and more as flexible, discriminating personalities. Our great heritage of literary experiences can
be fully enjoyed and understood only by such personalities.

These remarks concerning "stock responses" can be
translated into terms of the breadth or adequacy of the
individual life experience. Something in the reader's own
background or personality prevents him from understanding fully all that the work offers. His notions about possibilities of human character may be too limited, or his
moral code too rigid to encompass the complex human
situations and emotions presented in literature. In its
simplest terms, as we have seen, this inadequacy of experience may take the form of the city child's inability to
respond fully to country imagery; or a more extreme example is the Indian children's difficulties with Restoration
comedy. How much of the adolescent's indifference to
great literature is the result of inadequate experience?
How much of the shallowness or captiousness of his
opinions on books is a by-product of a similar approach
to situations in life?

Just as in medicine much of the knowledge about normal physiological processes is derived from the study of
pathological conditions, so in literature understanding of
what goes on when an individual reads a poem or a novel
or a play is illuminated by study of the causes for inadequate responses. They document the basic fact that any
sound response to literature is dependent on the quality
of the reader's personal contribution. He does violence to
a poem or a story when some obsession or blindness clouds
his vision of what the author has presented. He does

justice to it when his own temperament, his own experience, and a flexibly receptive attitude permit him to see clearly what the text itself offers and to perceive its significance. Precisely because it appeals to certain elements in his nature as his past experience has molded it, is the literary effect intense.

IF THE STUDENT'S STRUCTURE of attitudes and ideas is built on too narrow a base of experience, he should be helped to gain broader and deeper insight through literature itself. That is why throughout this discussion the emphasis has been on the interaction between the reader and the text. When the reader becomes aware of the dynamic nature of that interaction, he may gain some critical consciousness of the strength or weaknesses of the emotional and intellectual equipment with which he approaches literature (and life). Since he interprets the book or poem in terms of his fund of past experiences, it is equally possible and necessary that he come to reinterpret his old sense of things in the light of this new literary experience, in the light of the new ways of thinking and feeling offered by the work of art. Only when this happens has there been a full interplay between book and reader, and hence a complete and rewarding literary experience.

The work of art can have this effect because it does more than merely recall to us elements out of our own past insights and emotions. It will present them in new patterns and new contexts. It will give them new resonance and make of them the basis for new awarenesses and enriched understanding. It will tend to supplement and correct our own necessarily limited personal experience.

Through the work of art, our habitual responses, our pre-occupations and desires, may be given added significance. They will be related to the emotional and sensuous structure created by the author, and they will be brought into organic connection with broader and deeper streams of thought and feelings. Out of this will arise a wider perspective and a readjustment of the framework of values with which to meet further experiences in literature and life.

THESE CONSIDERATIONS reinforce the belief concerning the teacher's opportunities set forth at the end of Chapter 3. The fact that the personal contribution of the reader is an essential element in any vital reading of literature justifies the demand that the teacher create a setting that makes it possible for the student to have a spontaneous response to literature. But the preceding discussion makes more apparent the basis for the view that this represents only the first step, absolutely essential though that first step is. Once the student has responded freely, a process of growth can be initiated. He needs to learn to handle with intelligence and discrimination the personal factors that enter into his reaction to books. Through a critical scrutiny of his response to literary works, he can come to understand his personal attitudes and gain the perspective needed for a fuller and sounder response to literature.

This chapter has been concerned with the preoccupations and needs that the adolescent may bring to literature. To help the student critically to understand his own contribution to the literary experience becomes an aspect of helping him to do justice to the text. The thesis of

Chapter 1—that the teaching of literature necessarily involves helping the student to handle social, psychological, and ethical concepts—now falls into place. The next chapter will approach the problem of the clarification of the student's response more specifically in terms of the kinds of knowledge that will contribute to his understanding of the literary work.

Broadening
the Framework

A FREE EXCHANGE of ideas will lead each student to scrutinize his own sense of the literary work in the light of others' opinions. The very fact that other students stress aspects that he may have ignored, or report a different impression, will suggest that perhaps he has not done justice to the text. He will turn to it again in order to point out the elements that evoked his response and to see what can justify the other students' responses.

The preceding discussion of adolescent concerns has dealt with some of the factors that lead the individual to be especially receptive to some of the stimuli offered by the text, to ignore others, or even to "read into it" unfounded implications. All of this has assumed that a personal response can be either more or less relevant to the text itself. Therefore, in any teaching situation an awareness of the student's preoccupations and emotional needs should constantly be brought to bear upon the problem of insuring that the student has responded to what is actually offered by the text. The teacher aims to help the student evoke its sensuous, emotional, and intellectual import as fully as possible.

Those least in sympathy with the point of view of the preceding chapters will probably maintain that the only task of the teacher is to help the student understand what he has read, and that therefore the teacher need not be concerned with the personal preoccupations or reactions of the students. The crux of the whole problem lies in the word *understand*. The preceding chapter has shown that understanding is a much more complex personal process than many are willing to admit.

One oversimplified interpretation of understanding was rejected earlier when it was pointed out that the paraphrase is not the poem. A mere intellectualized definition of the meaning of a poem diminishes the work. The student will not be helped to understand if he is restricted to the plane of verbalization, of translation of the literary work into generalizations and abstractions. The ability to express the heart of an idea in clear terms that reveal its possible general application is indeed a rare and valuable one. But understanding does not begin on this level, certainly, nor does it necessarily culminate on this level.

Even if we take the word *understand* in a most limited sense, as it would apply to the definition of particular words, we ultimately become involved in elements of direct human experience that lead into all of the complex considerations concerning the social significance of English teaching. For to understand a word is to see implications in a context significant for human beings. In our everyday lives we often use words as mere empty counters swishing over the surface of the mind with little or no direct sense of what they point to. Thus it is that much of our speech and writing has only the vaguest significance. Certainly this habit will not be counteracted by having students translate one set of words thus vaguely sensed into another set equally devoid of outline and content.

Understanding implies the full impact of the sensuous, emotional, as well as intellectual force of a word. It requires linking the word with what it points to in the world of man or nature. This involves awareness of the sensations it symbolizes, the systems or categories into which it fits, the complex of experiences out of which it springs, the modes of feeling or practical situations with which it is associated, the actions it may imply. Above all, the word cannot be understood in isolation; it must be seen in the variety of its possible contexts. Moreover, we must relate it to our own experience in order that it may become part of our working equipment. Only then, as we place it in its relation to other sensations, ideas, attitudes, and patterns, all equally realized, shall we be in a position to say that we understand it.

The word *love*, for instance, cannot be defined without reference to some context. The varied experiences in life and literature that different individuals associate with the word will also affect the way in which they understand it. The words *virtue, justice,* or *democracy* would represent a similar necessity for encroaching upon the whole framework of ethical and social implications. Thus, even so narrow an aim as the understanding of words leads back to the field of human experiences. And that process becomes involved at once in implied assertions concerning human nature and society. In this vital sense, understanding of even one word demands a framework of ideas about man, nature, and society.

With like inevitability, the task of helping a student to understand a work of literature as a whole involves the context of the student's past experience as well as the historical, social, and ethical context into which he must fit the particular work. This will be true whether the work be "The Solitary Reaper" or *Paradise Lost, Hamlet* or *The Importance of Being Earnest, Anna Karenina* or *A Passage To India.*

Every time a reader experiences a work of art, it is in a sense created anew. *Fundamentally, the process of understanding a work implies a re-creation of it, an attempt to grasp completely the structured sensations and concepts through which the author seeks to convey the quality of his sense of life. Each must make a new synthesis of these elements with his own nature, but it is essential that he evoke those components of experience to which the text actually refers.*

Hence, even when limited to clarification of the student's understanding of the literary work, the teacher finds himself concerned with the student's personality and background, and with the whole range of facts, problems, and theories implied by the text. The student will not experience it (nor understand it) in a vacuum. The heightened sensuous observation, the keener and subtler perception of human emotions and actions, will not etch themselves on a blank page. There must take place an integration between the framework of interests, ideas, and

feelings that the student brings, and the structure of ideas
and emotions offered by the text. As the student is led to
clarify his own sense of it, the teacher will be able to lead
him to the various kinds of knowledge that will enable
him to achieve the experiences offered by this particular
text.

Thus, the clarification of the reader's personal understanding of the novel or poem or play carries with it a responsibility to the text itself. He seeks to recapture the
particular approach to nature or society that dominates
the work. He evokes the particular kind of awareness it
embodies—whether it be the stark terror of "The Pit and
the Pendulum" or the sense of time and slow change of
To the Lighthouse. He becomes self-critical in order to
see whether his own emphasis corresponds to what the
text actually presents. He returns to the text to make sure
that he has done justice to the particular words in their
particular order—sound and rhythm, image and metaphor, structure and point of view, indications of tone,
clues to character. The discovery of what he overlooked
will be as valuable in revealing his own blind spots and
emotional fixations as it will be in giving him a sounder
participation in the work itself.

The import of any work will remain thoroughly personal, since it is re-created by a specific personality with
its own sense of values. Thus there is not necessarily only
one "correct" interpretation of the significance of a given
work. Not even an author's statement of his aims can be
considered definitive. The text exists as a separate entity
that may or may not fulfill his intentions and can possess
for us more values than he foresaw. The work must carry

its own message to each of us. Nevertheless, the student should be led to discover that some interpretations are more defensible than others. A complex work such as *Hamlet* offers the basis for various interpretations; yet their acceptability will depend, first, on whether they take into account as many as possible of the elements present in the text, and second, on whether they do not imply elements that are not present in it.

An interpretation of *Hamlet*, no matter how subtle, that ignored his soliloquies or his conversations with his mother would obviously be inadequate. Similarly, an interpretation that assumed ideas and attitudes for which no basis could be found in the text, or ignored the fact that the language has changed since Elizabethan times, would certainly be capricious. Thus, understanding of the work can be nourished through study of what is sometimes called "background materials."

An undistorted vision of the work of art requires a consciousness of one's own preconceptions and prejudices concerning the situations presented in the work, in contrast to the basic attitudes toward life assumed in the text. Often the reader integrates the work into a context of psychological or moral theories different from those that the author probably possessed. Always, therefore, a full understanding of literature requires both a consciousness of the reader's own "angle of refraction" and any information that can illuminate the assumptions implicit in the text.

STUDENTS WILL BENEFIT from their cooperative attempt to embrace all phases of the work in their formulation of its dominant effect. An example of this is a discussion of Keats' "The Eve of St. Agnes." A number of the students first spoke of the poem as a delightfully gay and ornamental story of romantic love. Others, accepting this characterization of the poem, condemned as irrelevant and jarring the introduction of the old Beadsman, the tombs, the cold chapel, in the opening of the poem, and the death of old Angela and the Beadsman at the end. The group then found it necessary to decide what function these details might serve. They reread the text more carefully and decided that these elements provided an emotional background or undertone for the glowing colors and medieval atmosphere of the lovers' story. The contrast enhanced the warmth and sensuous vividness of the episode, threw over it an atmosphere of remoteness in time and space, and interwove the elegiac theme of death and the passing of all lovely things. The discussion stimulated the students to attend to all the components of the work, the minor chords as well as the major. Out of this came a fuller and more adequate response.

The effort to organize all the elements present in the text may also lead to considerations of human life and literary history. Thus the students' discussion of "The Eve of St. Agnes" helped to make them aware of the presence in much of Keats' poetry of the sense that

Ay, in the very temple of Delight
Veiled Melancholy has her sovran shrine.

They sought in Keats' letters and in the story of his brief life and literary enthusiasms, the source of this feeling for the fleetingness of joy and beauty. They placed the work in the context of the life and personality of the author. Note, however, that the movement here was from interpretation of the text to author's life. This is diametrically opposed to the usual procedure in textbooks and many classrooms. To derive an interpretation of a text from the author's life or stated intentions is, of course, critically indefensible.

To see the writer as part of a literary tradition can also clarify personal response, especially for the more sophisticated students. Melodramatic or inconsistent elements in the form and plots of Shakespeare's plays may no longer trouble the reader when placed in the setting of Elizabethan theatrical traditions. Similarly, the attempt to differentiate between the special type of sensibility of different members of the same literary movement, such as Wordsworth and Coleridge, or Conrad and James, will heighten perception of the special quality of the effects each sought to produce.

Thus students may find themselves embarked upon a study of the biographical and literary background of the work. They will come to understand better the particular medium of expression that the author selected. They may see how reactions against the dead weight of literary tradition or the exhaustion of an earlier vein of literary sensibility, as in the case of Wordsworth or T. S. Eliot, will have led him to his particular emphasis. They will thus gain a profounder sense of the communal basis of even the most highly individualized insights and emotions.

The desire to understand a particular work will produce ever widening circles of interest. Yet the focus of these concerns should continue to be the student's own sense of the work and his desire to clarify and refine his perception of it. Knowledge about the author's life and the literary influences acting upon him will create the need for understanding the intellectual and philosophical, the social and economic, conditions surrounding him. If the work is not a contemporary one, the contrasts and similarities between the conditions of that past age and the present will illuminate ways in which present-day reactions to the work may differ from those of the author's contemporaries.

Robinson Crusoe is for us the absorbing tale of man's ingenuity in wresting a livelihood from nature; the account of his religious meditations and conversion is much less stirring. The much pitied Pamela may seem to the young girl of today merely a shrewd and designing hussy. Hamlet's perplexities about whether the Ghost may be a benevolent visitant returned from Purgatory or an evil spirit who has assumed his father's form seem unimportant to those who question the existence of ghosts at all. Similarly, there is much in the work today that has special and perhaps hitherto unexploited overtones. Hamlet's hesitations and melancholy questionings in a world out of joint have a compelling significance for the twentieth-century reader.

Here again, there will be profit in seeing that the reader's own reactions, like the work of art, are the organic expression not only of a particular individual but also of a particular cultural setting. Literary history will not seem like a clear stream flowing between banks which enclose but do not affect it. Rather it will be seen that the literary stream is fed by thousands of rivulets which have their sources in the surrounding intellectual and social environment.

THESE CONCENTRIC CIRCLES of interest focused on the student's sense of a work will involve him in still deeper concern with human relations. He will see in the work a specific reflection of general ideas concerning good and evil. He will work out the scale of values that the writer applies to personalities and to relations between people. The student will apprehend Shakespeare's sense of the individual dominating even an adverse fate by the intensity and resonance of his nature. Or he will adjust to Jane Austen's "human scale," her characters measured against only the society and the world they have created. Or he will share Hardy's sense of individual man as a helpless atom in the cosmic stream.

The young reader will be especially alert to the treatment of character. The writer does more than present human beings in action; he offers clues to the motives and the repercussions of those actions. He shows, too, many of the forces that shape human personality and conduct. Pamela's constant reference to the moral and social code differs greatly from Tom Jones' uncalculating behavior. George Eliot, Thackeray, Aldous Huxley, and D. H. Lawrence each provide a different view of the determining traits of human character. Often, too, the writer reveals the broader influences at work in man's collective life. F. Scott Fitzgerald manifests the influence of social aspirations; Zola and Steinbeck show the force of economic pressures; Emily Brontë and D. H. Lawrence, each in a different way, evoke the power of human impulse and passion. Understanding of the individual sensibility or individual problems presented by the text may thus lead to understanding of the implicit system of values and sense of man's relation to the world.

Such analysis of the work, such acquisition of new insights and information, will have value only as it is linked up with the student's own primary response to the work. His own judgment on it will thus be thrown into sharper relief; for if he is indeed functioning freely and spontaneously, he will undoubtedly reflect not only on the work itself but also on the problems it presents and on the personalities and actions of the characters. The attempt to work out the author's system of values and assumptions about man and society should enable the student to discover the unspoken assumptions behind his own judgment. His conclusions about this particular work imply the unarticulated theories of human conduct and ideas of the good that shape his thinking.

During group discussions the students, in a spirit of friendly challenge, can lead one another to work out the implications of the positions they have taken. They may discover that they are making assertions based on fundamentally contradictory concepts. A student who espoused with equal vigor the causes of Pamela and Tess, and maintained that each of them was "virtuous," found herself involved in arriving at some consistent understanding of that term. Becky Sharp and her humbler daughter, Scarlett O'Hara, led another student into similar difficulties. By bringing their own generalizations into the open, students may be led to feel the need of putting their mental houses in order. They will see how often they have been dominated by ideas only because they have heard them repeated again and again. They will develop a more critical, questioning attitude and will see the need of a more reasoned foundation for their thoughts and judgments, a more consistent system of values.

The teacher's challenge, as well as the challenge of the other students, will stimulate each of them to search for knowledge that will clarify the problems he encounters and will supply the basis for valid judgments. Here the teacher of literature may legitimately see it as his function to point to the existence of helpful bodies of knowledge. He will have made a valuable contribution if the student leaves his experience of the literary work eager to learn what the psychologist, the sociologist, and the historian have to offer him. The core of direct emotional experience at the heart of the critical process outlined here should keep alive the sense of the immediate personal value of the objective knowledge these experts provide. Thus, a teacher of tenth-graders in an affluent and divorce-ridden community was nonplussed by their rejection of *Ethan Frome*. They refused to take it seriously: the whole story was contrived, they said, because to begin with, Ethan's meek acceptance of his lot was unthinkable. As the teacher led them to look more closely at the text, and as they grappled with their own reactions, they discovered how little they knew about recent history and about economic, social, and cultural climates different from their own. They learned something about these matters, but they also learned something about entering into the structure of assumptions of a literary work. They gained both literary and social perspective.

Just such spontaneous recourse to the other disciplines was illustrated by a group of freshmen in a woman's college who had read Ibsen's *A Doll's House*. One of the students attacked the play as profoundly insignificant since "Nora was a fool to have become so dependent on her husband." Others objected that she could do nothing else. You couldn't judge Nora, they pointed out, as you would a woman of today. Her relationship with her father and with Torvald reflected the position of women in the nineteenth century. Yet even those who recognized the historical background of the play could give very little accurate information about the status of women at that time. The students tried to find out what were women's legal and political rights in the nineteenth century as contrasted with the present. They discovered the differences among periods, countries, and even various states within the United States. They emphasized the extent of woman's emancipation since the date of the play, but admitted that some problems still persisted. They were also interested to discover the extent to which the greater emancipation of women had transformed their relationships with husband and children.

These insights deepened the students' sense of the play's significance. They no longer tended to regard Nora as an individual solving an individual problem. They considered her to a large extent the victim of a vast complex of conditions. They saw Torvald's attitude as the expression of a view of his rights sanctioned by the whole force of the society. To see the individual as shaped by a great many factors rooted in the society about him creates a broader perspective. The students also realized the value of suspending judgment until they had acquired a basis of information.

At certain points in the discussion the teacher had had pedantic twinges of conscience about the attention paid to subjects that could not be strictly defined as literary. He later realized that he need have had no qualms. Increased awareness of the complexities of human relationships led the students toward a fuller appreciation of the play itself. Some of the students became more aware of Ibsen's dramatic methods. Quite spontaneously, they discussed his extraordinary economy in conveying significant information about Nora's past relations with her father and her husband. They pointed out the clear structure of the play with its swift presentation of complex problems and its skillful creation of suspense. The final scene, although it presented no psychological or social solution, was judged to be theatrically effective because it involved overt action that clearly defined Nora's dilemma. Because they themselves raised the questions, there was nothing academically remote about these matters of form and technique; the students saw them as the author's choices, intimately related to what he was seeking to convey.

BACKGROUND MATERIALS ALREADY receive much attention in school and college literature programs. The danger, however, is that such study tends to become an end in itself. This chapter has proposed a major criterion of the usefulness of background information: it will have value only when the student feels the need of it and when it is assimilated into the student's experience of particular literary works.

Challenged to establish the validity of his interpretation and judgment of the work, he will be stimulated both to examine the text more closely and to scrutinize the adequacy of his own past experience and basic assumptions. He will test whether what he brings to the text has enabled him to do justice to all that it embodies. This may lead him to probe further into literary techniques and forms. It may also impel him to acquire various types of knowledge—literary and social history, biography, philosophy, psychology, anthropology—that may deepen his understanding of the work. Such a process of clarification and enrichment of successive literary experiences will foster sound critical habits. From this kind of literary study there should flow, too, enhanced understanding of himself and the life about him. The coming chapters will consider in greater detail how literary sensitivity may contribute to such insight.

PART III

Literary Sensitivity as the Source of Insight

Some Basic Social Concepts

TEACHERS OF LITERATURE deal inevitably with its human implications. Must they then become experts in the social sciences? The answer obviously is, No. But they are responsible for scrutinizing their own assumptions about human nature and society in the light of contemporary thought. This chapter will turn away from literature itself to clarify some of the concepts about human relations which underlie the preceding discussion of the relation of social insight to literary sensitivity and judgment. This may elucidate a few of the key ideas with which the teacher should be familiar, and which are more important than any of the specific findings of the various disciplines that study human behavior.

Some of these ideas have in recent years become generally current and are undoubtedly already known to the reader. They are formulated here in order to provide a coherent basis for considering their special relevance to the sphere of the teacher of literature. Chapters 7 and 8 will explore how basic social concepts may illuminate, and be illuminated by, the study of literature.

An axiom of contemporary educational thought is that, under the unprecedented and rapidly changing conditions of present-day life, to give the youth a rigid set of dogmatic ideas and habits is a certain method of producing insecurity and bewilderment. Members of the older generation know that many of the habitual attitudes and ideas they took most for granted have with changed conditions become inappropriate and even antisocial. Habits of thrift were much prized, only to have the economists decree that the socially valuable rule is to spend and invest, not hoard. Women dutifully restricted the scope of their interests to the home, only to find that the functions of the home itself had changed, and that as mothers, wives, and citizens they needed to develop broader interests and understanding. The traditional belief was that every American of any ability could rise unaided above the economic and social stratum into which he was born; now the ideal of equal opportunity is buttressed by a great network of laws. The doctrine that punitive measures prevent crime has been replaced by the view that the criminal is a symptom of weaknesses in our educational and social systems, and should be cured, not punished. In politics, in the relations between men and women, in the adjustments between parents and children, in all phases of our personal and social life, similar discrepancies between habitual attitudes and changed circumstances have developed. Everything points toward a prodigious acceleration of changes demanding such readjustments during the life-time of those who are adolescents and children today.

Obviously, a rigid set of dogmatic ideas and fixed responses to specific conditions is the worst kind of equipment for the contemporary youth. As soon as actual conditions prove that his passively acquired code is useless or even harmful, he has nothing else to cling to. Having been made dependent upon ready-made props, he will be precipitated into painful insecurity. This kind of insecurity, this craving for some easy, reassuring formula, makes the youth of other countries and sometimes of our own a ready prey to those enemies of democracy who hold out the delusive bait of ready-made solutions to all problems. Unprepared to think independently, the young man and woman seek to return to the infantile state in which there is no responsibility to make decisions; they are thus willing to blindly follow some "leader" whose tools and prey they become.

The conditions of human life, the complexities of the interaction of personality upon personality, the shifting images offered by human history, and the rapid flux of the life about us show how evasive of reality a dogmatic approach to human relations would be. Our literary heritage itself, with its reflections of the varied and contrasting forms of human life and personality, with its expression of so many different life goals and values, is eloquent rebuttal of any absolutistic approach to life. However satisfactory may be the system of values the teacher has worked out for himself, he is not justified in "teaching" it to his students, as one might "teach" a method of solving a problem in calculus. There is no proof that the conditions of life this generation of students will face, or the highly diverse personal problems they will have to solve, will be commensurable with any arbitrary measuring rod provided by the teacher.

The teacher, however, must do more than merely avoid explicit dogmatism. He must also avoid the insidious unconscious inculcation of dogma. Only a bundle of miscellaneous and unintegrated responses—in other words, not a functioning individual at all—could avoid conveying some attitudes toward experience. The teacher will inevitably possess some scheme of values, some particular way of approaching and judging people and situations. He should be critically aware of these attitudes instead of imposing them indirectly and unconsciously upon his students.

Nor should the teacher try to pose as a completely objective person. The assumption of a mask of unemotional objectivity or impartial omniscience is one reason why teachers and college professors sometimes seem not quite human to their students. A much more wholesome educational situation is created when the teacher is a really live person who has examined his own attitudes and assumptions and who, when appropriate, states them frankly and honestly. He does not have to seem to possess "all the answers," which the students then need only passively absorb. Admitting his own uncertainties and perplexities will stimulate the students to join him in the common task of seeking the knowledge that may clarify these problems.

But even this awareness of his own point of view and

his frankness are not enough. The teacher needs to see his own philosophy as only one of the possible approaches to life, from which his students should be given the opportunity to select for themselves. Tolerance of other points of view is extremely important for the teacher— an attitude those who are insecure and fearful of challenges to their authority find most difficult to maintain.

To rule out the conscious or unconscious transmission of an explicit set of ready-made answers to personal problems and ready-made judgments on people and society does not, however, mean an end to the teacher's responsibility, nor does it imply a nihilistic approach to life. Reluctance to impose a dogmatic philosophy may lead to an equally dangerous attitude of noncommittal relativism that refuses to admit any standards and tends to produce a paralysis of judgment on the part of the student. Such pseudo-liberalism can lead to the feeling that there is nothing to believe, that there are no values to be sought in this confused world. Wholesale negativism will leave youth completely unprepared. In times of crisis when the inevitable choices must be made, they will tend to fall back on the old, stereotyped attitudes, or to follow chance, irrational appeals.

Although no one code should be taught dogmatically, the need for the individual to work out his own principles and his own hierarchy of values is imperative. The task of education is to supply him with the knowledge, the mental habits, and the emotional impetus that will enable him to independently solve his problems—hence the teacher's need to clarify for himself the basic approaches to experience and the basic concepts concerning human nature and society that will be a useful preparation for the adolescent facing the uncertain future.

In order that the student may be prepared for the unpredictable demands that life will make upon him, our schools and universities must be transformed, as C. S. Peirce said many years ago, from "institutions for teaching" into "institutions for learning." The student should go to school and college, not for the purpose of being taught ready-made formulas and fixed attitudes, but in order that he may develop the will to learn. He must gain command of techniques that make possible a constantly closer approximation to the truth, and he must develop the flexibility of mind and temperament necessary for the translation of that sense of truth into actual behavior. Instead of judgments accepted in whole cloth, he must acquire a curiosity about the causes of human actions and social conditions; he must be ready to revise accepted hypotheses in the light of new information; he must learn where to turn for this information. He needs, in short, to develop a dynamic sense of life, a feeling that an understanding of causes makes for greater control of conditions. Instead of drifting with the stream of circumstance, he will be able to set up more rational personal and social goals and to understand better the conditions under which they can be achieved.

The implication here is that the social sciences have something positive to offer toward a solution of personal problems and toward a framework of ideas that will make possible constructive social action. In order to arouse in the student a desire for social understanding, the teacher of literature needs himself to be aware that such knowledge exists or at any rate that the foundation for it has been laid by the social sciences.

The literature teacher's responsibility toward the kind of information represented by the social sciences can be summed up in general terms: He should be aware of the existence of the various behavioral sciences and should possess a general understanding of what phases of man's life they treat. Even though he may not have a detailed knowledge of these fields, he should at least understand their methods of approach and the basic concepts concerning man and society which they have developed. Without such knowledge he will probably be very effectively undoing in the English classroom whatever the teachers of social studies may have succeeded in accomplishing. Moreover, there is no reason why the English teacher's knowledge should stop at this minimum level. The training of English teachers should include carefully planned work in the behavorial sciences, and the practicing teacher should recognize his responsibility for constantly adding to his knowledge in these fields as well as in the field of literature.

TEACHERS OF LITERATURE and the arts often think of themselves as saving the student from the stultifying effects of our present scientific age. The early romantic opposition to the scientist as one who "murders to dissect" lingers on. Teachers of English tend to consider themselves defenders of a lost cause, keepers of an imaginative or emotional oasis in the midst of our materialistic, science-ridden life.

This attitude toward science is to some extent due to a

prevalent confusion between the effects of science and the effect of the practical, materialistic emphasis of our society. It is not science, but the way in which it has been misused, to which the English teacher should feel himself opposed. More and more evidence is accruing to demonstrate that science, properly exploited, may eventually so reduce time devoted to work that the entire population will have the leisure and the energy for the rich imaginative life that literature and the arts offer.

Even some of those who will admit this continue to assume that there is a fundamental and irreconcilable opposition between science and literature.[1] It is still fashionable in some circles to stress the complexity of human personality and human affairs as an insuperable obstacle to the application of scientific method. The disagreements and conflicts among different schools of thought are pointed to as proof. Only lack of contact with the finest and soundest expressions of the scientific spirit, however, could enable opponents of the social sciences to make these unqualified claims.

An understanding of the spirit of scientific method and its application to human affairs is the most fundamental social concept that the teacher of literature should possess. A lively sense of the essential nature of scientific method will compensate for lack of detailed knowledge of the

[1] Another aspect of the literary person's antagonism to science is his reluctance to recognize that scientific works are often also works of literature. Cf. Huxley's *Man's Place in Nature,* Darwin's *Origin of Species,* Adam Smith's *Wealth of Nations,* Eddington's *Stars and Atoms,* William James' *Principles of Psychology,* Loren Eiseley's *The Immense Journey.*

social sciences. In fact, without this basic understanding of the scientific attitude, any specific facts or theories drawn from the social sciences which he might introduce into discussions of literature would very likely be confusing to his students.

The artist, we are reminded, always conveys the special quality, the peculiar attributes, the unique flavor, of some personality or situation. The scientist, his artistic opponents assert, reduces life to its lowest common denominators and centers attention on whatever in a particular object makes it like every other one of its class. The layman tends to think of the contribution of the scientist as being a body of laws or a system of classifications to be applied to nature and society. This on the surface would seem to negate the artistic approach to life, which seeks to individualize rather than to generalize. But this view of science does it gross injustice.

Wholesale application of broad categories, lumping together many personalities or situations under broad labels, adoption of stereotyped attitudes or sweeping judgments, are alien to the very spirit of science. Contemporary logic and theories of knowledge recognize the spontaneous quality of existence, the novel elements in nature, as much as do the arts. Part of the scientist's duty is to note in a given situation those factors that are unique or that are met here in new combinations which differentiate it from any other situations of the same type. Of course, the scientist recognizes that the human and physical world offers certain recurrent patterns upon which can be built theories concerning the correlation of their various elements. These theories, he hopes, will enable us to understand the consequences that flow from particular combinations of qualities or events.

This desire of the scientist to work out fundamentally recurrent patterns evidently has given rise to the idea that the scientific approach is inimical to the artistic.[2] It is essential to see how the scientist uses his generalizations or broad categories. His tentative generalizations are offered as a framework of ideas and guiding principles to be applied to specific situations. This framework will help to identify in a given situation those elements that possess a particular characteristic pattern. But, equally important, they help him to further discriminate wherein this situation differs from other situations.

This process in no way violates the approach of the artist to life; the artist is not only concerned with the unique. If every author were entirely different from every other human being, and if each of us were totally unique, there could be no art at all.

Fundamentally, comprehension of the author's theme must be based on the general or typical emotions or situations that are present in the work he is creating. At the

[2] Unfortunately, the social scientists themselves are largely responsible for the prevalent misconception. Their tendency has been to formulate their theories in such a way that their meaning for human lives is obscured. Economists, sociologists, political theorists, historians, have too often developed a technical jargon that makes their findings seem remote from ordinary life. They must deal with mass movements, statistical data, the broad sweep of events; yet this should not entail the neglect of the individual human behavior and personal motivations that give rise to these social phenomena. The more creative thinkers in all of these fields, however, are aware of the human import of their work. The view of the social sciences presented here rests on them, in the hope that it will be more and more generally operative. See also pp. 174 seq.

same time, he seeks to render its peculiar and special overtones, its subtle departures from the typical. For example,
there is much that is unusual in the personalities and
situations presented in Hardy's *Jude the Obscure;* yet
without the elements common to many human beings, no
matter how specially combined in the character of Jude
or Sue, we should not be able to understand the work at
all. Intent on the peculiar qualities or the strangeness of·
the situation created by the artist, we assume ideas concerning the general or the characteristic. The point of
view of the artist requires a recognition of recurrent patterns, paralleled by the recognition that every personality
and every situation has its own unique qualities.

The artist orders and classifies the data offered by life as
much as does the scientist. The artist aims to make us
experience imaginatively these common patterns and
special qualities; the scientist seeks to discover a framework of ideas concerning what is general and what is
unique that we may apply to such experiences. This
framework of knowledge, these guiding principles, offered
by the scientist are never irrelevant to the experience derived from either life or art.

SCIENCE STARTS WITH the complexity of human nature
and society, but conquers the variety and intricacy of its
subject matter by working out fruitful principles of explanation for limited phases of it. *Divide et impera,* the
old Roman principle for success in conquering enemies,
is the principle that science has used in overcoming the
complexity of its materials. By approaching human affairs
from different angles, anthropology, economics, psychol-

ogy, and sociology have been able to discover a considerable body of information that furnishes the basis for a provisional understanding of human beings.

Often the generalizations of the social sciences hold only for certain historical epochs, particular culture areas and cultural patterns. The scientist recognizes that his findings within these limited areas must be compared to findings drawn from other areas, such as civilizations other than the Western. The scientist works out a certain hypothesis concerning human personality and society, and then attempts to discover all the facts that will tend to prove or disprove it. He admits that his results are always tentative, that there are many gaps in his knowledge, and that new information may lead to the adoption of new theories.

This very tentativeness of the scientific attitude has been said to make it extremely unsettling to the child or the adolescent. It is feared that great mental insecurity will result from the fact that there is nothing absolutely certain, that all ideas are subject to future revision. Such insecurity evidently arises when the scientific spirit is not thoroughly presented. Though prepared to relinquish belief in any particular findings or conclusions of science, we can still hold firmly to our faith in the scientific method itself.

Scientific knowledge is essentially a cooperative product. Only as a fact or theory is tested and verified by many competent minds, often widely scattered in time and space, does that fact or theory come to be accepted. The important thing is not that one generation rejects a particular theory of psychology worked out by the preceding (paralleling, say, the substitution of an Einsteinian for a

Newtonian physics), but that there are innumerable minds all over the world working at these problems, building on what others have done before them, and contributing, each in his own way, to a greater approximation toward sound understanding. Bringing up young people to base their security upon the idea of absolute certainty has led only to disillusionment and insecurity. They will be much better equipped if they place their faith in the co-operative striving toward greater and greater exactitude and universality that is the essence of the scientific spirit.[3]

The social sciences already offer much that can be assimilated into the fabric of our everyday life. If they do not provide rigid formulas for action, it is precisely because the scientific spirit stresses the need for understanding the special conditions that qualify any particular situation. Our society is seeking more and more to take advantage of what the social sciences can already explain about the various factors involved in its operations. Understanding of the typical as well as the special

[3] "What is science? The dictionary will say that it is systematized knowledge. Dictionary definitions, however, are too apt to repose upon derivations; which is as much as to say that they neglect too much the later steps in the evolution of meanings. Mere knowledge, though it be systematized, may be a dead memory; while by science we all habitually mean a living and growing body of truth. . . . That which constitutes science, then, is not so much correct conclusions, as it is a correct method. But the method of science is itself a scientific result. It did not spring out of the brain of a beginner: it was a historic attainment and a scientific achievement. So that not even this method ought to be regarded as essential to the beginnings of science. That which is essential, however, is the scientific spirit, which is determined not to rest satisfied with existing opinions, but to press on to the real truth of nature. To science once enthroned in this sense, among any people, science in every other sense is heir apparent." Charles Sanders Peirce, *Collected Papers*, Vol. VI (Cambridge, Harvard University Press, 1935), p. 302.

characteristics of any problem is the prelude to more intelligent and more successful solutions. The teacher of literature should cling to this understanding of the flexible, questing nature of the scientific spirit—its readiness to utilize the insights which man's collective endeavors have thus far attained, and its dynamic sense of truth.

THESE OVERARCHING CONSIDERATIONS will protect the literary specialist from the danger of a dogmatic application of scientific theories or a substitution of scientific terminology for scientific insight. A bane of many discussions about human beings (and especially of much educational theory) is the use of a scientific jargon that masks from the speaker and the listener their lack of real understanding.

An illustration of this type of misuse of science is the employment of the jargon of psychological terminology. Recall, for instance, those people who swallow the Freudian or Adlerian theory unquestioningly and who use their various categories loosely and lavishly. Accepting such labels as the *Oedipus fixation* or the *inferiority complex,* they evidently feel that they have clarified their understanding of a personality when they have applied one of these labels to it. Their facile use of such terms merely reveals their lack of understanding of the psychoanalytic approach itself. Any of the accounts of particular analyses recorded by Freud or his disciples reflects their sense of how special each case is. The operation of any such general emotional patterns as the Oedipus fixation or the inferiority complex differs in its particulars in each case. Even the recognition of these broad, typical patterns was arrived at only after prolonged study of the specific cases.[4] Having determined the general pattern, the analyst's concern was to see how it had worked itself out in terms of the particular personality and the particular situation in which the person found himself. Only in this way, not by a mere process of labeling, could the psychiatrist offer any help. Equally valid illustrations of misuse of terminology might be drawn from other schools of psychology and other social sciences, e.g., the nineteenth-century use of *the survival of the fittest* or the indiscriminate application of phrases such as *the law of supply and demand, the class struggle* (economics), *the relativity of morals* (anthropology), *evolution and progress* (sociology), or *the inevitable decay of civilizations* (Spenglerian history).

That the teacher of literature inevitably deals with psychological problems does not argue that he should learn all the systems of classification of human types or all the theories of behavior. Nor should the discussion of literature necessarily be at all concerned with psychological classifications or terminology. Suppose a student docilely learned to classify literary characters according to whether they were extroverts or introverts, or according to whether they showed signs of an inferiority complex, or according to whether their actions could be phrased in Freudian or Jungian terms. Does it seem likely that such

[4] In fact, this recognition of human variability and the need for an ever broader base for generalization explains psychiatrists' current revision of their theories in the light of a study of other cultures. Cf. some early contributions: Karen Horney, *The Neurotic Personality of Our Time* (New York, W. W. Norton, 1937); James S. Plant, *Personality and the Cultural Pattern* (New York, The Commonwealth Fund, 1937); John Dollard, *Criteria for the Life History* (New Haven, Yale University Press, 1935).

a student would be much better off than one who had passively learned to think in terms of "the good people" and "the bad people" or to classify them as types, such as "the gossip," "the bully," "the old maid," or who might have been led to consider them only as "Aryan" and "non-Aryan"? Any rigid *a priori* classification used in this way merely becomes an obstacle to understanding people. As soon as he has labeled them, the student feels relieved of any further obligation to get at their inner qualities, to understand their special motivation, or to observe as many as possible of the factors that may enter into the external conditions influencing them.

Hence the teacher of literature should be conversant, not so much with the details, as with the spirit of psychological inquiry. If the teacher himself espouses any one school of psychology (and that might lend his teaching a consistency that the remarks about "human nature" uttered in most literature courses lack), he should be willing to recognize the existence of other schools and the student's right to know about them. For if the student is given a sense of the approach to human nature out of which psychological inquiry springs, he will be ready and eager to seek from the psychologists themselves the tentative answers they offer to his questions.

The same principle holds for the other behavioral sciences. The teacher of literature needs to convey the spirit of scrupulous inquiry and the flexible approach which is their characteristic. His contribution may be phrased largely in negative terms: he will not impose a dogmatic framework upon the concept of "human nature"; he will not allow conventional assumptions to go unchallenged; he will not permit his students to fall back upon pat, stereotyped formulas. In positive terms, he will awaken his students to an awareness of the complexity of human behavior and society and will stimulate them to seek the understanding that the social scientists are endeavoring to establish. He will share the psychologist's belief that knowledge concerning human nature must be the result of careful, controlled observation, that any hypothesis must be tested and retested, and that we must be particularly on our guard against imputing to human beings those traits or those psychological mechanisms that would justify or rationalize our own habitual method of dealing with them.

WHAT, THEN, ARE SOME of the basic concepts that should permeate the discussion when the reading of literature raises questions about human nature and experience? Perhaps an economical way of dealing with these questions within the limits of a chapter will be to start with certain ideas that often appear in the student's thinking and with which the English teacher must therefore deal. With these current conceptions as starting points, it will be possible to see what light the scientific approach can offer. This will have relevance to the problems that teachers constantly face in the classroom, and may indicate how certain concepts can function in ordinary thinking about people and society. The object will be to further illustrate the value of a firm hold on certain fundamental concepts and the importance of bringing such concepts to bear upon current attitudes.

One of the most glaring of the widespread assumptions

encountered in students' reactions to literature is the traditional voluntaristic conception of human nature and conduct mentioned briefly in the first chapter. This view is
based on the idea that any behavior can be interpreted as
having been willed by the actor. The assumption is that
in all situations the individual is free to accept or reject
various modes of behavior. If a person is pleasant or unpleasant, social or antisocial, it is largely because he
wishes to be so. One needs only to know the "rules," the
commandments of the society about one, in order to be
provided with a guide to one's own conduct and a code for
sitting in judgment on one's fellowmen. Although, stated
thus baldly, these assumptions seem almost to condemn
themselves, and although this view has lost its hold in
many areas of our political and social life, it still often
dominates the average man's thinking. We see this reflected in his actual judgments on people or in the attitudes toward whole groups of people.

Scientific investigation and analysis, particularly in the
fields of psychology, sociology, and anthropology, have
during the past quarter century generally undermined this
oversimplified theory of human nature and conduct. The
plasticity of the human creature is being recognized. The
human personality is thought of by the scientist as a
complex of qualities and habits which are the end result
of a great many different factors converging upon and
interacting with the individual organism. The innate physical and mental endowments of the individual are not
ignored, but the individual, as we meet him functioning in
society, is seen as the product of the particular ways in

which these innate elements have been molded, stimulated, or repressed by external conditions.

The conception of the child as a little savage whose rebellious will must be broken and who must be coerced into civilized ways lost its currency at least a century ago. Equally mythical is the romantic conception of the child as an unspoiled angel who is corrupted into the ways of the world as its "prison walls" close about him. Instead, the human creature is seen to possess potentialities for an infinite variety of behavior. The circumstances into which he is born, the temperaments that act upon him in his earlier years, the kinds of stimulation or repression to which he is subjected, and the satisfactions or frustrations he meets will have a powerful influence in patterning the mental and physical potentialities with which he is born.

Present-day psychology is devoting a great deal of attention to attempting to discover significant forces that contribute to molding the personality. These forces are attributed differing degrees of importance by the various schools of psychology. Some focus their attention upon such seemingly external factors as methods of feeding during babyhood. Others stress more the emotional relationships with the parents and with brothers and sisters as important factors in patterning the child's personality. Still others stress the environment in which the child grows up; the economic conditions that surround him, whether an affluent environment permits unhampered activity or whether, as in the city slums, he is often forced to seek an outlet for his energy in destructive and underhand activities.

No matter which aspect of the forces acting upon the child is stressed, and no matter how much contemporary schools of psychology may differ concerning the methods, behavioristic or introspective, of studying the individual, they share this basic approach to human development. The behavior, the emotional patterns, the ideas and dominant drives that make up a personality, are seen as the result of a process by which the particular mental and emotional habits are, so to speak, learned. Thus, a particular temperament or a particular action cannot be judged in itself. It has to be seen in relation to the whole stream of the individual's life, the various influences to which he has been subjected, the situations and events through which he has passed. This does not eliminate the concept of the will. But it does mean that we have to get back of any particular action to see the context within which "the will" operates.

This view of the plasticity of human nature has been strengthened by the sociologists and the anthropologists, attacking the problem from other angles. From the immediate environment, particularly from the family group, the child acquires not only such things as physical mannerisms, habits of gesture and language, but also emotional habits and major ideas concerning behavior. Similarly, the particular social group of which the child is a part contributes certain elements to his personality patterns and his mental and emotional habits. One illustration of how the ideas and attitudes of the surrounding society are incorporated into the individual personality is the acquisition from the environment of ideas of masculinity and femininity. These mold the individual's own behavior and his expectations concerning the behavior of others. In the same way are built up the patterns of feeling and behavior, the expectations and values that constitute the content of the individual's personality and sense of life.

In our own heterogeneous society this concept of the influence of the family and social environment upon the individual is particularly important. The effort to fully carry out the democratic dream has brought the realization that in our highly complex civilization, people may be the products of practically different subcultures. In our cities, for instance, we find people who superficially seem to be conforming to the ways of life of the average city dweller, and yet who, coming from different parts of the country and from different family, social, and ethnic backgrounds, may be motivated by entirely different conceptions of personal relationships. The young couple who have met and married in the city may represent the conjunction of two different patterns; the young husband coming from a small New England town with its leisurely tempo and thrifty, disciplined, undemonstrative way of life will have very different images of behavior from his wife who may have grown up in the easygoing atmosphere of a Western town where heartiness and vigorous action are valued more than discipline and decorum. Or they may have very different images of what constitutes the family, one perhaps used to a household in which several generations shared their activities and their pleasures and troubles, and the other thinking of the family in terms of the biological unit of parents and children, seeing all others as outsiders toward whom no responsibility need be felt. Other patterns may reflect the high incidence of divorce or perhaps the home built around an unmarried mother.

Beyond such broad patterning factors exists an even more complex and perhaps even more powerful set of influences. The boy who has grown up as the subject of the excessive care and emotional attentions of a doting mother may seek in any other relationships as, for instance, in marriage, similar cherishing protection and emotional dependence. This may be so powerful as to prevent his assuming the emotional responsibilities that are usually associated with marriage and parenthood.

THE ANTHROPOLOGISTS have contributed still another and broader framework within which to place this basic concept of psychological conditioning. By studying a great variety of societies or, to use the anthropological term, *cultures*, they have revealed the diversity of patterns into which man has poured his personal and group life. Around the universal activities of food-getting, propagation, child-rearing, have been developed modes of behavior, types of personal relationships, ideas of good and evil, religious beliefs, social organizations, economic and political mechanisms, that result in cultures with seemingly nothing in common.

Some cultures may organize their economic life on the basis of the individualism of the Eskimo or on the basis of the economic communalism of the Zuni. Kinship may be reckoned according to matrilineal or patrilineal lines. The family may be organized on the basis of the biological unit of parents and children, or on the system whereby a whole community constitutes the family group, or in such a way that the child looks to his mother's brother as his guardian and protector rather than his biological father. One folk may people the universe about them with malevolent spirits, another with benign spirits. Ethical codes may be set up that require the ruthless taking of human life, or that deem it an unpardonable sin, or as in our own society, that make the taking of human life at times sinful murder and at other times (in war) a glorious social deed.

One culture may make the generous bestowal of property upon others the means of social prestige, or as in our own society, prestige may depend upon the ability to accumulate and retain possessions. Some peoples may rear their children from the earliest age as a functioning part of the economic and social group, as among the Samoans; others may let them grow up almost completely outside the adult pattern, as among the Manus; or still others, like the Batciga, may let them create an organized "child society" of their own. For each item of social and personal relationships within any culture, other societies have erected not only contrasting and contradictory but almost incommensurable ideas and arrangements. Everything, from the structure of language or the ways of measuring time and indicating direction, to social and economic organizations or ethical and religious codes, will reveal this extraordinary capacity of the human race to create diverse cultures on the basis of the biological needs of the individual and the group.

In terms of the individual, this implies, of course, that his personality, his needs and aims, will be molded by the particular cultural group in which he has been reared.

Each culture tends to stimulate or nourish certain aspects of personality and to repress others. There would be a great difference in the resulting personality according to whether a particular human organism, whatever its innate tendencies, was born into a cultural pattern that values gentleness, moderation, and cooperativeness, or into a culture . that values aggressiveness, violence, and individualism. In one society the pugnacious, acquisitive man will be an admired leader; in another society he will be a misfit or an outcast. Everything from physical traits to the ability to dream dreams and see visions may receive different valuations in different cultures. An illustration of this from within our own cultural stream is the social value placed by medieval society upon the seers of visions as opposed to our present-day interpretation of them as abnormal. In other words, what is considered the approved or "normal" temperament or behavior in one culture, or even at one epoch in a civilization, may be disapproved of as abnormal in another.

The anthropological approach to the concept of normality is particularly useful to teachers of adolescents, since this is a problem that troubles many of them. Within the broad scale of temperaments and actions of which the human creature is potentially capable, different societies have placed the range of normality very differently. We especially need to recognize how powerful a hold the norms of our own group have on us. Whatever the concept of the normal, it is to a certain extent the result of historical causes, since ideas of normality have changed from country to country and from age to age. Therefore our own ideas of the normal have no particular divine sanction, but must be judged rationally by their social effects.

Teachers sometimes fear that such a sense of the cultural "relativity of norms" will be unsettling to the adolescent. Will he not feel that there are no standards—that anything, any kind of behavior, is "as good" as any other? This, of course, is an attitude that could only lead to moral and intellectual chaos, and should be carefully guarded against. Such a conclusion, however, can arise only out of a stress on one part of the anthropological facts. For if anthropology shows us the diversity of norms, it also shows us how closely personality and behavior are related to the whole framework of the culture.

The concept of the relativity of standards must be related to the anthropologists' emphasis on the need for seeing the culture as a whole. They warn against the tendency to think of different phases of society as distinct and unrelated. The ideas about physical beauty or attitudes toward property or the possession of intuitive powers in any one society will often tend to be colored by certain underlying drives, certain basic ways of envisioning human nature, certain values typical of the culture. Although it is unlikely that any culture is completely integrated, the elements of culture influence one another.

> All the miscellaneous behavior directed toward getting a living, mating, warring, and worshipping the gods, is made over into consistent patterns in accordance with unconscious canons of choice that develop within the culture. Some cultures, like some periods of art, fail of such integration, and about many others we know too little to understand the motives that actuate them. But cultures at every level of complexity, even the simplest, have achieved it.[5]

[5] Ruth Benedict, *Patterns of Culture* (Boston, Houghton Mifflin Company, 1934), p. 48.

Hence, we must not view in isolation any detail of behavior in our own or any other society but must study it against the background of the motives and emotions institutionalized in that culture. The individual will be liberated from blind subservience to the norms of his group, not by throwing overboard all standards, but by seeing them in relation to the whole complex of attitudes and values into which they fit.

Thus, it was not enough for women to resent the norms set up by the Victorian image of the submissive, self-effacing female. They had to learn in what ways this image was linked with economic dependence and the habits of mind derived from acceptance of political and intellectual authoritarianism. It is not enough for the artist to chafe at the indifference or scorn of the average American. When the artist sees that indifference as a corollary of the dominant emphasis upon practical action, he is ready to inquire into the historical sources and economic and social causes of these attitudes. The very fact that our society places such emphasis upon being an average "good fellow," the fact that so often our college professors consciously seek to look and talk like solid businessmen, the fact that we are so painfully aware of an unusual individuality in dress or belief, require similar explanation. How often is personality or achievement valued according to its translatability into terms of potential income? To what extent have these dominant attitudes been qualified during the past fifty years by recognition of contributions to general social welfare and by a growing emphasis on the value of every individual human being?

If we consider the norms concerning the relations between husband and wife, or parents and children, for example, we must again see how pervasive are the fundamental drives of our culture. The institution of the family, which concentrates within itself so many economic and social functions, will necessarily be affected by the emphasis on material possessions or the extent to which cooperation or rugged individualism is socially approved. Thus it is futile to discuss recent changes in family relations or to forecast their future development without considering recent economic and social changes or what possible direction our whole society will take. If we are going in the direction of greater valuation of individual personality, family relations will be very different from what they would be if we moved toward approval of conformity and the suppression of the individual. Labels such as "the organization man" and "the hippie" reflect current extremes.

Far from furthering the rejection of all standards, an understanding of cultural conditioning illuminates the intimate relation between individual lives and the whole social fabric. The adolescent is thus provided with a broader perspective from which to view his own struggle to conform to or to modify the dominant norms. He must live within the framework of our own culture, of course. But he need no longer give unthinking adherence to its images of success. Unthinking total rejection should also be seen as conformity, a conformity in reverse, so to speak.

The youth can be liberated from submission to standards that may be peculiar to the particular environment in which he finds himself. If he is brought up in some limited geographic or social setting, or if he is aware only of the most generally accepted standards, he may be equally in danger of too narrow a view. Our society is strikingly heterogeneous; a number of cultural subpatterns exist side by side. Ethnic, regional, and economic groups have developed very different images of the approved kinds of temperament, behavior, or social success. Often the individual born within one of these groups and measuring himself against its particular norms develops a feeling of inferiority which would disappear if he could become aware of the standards developed by other groups.

AS OUR SOCIETY DEMONSTRATES, the concept of cultural patterns and group norms does not rule out the possibility of individual differences within groups. Every society permits a certain degree of acceptable variation. Early childhood experiences and the particular society within which the individual finds himself set certain general patterns, but after all, the experience of no two people, not even of two children within the same family, is identical. That in itself, even without the factor of congenital differences, would lead us to expect a diversity of personalities.

The study of the influences acting on the individual is therefore also concerned with the attempt to see at what points or in what ways emotional and mental habits are set up and the personality becomes crystallized. Despite the original plasticity of the human creature, once the personality pattern is formed, there is a certain resistance to change. Present-day psychology considers early childhood the most important period in the formation of basic tendencies and mechanisms. The psychoanalytic school especially emphasizes this phase of the individual's development and considers that if any remolding of the personality is attempted, it is necessary to penetrate the deep strata of feeling and habit shaped by early experiences in the family. Other schools of psychology postulate that under favorable conditions the structure of personality can be decisively affected in adolescence and adulthood, although such conditions are more likely to occur in childhood. This theoretical position leads to methods of inducing change in personality different from the prolonged analyses carried on by the depth psychologists.

The study of personality should prevent us from falling into the view directly opposed to the voluntaristic one, but equally erroneous: namely, that the individual is merely a kind of automaton entirely at the mercy of external pressures. Too often the youth is given only one side of the picture. He is encouraged to think of man either as an entirely free agent or as the helpless pawn in a completely deterministic system.

The concept of cultural conditioning in no way implies a fatalistic notion that man is a puppet in the hands of some mythical, external power called the "environment" or the "culture." Rather, the anthropologists view the human organism as interacting with the cultural environment. Every child is born into some kind of social environment, and this immediately exerts a patterning influence. But the individual in turn reacts upon the physical and cultural environment and hence influences it in some manner. The process of conscious cultural change can be conceived in such terms. The more conscious the individual is of the nature of the cultural forces with which he is interacting, the more intelligently can he accept or resist them, and the more intelligently can he modify their power and their direction.[6]

The influence of the cultural environment can be envisioned as setting the broad limits within which the individual can develop and within which he has freedom of choice. This may apply to choices permitted by his physical and temperamental development. It may apply to such choices as whether or not he will read a new book and whether or not he will attempt to change the surrounding society through the advocacy of new laws. In other words, in terms of his own temperamental bent, he can accept or resist environmental pressures and can choose one line of behavior rather than another.

The more unthinkingly and mechanically the human being follows the patterns set for him by his environment, the nearer he approaches the state of the automaton. If the individual understands the important molding influences in his own past and in the history of mankind, if he becomes aware of alternative social patterns or of alternative types of happiness, he will be better able to make choices, to dominate, and if necessary, to remold his environment. Thus he will be in a position to exercise his

[6] The psychoanalysts utilize the same principle in their technique of helping the individual to gain insight into the nature and influence of his past experiences. When these are brought into his consciousness and their relation to his present anxieties and obsessions is understood, he becomes capable of dealing with them rationally, and is thus enabled to remold or readjust his personality. (This analogy was pointed out by Lawrence K. Frank in a letter to the writer.)

Other schools of psychology have applied this principle in the development of different techniques, e.g., David C. McClelland's work in achievement motivation.

"will" and to consciously influence his own future and the future of the society about him.

The anthropologist and the psychologist offer a critical approach to another widespread tendency: to accept the familiar or the traditional as possessing a fundamental rightness and, conversely, to consider the strange and the unfamiliar as necessarily inferior or reprehensible. Since the individual unconsciously absorbs the particular modes of behavior, views of human nature, and ideas about socio-economic arrangements, of the culture into which he is born, he takes them for granted and often cannot even imagine any possible alternatives or variations. Hence, when he does encounter another cultural pattern, as when the white man comes into contact with the African or the Samoan, he tends to look upon it as inferior. An extreme illustration of this is the fact that many primitive peoples have as the name for their cultural group only the word in their language that signifies "human being." Any who do not belong to their cultural group automatically fall outside that category.

The anthropologist helps us to realize that merely because we have grown up in a particular cultural pattern, we have no legitimate basis for considering it, *ipso facto,* the only possible, or even best possible, pattern. Much is to be gained from the knowledge that other cultures have developed working alternatives to the customs and institutions with which we are familiar. Similarly, we can compare the ethical and social ideals of our culture with those created by other cultures or other possible cultures.

Different societies, then, set up different images of the

most highly desirable human satisfactions—as in the contrast cited above between those valuing violent competitive behavior and those valuing peaceful cooperation. Societies also differ in the degree to which their various institutions and customs make the valued satisfactions either more or less easily attainable. Sometimes there is a decided discrepancy between those two aspects of a culture. An example is the gradual elimination of such a discrepancy from our own society during the past few generations: sexual experience was valued, yet a frustrating atmosphere of guilt or shame was cast about it. The satisfaction of this strong culturally reinforced need is more and more being freed from culturally imposed feelings of guilt or shame. Another example from our own society: individual self-determination, freedom of thought and speech, and self-respect are values that have received cultural sanction and have therefore become needs for which the individual craves satisfaction. Our political institutions were designed to fulfill them, but in the lives of many people conditions tended to frustrate these demands. Government has played an increasing role in fostering economic and social changes designed to narrow this gap between ideal and reality. The civil rights movement comes as the culmination of a whole series of steps in this direction. That this struggle has not been immediately successful, and that unremitting effort will be needed to bring lasting results, does not contradict the fact of a great shift in institutionalized attitudes and expectations.

We can judge the society about us, then, in terms of the kinds of basic satisfactions it values and the degree to which it permits or stifles the attainment of those satisfactions. Self-consciousness about our cultural pattern means that we no longer need accept it as unthinkingly as the air we breathe. Probably more than any other cultural group before, we have the knowledge to consciously influence the future development of our customs and institutions.

The concept of the cultural pattern can also counteract the tendency to look upon different phases of the society or different groups as distinct and unrelated. In so complex a civilization as ours, anything affecting one element in it—whether that be a geographic or economic section, an ethnic minority, or a particular category such as women or coal miners—will tend to have repercussions upon the rest of society.[7]

This view of the interaction between different aspects of the culture has been given a special interpretation by those who believe that man's economic life—his particular methods of food-getting, manufacture, distribution of goods, and property regulation—tends to determine the nature of all the other aspects of his life, such as social

---

[7] The concept of the cultural pattern is particularly rich in implications for the study of literature. Through literature we are constantly coming into contact with cultural patterns of the past or of other societies. Often, literature gives clear expression to the characteristic ways of feeling, the types of temperament and behavior valued by the society as a whole. It would be unfortunate if, in the study of literature, the student were permitted to forget that man's life is lived in a web of crosscurrents that tend to take on a basic pattern. Literature itself cannot be viewed in isolation from other aspects of man's activity in society. Moreover, the particular images of life presented in literature should be approached with a sense of the complexity of man's life and an awareness of its tendency to reflect some dominant pattern. These questions will be discussed more fully in Chapter 8.

organization, religion, and art. Although this theory of economic determinism has often been applied in a crudely oversimplified way by the "economic determinists," the economic factor is generally recognized by social scientists. The distribution of wealth among various classes in a society, for example, affects a great many different phases of life. Thus, even in the history of literature, it surely was not an accident that the type of fiction represented by the novels of Richardson, Fielding, and their literary descendants began to flourish at the time when the middle class in England was attaining increasing economic power. Moreover, the particular economic group from which a writer springs surely plays some part in his view of life, his sense of values, and his particular choice of subjects. The teacher of literature, like any other student of the products of man's social life, cannot ignore economic influences.

THE PRECEDING PAGES have sketched only a few of the topics that enter into the problem of the patterning of human personality and human society. A great many subjects and considerations that are live concerns of present-day social scientists have not even been broached. In psychology, for instance, a center of much illumination and controversy, psychoanalytic theories concerning the role of unconscious processes and the ways in which they find expression have only been touched upon. Numerous other omissions can be listed: in anthropology, the studies that undermine belief in racial superiority or inferiority, or the problems involved in understanding cultural contact and change; in sociology, studies of the results of increasing industrialization and urbanization; in economics, the development of a "welfare capitalism" and the elimination of the cyclic nature of unregulated competitive enterprise.

The discussion may suffice at least to suggest the general way in which an acquaintance with certain basic concepts in psychology, sociology, and anthropology have a direct bearing upon the subject of human personality and conduct—a subject that is an integral part of any consideration of literature. Such a structure of ideas should make it possible to turn to the literature of other ages and other societies with an open mind, and to look upon the expressions of our own world with critical freedom.

It is not surprising that the older approaches to human nature and society tend to persist. Even those who have come into contact with the newer theories often fail to assimilate them into their attitudes in actual life, and in their personal relationships are still dominated by automatically absorbed prejudices and expectations. Marriage consultants, for instance, reveal that often relationships are shattered by the inability of each of the partners to recognize the causes of the behavior they dislike. The reaction is entirely one of rejection and blame. There is no sense that behavior grows out of a complex network of factors, some of them environmental, some physical, and some the result of emotional attitudes and habits whose source is in the early psychic frustrations of the individual. Each spouse also fails to understand his own motivations and to see that perhaps his own resentments and irritations may be due to certain factors in his environment or past history which have no validity in themselves. An attempt to understand the possible origins of the disapproved behavior may lead to modification of these causes;

a changed external situation and temperamental readjustments may be brought about.

Contemporary behavioral scientists have substituted for the older, voluntaristic approach the effort to understand the factors that generate behavior. Given such habits of mind, the possibility of the adjustment of personalities to one another is greatly enhanced. Such an approach might also tend to prevent people from entering into relationships in which there were fundamental elements that would probably lead to misunderstanding and maladjustment.

During the past quarter-century, many of the concepts presented in these pages have received wide currency in college courses, in newspaper columns on child-rearing, and in legal judgments and actions. On all sides, nevertheless, the student is still being bombarded with expressions of the old approach to people and affairs. In the mass media, in our governmental practices, in our law courts, and above all, in the average home itself, this view often prevails. Hence, it is particularly important that any phase of the student's educational experience concerned with human relations should responsibly present attitudes growing out of the newer approaches to personality. The potential influence of the teacher of English is therefore considerable. Only if the teacher is himself imbued with a more reasoned approach to human personality and society, will he be able to help the student build the attitudes toward people that the psychologists and others concerned with mental health have demonstrated to be most constructive. Instead of the old defeatist notion that "human nature is what it is and will never be changed," there should arise the vision of human beings as responding to many forces that can be modified and directed.

The view that insights offered by the social sciences may lead to more successful living or to a redirection of life or a remolding of society, immediately raises the problem of values. For as both the moralists and the opponents of science are eager to remind us, science may give us the facts, but it cannot give us the standards of what is desirable or undesirable, good or evil. Indeed, long before the invention of nuclear bombs, it was clear that the use of scientific knowledge could raise crucial moral questions. A lesser illustration is the application of psychological knowledge to advertising that creates a demand for useless or harmful things.

The social sciences, then, are slowly building up a body of knowledge concerning important factors in the development of human personality and in the patterning of human society. But where shall we turn for some scale of values that will help us to judge what kinds of personality and what kind of society are desirable?

This problem does not consciously present itself to great masses of people (and they include many of the "educated"). They have unthinkingly acquired from the cultural atmosphere their ideas concerning desirable and undesirable ends, moral or immoral acts, acceptable or unacceptable social arrangements. In other words, they are completely guided by the dominant system of values assimilated from their environment. Almost automatically they have at their disposal a yardstick by which to measure their own and others' conduct and a basis for rejecting personal or general social arrangements that deviate from the customary.

Such unthinking acceptance of any system of values is undesirable. The anthropologist, the historian, and the sociologist (as well as the philosopher) point out that many alternative systems of values are possible. This constitutes a challenge to inquire objectively into the varying effects of these different social and moral codes upon the human beings whose lives they regulate.

Those who find the task of working out their own philosophy too difficult, or are not sufficiently mature to assume the responsibility for their own choice of goals and moral code, turn to authority—to some institution such as a church or to an individual such as a dictator. Comfortable as throwing off the burden of decision might seem to be, the social sciences reveal that institutions often tend merely to reinforce and crystallize the particular customs and traditional values built up by the past. They are not necessarily safe guides in a changing world. In fact, historically they often seem to stand in the way of any adjustment of old values to new conditions. Hence, a blind following of their postulates may lead to painful maladjustment and conflict, and perhaps defeat the very ends of human happiness or social peace for which they first were formulated. Within such institutions today, as, for instance, in the churches and the educational enterprise, there are individuals with sufficient perspective to question whether the traditionally perpetuated codes and practices are relevant to changed conditions.

A sound system of values must guide the search for a

more adequate moral code and social philosophy. The students of other societies will give us information about the personality types, the social institutions, that other cultural groups may have developed. The historians of philosophy will explain to us the various value systems that men have applied in the past or in the present age. And today's social philosophers will be suggesting new guidelines. Our ultimate choice will be influenced by all these, particularly by the philosophies that have directly contributed to our own cultural stream. Certainly, present-day attempts to solve this problem of values would be very different if the Greek and the Judeo-Christian philosophies and the ethical theories developed under feudal and capitalistic social organizations were not part of our cultural heritage. The individual will thus have available alternative schemes of value which his own culture has produced, and he may sometimes seek to import a hierarchy of values derived from another culture. The very fact that he reacts forcibly against some of the points of view in his own society may lead him to emphasize those values and ideals that they neglect. The current interest in Oriental thought—in, for instance, Zen Buddhism—suggests such a quest for alternative possibilities.

One basic value judgment has been implied throughout this discussion: Any system of values can be scrutinized in terms of its consequences for human life. Any form of conduct, any social mechanism, any custom or institution, should be measured in terms of its actual effect on the individual personalities that make up the society. To use the culturally sanctioned terminology, every human being is entitled to "life, liberty, and the pursuit of happiness."

This means that the human being is recognized as having value in himself and that anything which reduces him to the status of a thing, instrument, or automaton is condemned. It sets up as an ideal the social situation in which each member of society is given the opportunity for the greatest fulfillment of those culturally valued satisfactions of which he is potentially capable. The corollary of this is that if a conflict of interest should arise, no individual and no group would be justified in gaining their own satisfactions through exploitation of any other individuals or groups.

This rests upon belief in the fundamental dignity and worth of the human being. It sets up the well-being and fulfillment of the individual in opposition to any abstractions for which might be claimed a superior reality or value such as the Elect, the Supermen, the Proletariat, the Nation, the Race, or the State. This basic postulate of value is obviously one that receives support from many elements present in our cultural heritage. Implicit in various religious philosophies and in the democratic philosophy, it applies not only to our political but also to our social and economic life.

This fundamental principle provides a measure for individual lives, as well as the customs and institutions, the ideas and assumptions that make up our culture. It provides a standard, too, for utilizing and applying the knowledge that the scientists are so laboriously cooperating to acquire. Often, only the scientist can tell us what is best for man's physical and mental health. The sciences that propose to study man as a biological organism and as a social creature are slowly becoming aware of their common function, their responsibility to contribute to this core of knowledge about the factors that enter into the creation of freely and fully functioning human beings. Thus the physician finds that he cannot think of man as a biological organism in a vacuum but must concern himself with the particular social and economic setting within which that biological organism functions. The sociologist, studying man's behavior under the varying conditions created by our social and economic system, can provide information to be judged in terms of successful or unsuccessful human lives. The psychologists are increasingly aware of the fact that psychology of the individual is part of what is known as social psychology. Various specialists in the field of mental hygiene have already reached the point of being dissatisfied to merely readjust scattered individuals among the increasing numbers who are known to be suffering from nervous maladjustment and disorder. On the basis of psychiatric study of these individuals, experts will be better and better able to tell us at what points our particular cultural pattern sets up deep psychic disturbances or stifles and condemns fundamental human drives. In the field of psychology, too, preventative therapy will develop a body of information by which we can apply the basic value judgment indicated above. We shall probably be increasingly able to judge the degree to which any particular cultural pattern satisfies the requirement that it permit the greatest possible fulfillment and enrichment of human lives. Then, too, economists are studying the functioning of methods of production and distribution and of regulations concerning property in various societies, so that these practices may be judged by the standard of the maximum social welfare.

Those who are principally students or practitioners of an art, such as literature, can also place their knowledge and interests within the context of this broader system of values. Surely it is hardly necessary to speak of the joy of artistic activity and the satisfactions of the experience of art. Moreover, the artist can tell us much about man himself. Many of the subtler potentialities of human feelings and behavior that could have been given common utterance in no other way are revealed and embodied in artistic form.

The fundamental values of democracy, the criteria of the dignity and the worth of the human being, require the corollary of freedom for the artist. For not only does the artist give expression to innumerable facets of the life about him. He also has served an important function by recalling his fellowmen to a sense of basic human needs when they forgot them under the sway of destructive symbols and slogans or the compulsion of materialistic ambitions. The opportunity for this kind of activity, at once creative and critical, is essential. Equally essential is freedom for youth—and indeed all citizens—to experience those works of art that reveal weaknesses in the contemporary world or that create a vision of greater fulfillment of human values.

YET IT MAY BE ASKED, why should the school or college be concerned with the development of emotional attitudes or with preparing the student for his personal as well as his broader social relationships? Are there not many other social agencies concerned with precisely these problems? Indeed, has not the importance of the family and community environment just been pointed out? Why then place this additional burden upon the school, which in our society already has so large a task in giving information and developing skills? Why, above all, involve literature, which offers experiences that would be precious in themselves even if they had no further practical justification?

The answer is that the generations of young people now in school and college will have to meet conditions and problems very different from those their parents and grandparents faced. During periods of relative stability or extremely slow social change, the home and the community could be relied upon to furnish the emotional conditioning and attitudes that would automatically fit the kind of society the child was eventually to enter. At no time, of course, has the school been entirely free from the responsibility of influencing character and mental habits. In a stable society, however, that influence would principally be a reinforcement of attitudes acquired by the child outside the school.

Present-day conditions no longer automatically provide the youth with the habits of mind and images of behavior that will be appropriate to future social conditions. The development of an urban industrial society, with all its changes in technology, and the emergence of the "one world" of the "space age" have produced a welter of new relationships and new images of the values to be sought for. The multiplicity of alternative choices in personal relations and social philosophy is particularly characteristic of American society. The old habitual responses, the old images of what is to be taken for granted in relations between people, can no longer be followed unquestioningly. Many of the old attitudes continue, of course, to be valid. No matter how drastic and revolutionary social change may seem, the anthropologist and the historian will remind us that the new elements are infinitesimal in comparison with the mass of cultural attitudes that persist. Nevertheless, failure to cope emotionally and intellectually with the changing political, economic, and social situation can produce much unhappiness and frustration. In a world of such vast technological change, of such a desperate sense of international tensions, the individual needs to build for himself a mental and emotional base from which to meet the fluctuating currents about him.

Since the old attitudes, the old habits of response, the old goals and images of success can no longer be automatically relied upon, youth are increasingly plunged into an unprecedented self-consciousness in the choice of their patterns of life. They must be prepared to test and perhaps to modify the emotional responses their childhood environment transmits to them from the past. The home and the community, whose educational influence operates principally in undirected and unconscious ways, are being called upon to contribute to such flexibility but cannot be expected to do this alone. The school, also, must step in to deliberately provide preparation for the unpredictable future.

Because in so many areas old patterns have crumbled and no clearly defined new patterns have crystallized, young people more than ever before must be sufficiently mature to assume responsibility for making their own judgments and working out their own solutions. The concept of "maturity" is stressed in the disciplines concerned with mental health. They see in our failure to develop a population of mature, self-reliant individuals the explanation of much of the unhappiness, the frustrations, the cruelties, often characteristic of personal relationships in our society. The same lack of emotional maturity explains many of the weaknesses in the functioning of our democratic system of government. The individual who is still in the infantile state of needing an outside authority to make his decisions for him cannot be expected to participate constructively in the creation of a rational society.

The concept of emotional security is closely related to this problem of maturity. Because the surrounding intellectual and social atmosphere is in such a state of flux, the youth needs help in attaining his own intellectual and emotional base. The aim of providing employment and economic security for all, and hence eliminating one great source of insecurity, no longer seems visionary.

But there is another source of security that each individual in our culture should be able to draw upon. This, the behavioral scientists tell us, depends very much on childhood experiences. If the child has been given a feeling of being wanted and loved, if he has been able to feel that he is an accepted member of the family and social group, he will tend to develop the kind of inner security that will enable him to meet constructively much of the external insecurity and struggle of later life. The less he is given assurance of affection and concern, the less strength of character and sense of self-esteem he is likely to develop. These insecurities will color his approach to the people and the world about him. The feeling of being worthless or inadequate or unloved may express itself in hostility to others and in the resort to physical force as a way of meeting the threat of life. So far as present studies indicate, the most important factor seems to be the degree of warmth experienced by the child, rather than any particular techniques of child training.

During the past quarter-century, many parents and teachers have been made intensely aware of the far-reaching influence they can have on the child's personality development. They recognize that he should not be made to feel guilty because he is a child and therefore cannot always live up to adult demands. Life should not be for him a formidable series of rules and prohibitions against which he is naturally a sinner. Throughout the whole course of his home and school life, he should be given the feeling that he is a person worthy of consideration. As in so many instances, the reaction against earlier authoritarianism and rigidity has sometimes led to what is now considered an excessive permissiveness. Evidence seems to suggest that the absence of rigid controls is not in itself enough. For example, inconsistency in the demands made on the child by different parents, or by the home and the school, may be a more important factor than the degree of authority or permissiveness.

Problems of maturity and mental security—much too complex to be adequately treated here—ultimately involve our whole economic and social setup, as well as the methods of child-rearing in the home and the fundamental characteristics of our educational system. A recognition of the importance of these problems strengthens one of the main ideas upon which the foregoing chapters have been based: that although the school should not force upon the student subject matter and materials beyond his intellectual and emotional level of comprehension, it should permit him to function at his fullest emotional and intellectual capacity.

Particularly in the adolescent years, students are often confined to too childish a plane of thought and feeling. They too frequently are encouraged to passively accept what the teacher wishes them to think and feel, without becoming aware of themselves as personalities with definite patterns of their own. The emphasis in earlier chapters on the importance of the personal relationship between the student and the literary work, which grew out of an attempt to understand the literary experience realistically, can be related to this broader concern with the need for fostering the individual's attainment of greater maturity.

American society today—often with too-unquestioning cooperation of school and university—is increasing its demands on youth, "accelerating" the educational pace, and extending the number of years of preparation for adulthood and career. Much effort, often successful, is being expended on tapping the latent intellectual potentialities of children and youth. But there is a glaring lack of general concern, to say nothing of concerted efforts, to provide the basis for an equally successful emotional life. Both in the preadolescent and adolescent years, an emphasis on emotional development should parallel the current emphasis on the intellectual. Here literature and the other arts can make an important contribution.

Such pressures and overintellectualized demands on the post-Sputnik generation have had repercussions in the extreme reactions of some and in the sense of disorientation of many. It is sheer abdication of responsibility on the part of the older generation, for example, either to ignore or to condemn adolescent efforts to discover for themselves the meaning of sex and love—efforts necessarily confused and often self-defeating in a world that offers no clearly defined satisfactory patterns and assumes that an emotional life can be postponed as easily as a profession or a career. The social scientists—the historian, the sociologist, the economist, the psychologist—deal with subjects about which cling strongly emotional, culturally transmitted attitudes. Political and economic questions, topics involving racial or national prejudices, or such matters as the relations between parents and children, or husband and wife, almost automatically arouse strong feeling. The social scientist must therefore clear the ground for rational discussion by first eliminating or reducing any prejudices or fixed emotional attitudes that may obscure a clear view of the facts. He has striven for unemotional treatment of these explosive subjects. The general effect has been to "de-emotionalize" not only the scholarly investigations in the social sciences but also the teaching in those fields.

To bring the student under the dominance of the scientific spirit is a most valid aim. The means by which this is to be accomplished is another matter. One may question whether plunging the student at once into abstract considerations of generalized social conditions and problems is the best way to lead him to adopt a scientific approach to individual life and to society. May this not strengthen the tendency to deal with words as empty counters, to brush lightly over their surface meanings without any vivid perception of the actual material and emotional elements to which they point? This abstracting, generalizing, and devivifying tendency will not be counteracted by the type of materials usual in social science courses. In reading his psychology textbooks, for instance, the student may tend to dissociate theories or phenomena from the thought of actual human beings. In his history classes, mass movements and national changes may be thought of without ever translating them into terms of the individual human lives that made up these vast historical sums. The information drawn from sociology and economics courses may also be kept on the plane of the general and the impersonal.[8]

If the purpose of the social science courses in high school and in college were solely to give information, complete objectivity might be an end in itself. The teaching of such courses, however, seems to imply a more practical aim than information for its own sake. The assumption seems

---

[8] This tendency to deal with abstractions called "social forces" apart from any sense of the human beings who embody these forces may explain why so many adolescents seem to have derived only a pessimistic view of the individual and society from their social studies. They have developed the feeling that the individual is merely an impotent puppet at the mercy of inexorable "forces." This result might largely be averted through a more human presentation of social theory. This is an illustration of the extent to which the so-called form in which ideas are presented actually determines the meaning that they will have for the student.

to be that such understanding will enable students to handle better their own observations and experiences. Should it not be assumed that a comprehension of the forces at work in society may help them to play a more socially useful role? Therefore, without abandoning the emphasis on objective scientific knowledge, the educator still has to inquire whether such understanding is being conveyed in a form that will affect social attitudes and influence social behavior.

The aim, surely, is to enable the student to make intelligent judgments. In the choices open to him, he needs to be guided not by the blind reflex of unconsciously absorbed prejudices but by ideas based on scientifically valid facts. Can the unemotional, impersonal recital of facts and the objective scientific analysis of problems be counted on in themselves to give the youth the power of rational choice? Will the information thus acquired outweigh the force of irrational attitudes absorbed from the lagging social atmosphere? In its simplest terms, the question is: Will this objective knowledge affect his actions, inside and outside the school today, and will it influence his actions in later adult life as a member of a family and as a member of a national and world community?

Investigations of changes in attitude resulting, for example, from courses in the social sciences have usually proved nothing more than that the students changed their articulate opinions. They no longer echoed jingoistic sentiments but approved international cooperation; they advocated racial tolerance; they rejected the "devil take the hindmost" theory in favor of the idea of community responsibility. Whether these opinions had struck deep enough to affect emotional response and actual conduct under the pressure of practical circumstances is a highly debatable matter and a question seldom investigated.

Impersonally presented information, thoroughly understood, may influence behavior. For one thing, there are individuals who respond most readily to abstract ideas. Yet, even in this case, those abstract ideas are practically worthless unless the student is led to recognize their application to specific, concrete situations. The fact remains that the influence of this type of impersonal, theoretical instruction is not as obviously visible or as profound as one might hope. How often even high school and college graduates seem unable to resist the pull of disingenuous slogans, specious appeals to emotion, or the contagion of mob hysteria!

It must not be forgotten that the student—no matter whether he is a young child or a college boy soon to enter adult life—is already functioning in society. He has to make choices; he must set up goals for himself in his daily life; he must develop a sense of values. And these demands he will continue to meet throughout his life. The pressure of actual living does not permit prolonged meditation and analysis in precisely those person-to-person and general social situations where such reflection is most needed. Hence, in moments of indecision the emotionally rooted attitudes come to the surface to guide behavior.

The young man in school or at college may have become thoroughly acquainted in his courses in history or sociology with, for instance, the more modern ideas concerning woman's potential equality with man. He may even have become convinced of the desirability of the new ideal of marriage as a partnership and a mutual give-and-take, in which sometimes one and sometimes the other will be dependent or dominant. The success with which he carries out his program for a modern marriage, however, will largely depend on the degree to which these intellectual convictions have been translated into emotional attitudes and have displaced the old automatic sets. Probably, from his family background and many other sources in the society about him, he would earlier have absorbed the image of woman as weaker, more dependent, more emotional than man. He is still being indoctrinated with this image daily in the society about him. If these older, deeply ingrained images still persist, he will unconsciously demand those qualities from the women with whom he comes in contact. He may often find himself irritated at the absence of the conventional feminine qualities in his mate. Particularly in moments of tension, the older, culturally weighted attitudes will tend to assert themselves. He may find himself seeking the sense of dominance and superiority associated with the early acquired image of the husband.

When such moments of conflict and irritation arise, they can be handled successfully only if he and his wife are able to recognize his reaction as the irrational following of deeply grooved patterns which may no longer be justifiable. In order to overcome this, he must possess some strong emotional impulsion toward achieving the kind of marriage that his reason approves.

The gap between the individual's intellectual perceptions on the one hand and his emotional attitudes on the other must be bridged. If such a linkage of opinion with

the emotional springs of action does not occur, there are
two dangers. First, in moments of crisis the individual may
be dominated, not by his rationally worked out opinions,
but by the no longer appropriate attitudes absorbed from
his childhood environment. Or, if the critical point of view
has succeeded in breaking down the old attitude, he may
be capable of only a negative approach to the situation.
To revert to the illustration, the family: Have we not all
encountered the "emancipated" man or woman, whose
only attitude toward marriage was a sense of all the things
it must *not* be?

The objective study of man in society should do more
than illustrate the absence of a valid basis for many of the
attitudes and images surviving from former social conditions.   There should also be provided a valid emotional
basis upon which to build more appropriate and more successful patterns of thought and behavior. Only then can
we hope that the present knowledge concerning man and
society will bear fruit in more rational social development
and in happier, more complete human beings.

This phase of the problem, the transmutation of scientific knowledge and critical opinion into emotional attitudes
guiding behavior, has usually been either neglected or
evaded by the social science teacher as well as by the
others. Obviously it offers difficulties and even some possibilities of abuse. Yet to go on blithely with objective "de-
emotionalized" procedures is a betrayal of the practical
value of social understanding. The young boy or girl still
under the sway of anachronistic compulsions will be
a ready victim of the emotional appeals made by less
scrupulous, less disinterested social agencies, such as the

biased press or partisan groups. The cause of youth's confusion and sense of futility today is often that they recognize the inadequacy of the old images and yet lack any clearly felt emotional drive toward new choices and new patterns of behavior. The quest for new images and social goals must be given sufficient emotional sanction to carry the younger generations through to a more successful solution of their problems.

EDUCATION IN THIS ERA of social transformation must serve both critical and constructive ends. On the one hand, youth need the knowledge and the intellectual tools required for objective appraisal of ideals and social mechanisms—new and old. On the other hand, youth need to develop positive emotional drives that will quicken intellectual insight. Thus they will be enabled to free themselves from antisocial attitudes and will be impelled to achieve a world that will safeguard human values.

Teachers of literature share these responsibilities with all others in the educational enterprise. The theory of literary experience presented earlier explains why the literature classroom can serve these broader aims while fulfilling its esthetic purposes. The following chapters will consider some of the ways in which this can be accomplished.

Personality

LITERARY MATERIALS—the poem, the short story, the novel, the drama, and by extension, the motion picture and television—can contribute powerfully to both phases of the twofold educational process that we have outlined. Contemporary psychology encourages the belief that "the really important things in the education of youth cannot be taught in the formal didactic manner; they are things which are experienced, absorbed, accepted, incorporated into the personality through emotional and esthetic experiences."[1]

Of all the elements that enter into the educational process—except, of course, the actual personal relationships and activities which make up the community life of the school—literature possesses the greatest potential for that kind of assimilation of ideas and attitudes. For literature

[1] Lawrence K. Frank, "Some Aspects of Education for Home and Family Life," *Journal of Home Economics*, Vol. 23, No. 3 (March 1931), p. 214.

enables the youth to "live through"—and to reflect on—
much that in abstract terms would be meaningless to him.
He comes to know intimately, more intimately perhaps
than would be possible in actual life, many personalities.
He vicariously shares their struggles and perplexities and
achievements. He becomes a part of strange environments,
or he sees with new emotions the conditions and the lives
about him. And these vicarious experiences have at least
something of the warmth and color and immediacy of life.

Any insight or clarification the youth derives from the
literary work will grow out of its relevance to certain
facets of his emotional or intellectual nature. The whole
personality tends to become involved in the literary experience. That a literary work may bring into play and
be related to profoundly personal needs and preoccupations makes it a powerful potential educational force. For
it is out of these basic needs and attitudes that behavior
springs. Hence, literature can foster the linkage between
intellectual perception and emotional drive that is
essential to any vital learning process.

The criterion for judging the success of any educational
process must be its effect on the actual life of the student;
its ultimate value depends on its assimilation into the very
marrow of personality. What, then, are the results in terms
of personality and behavior to be expected from the kind
of literary experience and training that has been defined
as desirable?

This question will be answered first in the light of the
individual student's relation to books. The present chapter
will thus deal with the potential influence on personality
inherent in literary experiences themselves. Chapter 8 will

then apply this question to the type of literature study outlined in the first half of this book Both of these chapters will reflect the view of personality development sketched in the preceding chapter and will indicate how an awareness of the suggested approach to human relations may grow out of the experience and study of literature.

We are now venturing on ground that is thorny with unexplored difficulties. Much emotion has been expended upon this problem of the influence of literature, but little careful or controlled study has been made of it. The following discussion is offered principally for the purpose of focusing attention on this extremely important problem. The aim is to arouse an increased awareness of some of the elements that enter into this question, rather than to suggest a set of neat formulas. As teachers themselves become aware of the dynamic and complex nature of the literary experience, and as students of literature give it added attention, a body of more accurate information on this phase of the problem will slowly be built up.

If we keep this view of the interaction between the individual mind and the literary work in the center of our attention, we shall not be misled into thinking that only books read in the most solemn and pedantic manner will have an influence. The power of literature to offer entertainment and recreation is, despite the pedants and moralists, still its prime reason for survival. Books read solely for entertainment satisfy, after all, definite needs and answer definite preoccupations. Such works have therefore a potential capacity to influence the reader's personality and behavior, perhaps even more than those he may read in the course of the school routine. The discussion that follows envisages any writings that elicit a vivid personal response from the young reader.

PROLONGED CONTACT WITH LITERATURE may result in increased social sensitivity. Through poems and stories and plays, the child becomes aware of the personalities of different kinds of people. He learns to imaginatively "put himself into the place of the other fellow." He becomes better able to foresee the possible repercussions of his own actions in the life of others. In his daily relations with other people, such sensitivity is precious. Through literature the individual may develop the habit of sensing the subtle interactions of temperament upon temperament; he may come to understand the needs and aspirations of others; and he may thus make more successful adjustments in his daily relations with them.

This increased ability to imagine the human implications of any situation is just as important for the individual in his broader political and social relationships. Many political blunders or social injustices seem to be the result not so much of maliciousness or conscious cruelty as of the inability of citizens to translate into human terms the laws or political platforms they support. Political slogans tend to take on an emotional coerciveness regardless of their human implications. Whole nations have been, and indeed are today, so dominated by such dogma in their political and social life that they follow its dictates no matter how disastrous the consequences to themselves or others. A democratic society, whose institutions and political and economic procedures are constantly being developed and remolded, needs citizens with the imagination to see what political doctrines mean for human beings.

It has been said that if our imaginations functioned actively, nowhere in the world would there be a child who was starving. Our vicarious suffering would force us to do something to alleviate it. The reading of the morning newspaper with its accounts, say, of war, famine, the suppression of human freedoms, the death of scores of people here and there in automobile accidents, may take place with hardly an emotional quiver on the reader's part. He registers only the abstract sense of the words and may never even glimpse what they mean in actual human experience. This habit of mind has its immediate value, of course, as a form of self-protection. Yet this callous shell is there to be dealt with in any attempt to inculcate new understanding and new attitudes. Because of the reluctance of the average mind to make this translation into human terms, the teacher must at times feel the responsibility for stimulating it.

Many young people today seem to have withdrawn into some such defensive attitude of callousness. Not to feel anything very deeply, not to care about anything too much, is one way of dulling the effect of quite possible defeat or disillusionment. In a highly competitive world, it also seems necessary not to think too much about the feelings and needs of others. The way the youth in many countries has lent itself to a philosophy of force and brutal sadism is proof of the great social dangers inherent in that kind of disillusioned cynicism and flight from altruistic feeling. The totalitarian ideologies capitalize on this when they callously preach that their ends justify any means, no matter how brutal.

Lack of such imaginative sympathy is probably back of many of our present-day difficulties. No matter whether the problem is just distribution of taxation or universal civil rights or federal-state relations, the basis of any ultimate decision should be its meaning for actual human lives. It is easy enough to understand the possible effect of a point of view upon ourselves and upon the human beings with whom we feel the kinship of family, class, nation, or race. We must also develop the capacity to feel intensely the needs and sufferings and aspirations of people whose personal interests are distinct from our own, people with whom we may have no bond other than our common humanity.

If there has been any "progress" during the past few centuries, it has fundamentally resulted from a certain extension of this kind of imagination. For is not "humanitarianism" ultimately the result of this sense of the prime importance of the human being, based on the ability to transcend selfish interests and to feel the needs of others? Despite the horrible persistence of war, the record shows an extension of increasingly humane social practices.

It would be absurd to suggest that literature was the cause of this (*Oliver Twist* and *Uncle Tom's Cabin* notwithstanding!), for the writing of such works was in itself the result of social conditions conducive to increased humanitarianism. Yet it can be maintained that literature undoubtedly contributes to the diffusion of more humane sentiment. And this applies not only to works like *Oliver*

Twist that preach such sensitivity but also to works written without propagandistic social or moral aims. The ability to enter vicariously into the experience of others can be fostered by a great many different kinds of literary experience.

Constant reading of a wide range of literature may in itself, without any contribution from the teacher, tend to develop social sensitivity. The teacher, however, can have an influence: he can help the student retain his living sense of the experiences through which he has just passed or, by pedantic "literature study," lead him to dismiss them as unimportant. By helping to focus the student's attention upon the actual emotions through which he has entered into the lives of others, the teacher can reinforce the power of literature to develop social imagination. Hence, in attempting to foster a vital personal relationship between the student and the literary work, the teacher will also be making an important social contribution.

LITERATURE CAN PLAY an important part in the process through which the individual becomes assimilated into the cultural pattern. Just as the young child and the adolescent acquire images of behavior and ways of thinking and feeling from the actions and lives of the people about them, so they may assimilate such images from the experience offered by books—from sharing the emotions and ideas of the poet, from participating in the lives of the people created by the novelist, the dramatist, or the biographer. The child and the adolescent often learn from books the culturally appropriate emotional response to types of situations or people (cf. p. 90). Similarly, they may absorb from their reading ideas concerning the kinds of behavior or types of achievement to be valued, and they may acquire the moral standards to be followed under various circumstances.

Undoubtedly, the human influences encountered in the family, the school, and the community tend to be the most powerful and lasting. In recent years, however, it has been increasingly recognized that television, the radio, the motion picture, the newspaper, and the literary work often take their place beside other social agencies in the important task of molding the individual. Probably not enough attention has been given to the fact that literature is one of the important media through which our cultural pattern is transmitted.

Any individual born into a society must somehow learn not only its language, its gestures, its mechanics, but also the various superstructures of ideas, emotions, modes of behavior, and moral values that this society has built on the basic human relationships. It has been maintained, for instance, that if it were not for literature most people would never even have suspected the possibility of romantic love. The whole superstructure of affection, admiration, idealization of the loved one, desire to sacrifice oneself for his or her welfare, and all the other attributes of the romantic relationship, does not inevitably and automatically grow out of the basic fact of sexual attraction. These are ways of feeling and behaving that in some parts of our culture have become associated with this basic physical factor. After all, even within Western culture there are groups who dispense with much of this idealizing aura cast about the sex relationship. They see it associated with the need for a mate who can bear healthy children, or cooperate in the business of life on a farm, or bring the necessary wealth or social prestige. In any case, the feelings and attitudes associated with the basic fact of sexual attraction will have been learned.

Even in the case of romantic love, it would be ridiculous to suppose literature the sole agency through which it was propagated. It would never have found expression in literature if there had not been present in the society the social and economic conditions out of which such a complex of attitudes could have flowered. And there are many other agencies through which this view of love can be inculcated. Yet undoubtedly literature, oral and written, has played an important part in its perpetuation.

This theory does, at any rate, emphasize one of the social effects of literature—its inculcation of images of behavior and accompanying emotional attitudes. This applies potentially to all the phases of man's life and aspirations that have found expression in literature. With the increase of literacy and the wider dissemination of books, it can be expected that literature may play an increasingly important role in helping the individual to assimilate the superstructure of attitudes that he must erect on the basis of his fundamental human impulses.

In contrast to abstractly phrased statements concerning mankind or abstract formulations of moral codes that may be encountered in books, the peculiar power of the literary work of art resides in its influence on an emotional level, analogous to the kind of influence exerted by people and situations in life. Much more important than the explicit general ideas are the kinds of personalities and the emotional overtones ascribed to particular situations or conduct.

The very things most taken for granted in a work may have the most powerful influence on the adolescent reader. He is avidly curious about what it means in intimate personal terms to fulfill various adult roles. In literature the adolescent finds, for instance, certain traits of temperament, certain kinds of emotions, certain ways of achieving prestige, associated with women characters that are very different from the traits or satisfactions associated with the concept of the male character. Again, certain kinds of physical expressions of emotions such as fear, anger, or love are encountered, or certain emotional reactions are presented as appropriate to specific situations. Because of the personal quality of literary experience, it can be an important force in the transmission of the culturally shaped images and options of behavior.

The power of literature to transmit those elements of our culture that are most taken for granted may be more easily seen operating in a past age. The image of the delicate Pamela with her tiny waist and her hands too tender to scour a pewter dish had many even more exaggerated counterparts in eighteenth-century literature. Innumerable maidens of fragile physique, too ladylike to engage in even the slightest practical activity, sighed and wept and fainted their way through the pages of interminable eighteenth-century novels. Letters and biographies of women of the time, particularly of those women who came to revolt against this image, demonstrate how inextricably these attributes came to be associated with the idea of being a lady.

Veblen, in his *Theory of the Leisure Class*, treats some of the social and economic factors that probably produced this ideal of the lady; the novelist did not create her out of whole cloth, for obviously he was reflecting standards in process of crystallization. The novelists, however, clearly did much to perpetuate and disseminate this image. It has tended to persist in slightly modified form long after the conditions that produced it had changed. It began as a picture of the aristocratic or upper middle-class woman, but with changing social conditions and with the extention of literacy, women of the lower classes sought also to approximate this picture in their appearance and behavior. That this was not necessarily the aim of the novelists who created such heroines does not minimize the incidental influence of this image.

Thus, notions of complex patterns of behavior, such as courtship, or moral and social attitudes can be assimilated from books. Goethe's *Werther* and Byron's poems influenced whole generations. Scott's novels undoubtedly played a part in the hold of feudalistic ideas on the South. This kind of influence may reinforce acceptance of rigid class differences or suggest the possibility of overcoming them. Books may propagate stereotypes; consider the influence, for instance, of the fact that for so many generations the child usually encountered the Negro presented as an object for laughter or at best a prized servant, as in so many of the novels of the South purporting to show the kindness of masters. The repeated impact of such images in poems, novels, plays, and biographies surely added to the complex pressures acting on the individual and leading him to crystallize his sense of the world about him and of the appropriate attitudes to assume toward it.

THUS FAR, parallels have been drawn between the nature of the influence exerted by literature and the nature of the influence of the family or community environment. Literature, however, possesses special characteristics of its own. In so-called primitive societies, only those elements of the culture present in the minds of specific human beings at that time can possibly be transmitted to the child born into the culture. The only chance for him to suspect the existence of any other way of life is through particular individuals in the society who may have had contact with other cultural groups. The basic factor that distinguishes our own society from primitive societies is that we possess a written literature. Books are a means of getting outside the limited cultural group into which the individual is born. They are, in a sense, elements of societies distant in time and space made personally available to the reader.

Books are one important means of transmitting a much more complex cultural pattern than could be derived from any particular family or community environment. Without the additional contribution offered by the written or printed word, it would be impossible for the personal or community agencies of cultural transmission to give to youth an adequate sense of the complex fabric of our society. (Any kind of systematic education through the electronic image still remains a hypothetical thing of the future, and even this would undoubtedly incorporate the printed word.) Hence, the illiterate or unread person usu-

ally participates only in a very narrow and limited sub-
culture in our society.

Literature offers a release from the provincialism of
time and space. In this way it may exert a powerful influence upon the youth's future behavior. In a heterogeneous, democratic society more and more explicitly seeking
to create new social and economic patterns, literature can
perform an increasingly important function. Any new
synthesis, any integrated American culture, must be more
than a mere aggregate of its many, often conflicting, social
and economic groups. More than ever before it is essential
that the individual be liberated from the provincialism
of his own particular family, community, or even national
background. Democracy requires a body of citizens capable of making their own personal and social choices. The
corollary of this is that they should be emotionally and
intellectually aware of the possible alternatives from
which to choose.

A third generalization concerning the potential influence of literature is, then, that literature offers an important source of awareness of possible alternatives. This constitutes the social value of that "enlargement of experience" which the college girls quoted in Chapter 2 attributed to literature.

Books can be a liberating influence in many ways. They
may reveal to the boy and girl that there can be modes of
life different from the ones into which they have happened to be born. They can learn about the extraordinary
diversity of subcultures to be found within the framework
of our society, with its sectional, economic, and social

differences. Their reading can early make them aware that there are families organized very differently from their own. They will discover in our complex society culturally accepted patterns of behavior and socially approved formulations of personal and social goals completely alien to their own background.

Particularly important is this discovery that various groups within our society hold up diverse images of success, and that there are kinds of work despised or ignored by his own group that others consider socially valuable. This diversity of patterns is undoubtedly one of the most valuable aspects of American society. The craftsmen, the technologists, the artists, the scientists, the scholars, offer personal goals and systems of value often strongly in contrast to those represented by the dominant image of the successful businessman. Literature may often provide the first emotionally vivid realization of these facts. Young readers glimpse types of temperament, kinds of work, intellectual and moral atmospheres, very different from anything they have known. They come to realize that there are wide possibilities for choice open to them within the framework of American society.

Vicarious participation in different ways of life may have an even more broadly liberating influence. The image of past civilizations or of past periods within our Western civilization, as well as images of life in other countries today, can help the youth to realize that ours is only one of a great variety of possible social structures. The individual is thus able to look at the society about him more rationally. He can evaluate it, judge what elements should be perpetuated and what elements should be modified or rejected.

Literature not only makes possible the experience of diverse patterns of the past and present; it also offers the opportunity to envisage new and more desirable patterns. Wilde's dictum that "nature imitates art" is after all only a paradoxical expression of the fact that the artist often makes his fellowman aware of new aspects of life and new angles from which to view it. Perhaps Wilde was quite accurate in calling a sunset a poor Turner painting. Without Turner his contemporaries might never have learned to look for and perceive certain effects of light and color in that sunset. Surely the same thing applies to what the artist and particularly the writer can reveal about new emotional overtones in relations between human beings, new aspirations toward greater fulfillment of human personality, or new points of view, moral and esthetic, from which to judge experience.

Thus the writer often becomes the medium through which the future is forecast. Often especially sensitive to the new tendencies at work in the society about him, he disseminates images of new goals. These may kindle in his readers emotional drives toward setting up new patterns of conduct and new social structures. As the history of literature reminds us, writers have set forth scathing revelations of the life about them or have created attractive images of alternative ways of life. Of course, their writings have had influence because many other factors in the society at that time were conducive to it. Conversely, writers have many times created images of life that their own age and succeeding ones were not yet ready to understand or to assimilate.

THIS LATTER CONSIDERATION should allay the typical fear that literary works may incite the youth to rush into all sorts of untried modes of behavior. This view is based on the unrealistic idea of the social effects of literature that is usually associated with Victorian moralism. The Victorian critic often seemed to believe that the mere reading about particular actions in a book would in itself lead to the performance of the same actions in life.

Fortunately or unfortunately, the human being is not plastic enough to be easily moved to any new action simply by reading representations of it. The Victorians mistakenly thought of the reader as a blank photographic plate upon which was projected the series of images offered by a literary work. Some of the factors that make the individual reader anything but such a blank photographic plate have been noted in earlier chapters. Various influences in his environment have already left their imprint on him. For the youth especially, literature can be only one of the many elements that help to channel the intensely dramatic process which is so casually called "growing up." Books contribute an additional influence that must take its place beside the others.

In the interplay of forces acting upon the individual, the literary work, unaided, will probably have little weight if its emphasis is opposed to images that many of the agencies in the society about him are reiterating. If the work does not fit in with dominant conceptions, the reader may indignantly reject what the book offers. In fact, the great body of literature probably exerts its most powerful influence in reinforcing and perpetuating the cultural pattern. Therefore the images or ideas presented by literature function in the context of other environmental influences.

The reading of a book, it is true, has sometimes changed a person's entire life. When that occurs, the book has undoubtedly come as a culminating experience that crystallizes a long, subconscious development. In such cases the book usually opens up a new view of life or a new sense of the potentialities of human nature and thus resolves some profound need or struggle. The probability of any particular work having so profound and transfiguring an effect cannot, however, be predicted or planned for. It would result from the convergence of a great many intangible factors. The possibility that literature may offer such inspiration should, nevertheless, make us eager to stimulate our students to roam freely through a great many types of literary experience.

Literature characteristically operates in less direct and sudden ways. The "influence of literature" will usually be the result of the cumulative effect of a long series of literary experiences, interacting with, or parallel to, the many other forces acting upon the young person.

Only in rare cases would the literary image of a new and aberrant interpretation of a personal role outweigh the influence of frequently encountered conventional images of that role. When the power of the old patterns sanctioned by society is surmounted, it is probably because conditions have so changed that there is a pressing need for a new adjustment. Moreover, even then the new image probably must be reinforced by constant repetition over a long period of time. The emancipated woman, for instance, appears in literature at least from the time of Shelley and Mary Wollstonecraft, very infrequently at first and only with any significant frequency after about 1880. Yet it was not until early in the twentieth century that that image caught the imaginations and was translated into the practical lives of an appreciable number of women.

This may seem a decidedly pessimistic estimate of the possible contribution of literature to constructive social change. That is not the case. Yet it is evident that no over-simplified theories about its influence can be accepted. Since any one literary work is only a strand in a complex fabric of influences, the social situation out of which the reader turns to a particular book will, in large part, determine its possible impact on him.

The rather negative implications of the preceding paragraph are counterbalanced by the overarching fact about our age: we are living in a time of extraordinary social flux. Because there is such a lack of unanimity in our society, because even the agencies committed to transmitting the conventional images are often self-contradictory or at cross purposes, the individual is freer than in other periods to accept or to reject the images offered by literature. Hence the insight of the adolescents who claimed that "enlargement of experience" is an important function of literature. Because conditions are ripe for it, people today are eager for the new vision and new sensitivities that books may stimulate.

Someone has said, "The fool learns only through experience. The wise man anticipates experience." This suggests two essential traits of literature: its power to give vicarious experience and its delineation of a great diversity of personalities and conduct. Is not the capacity for imagination—the ability to picture oneself in a variety of situations and to envisage alternative modes of behavior and their consequences—the thing that gives the "wise man" his advantage? C. S. Peirce, in stressing the value of "ideal experimentation," was referring to the same thing. In imagination we rehearse various possibilities of action in a given situation. We go through a process of imaginative trial and error, trying out different modes of behavior and working out their probable effects. When the situation arises in actual life, we are better prepared to act successfully.

Literature permits something resembling "ideal experimentation" because it offers such a wide range of vicarious experiences. We can live different kinds of lives; we can anticipate future periods in our own life; we can participate in different social settings; we can try out solutions to personal problems. We are able to apprehend the practical and emotional results, the reactions of others, the social praise or blame, that may flow from such conduct; we find some of these temperamentally more satisfactory than others. Literature may thus offer us a means of carrying on some of the trial-and-error experimentation that might be disastrous in real life. *Hence the emphasis in earlier chapters on the necessity for equipping the student to evaluate the diverse images of life that he encounters in books.*[2]

THE VICARIOUS EXPERIENCES OFFERED BY LITERATURE can have a particularly significant effect when they are related to problems and conflicts intimately involving the reader. The students mentioned in Chapter 2 remarked that often in books one comes across people like oneself or people with problems similar to one's own: Other adolescents carry on the struggle to achieve a new working relationship with their families; other husbands and wives live through irritations and misunderstandings; other men and women seek recognition and the opportunity to exercise their talents in an indifferent world. The very fact that the reader's situation is not unique, that it at least parallels what others evidently understand and have lived through, gives him some perspective. Through seeing his problems apart from himself, he is helped to think and feel more clearly about them. This constitutes another phase of the potential influence of literature.

Lawrence K. Frank has suggested [3] that ideally a series of literary experiences could perform something approaching a psychoanalysis if the reader were encouraged to react fully and freely. In large part, the psychiatrist serves his patient by helping him to bring into consciousness various experiences, attitudes, or impulses that have been repressed or "censored." The patient is then encouraged to

[2] See also page 262 for comment on the fact that literature does not simply mirror life.
[3] In a letter to the writer.

look upon them as rationally explicable and hence manage-
able. Thus he is led to free himself from his fears and
obsessions. In order that he may readjust his environment
as well as himself, he is also helped to see at what points
his environment imposes unnecessary frustrations. The
experience of literature may effect a similar liberation.
Vicariously experiencing the life of a character in fiction
or participating in another's emotion expressed in a poem
may enable the reader to bring into consciousness similar
elements in his own nature and emotional life. This may
provide the basis for a release from unconscious fears and
guilt.

The adolescent particularly may be helped to interpret
his own acutely self-conscious emotions and motivations.
As a child he has built up a sense of himself in relation
to other people. Now he finds that "self" undergoing
various modifications and expansions. Often he feels that
he must be abnormal because of unsuspected tendencies
within him. Often, too, he develops a sense of guilt, a
feeling that he is highly sinful because his fantasies lead
him into forbidden fields or because he resents restrictions on his behavior. If he has been brought up to have
religious belief, the growth of agnosticism may lead to
intense inner turmoil and disillusionment. The young boy
or girl frequently hesitates to confide these conflicts or
fears to adults because they might view them as rejections
of their standards. Sometimes such anxieties create nervous tension and neurotic distortions of the personality.
Literary experiences may at least militate against the
growth of neurotic tendencies.

Books may help the adolescent perceive the validity of

his own temperamental bent, even when that may not be
valued by his own environment. Thus, the young boy and
girl may find encouragement to set up for themselves
goals undreamed of in their own families. For example,
a contemplative youth in a family of extroverted businessmen or a mechanically minded boy in a family with intellectual traditions might be particularly in need of reas-
surance that he is not eccentric or a failure. This sense
of aloneness or estrangement creates much adolescent insecurity. Through books each of these boys might learn
that other milieus valued his kind of temperament and
ability. For the first boy, works such as Willa Cather's or
Thomas Mann's stories or Joyce's *Portrait,* for the second
boy, works such as Michael Pupin's autobiography or the
books about George Washington Carver, might offer the
sense of sharing common values and goals. In the literature of both the past and the present they might have
found strong contrasts to the norms of their environments.

The range of human temperaments that have been admired and held up as a standard are perhaps best revealed
through literature. The autobiography of a Franklin with
its disciplined, prudent narrator may be contrasted with
the reckless, swashbuckling heroes of romance or with the
sensitive, introspective characters in a Henry James novel.
The passionate, impulsive folk of Elizabethan drama may
be compared with the intellectualized, cynical creatures
of Restoration plays, their most vigorous act some sharp
thrust of phrase, or with the characters in contemporary
dramas such as Shaw's, O'Neill's, or Arthur Miller's, where
dramatic conflicts often take place within the mind and
are revealed through a technical device. Portrayals of the

successful man of power may be placed beside characters whose success lay in self-abnegation or in spiritual and intellectual achievement. The poets, too, offer a wide gamut of temperaments that we can come to know intimately.

The young girl may need to be liberated from the narrow view of the feminine role imposed by her milieu. It hardly seems necessary to point out that through literature an extraordinarily broad range of feminine temperaments and a great variety of views of woman's place in society may be encountered: Pamela's determination not to offend the social code, the common sense conformity of Elizabeth Bennet, the passionate struggles of Meredith's Diana, the striving for independence of Hardy's Sue, or the merging of feminist aspirations with the broader struggle for human rights that characterizes lesser-known heroines of recent fiction. The adolescent worry over the need to conform to the culturally dominant pictures of the temperamental traits, types of work, and modes of behavior appropriate to each of the sexes can be lessened through a wide circle of literary acquaintances.

For the younger adolescent, we have seen, the concern with normality extends even to the problem of conformity to a particular physical type. Here, again, literature may show what a great diversity of physical traits have been admired, and that physical characteristics, even those considered handicaps, need not prevent successful and happy lives. If one approaches fiction from this rather special angle, one is amazed to find how many novels and stories do reflect this concern with conformity to physical standards. Cyrano de Bergerac and Falstaff by no means stand alone. In our own day, Thomas Wolfe recounts the experiences of an extremely tall man, or Vardis Fisher, in *April*, tells the story of a girl who thinks herself hopelessly unattractive.

Frequently literature is the means by which the youth discovers that his own inner life reflects a common experience of others in his society. He finds that the impulses and reactions he feared are "normal," that they are shared by many others in our society, and that there may merely be a convention (or a conspiracy) of silence about them. In this way, a particular poem or an autobiographical novel may provide liberation from blind fears or guilt. Having learned that others have lived through and dominated these supposedly strange impulses, the adolescent can achieve sufficient objectivity to proceed to work out an integrated sense of his own emotional nature. This kind of influence is especially difficult to document. All that psychologists and psychiatrists have been telling us recently about adolescent conflicts, however, tends to suggest that it may be very important.

A point introduced earlier in another connection is especially relevant. Often the reader, without necessarily being aware of it, projects his own present emotional preoccupations on fictional situations and personalities that seem on the surface very remote. The reader responds not so much to the situation presented in the work as to the structure of emotional relationships it implies. Thus, *Mutiny on the Bounty* or *Catcher in the Rye* might strike a responsive chord because a boy was passing through the process of psychological weaning from the authority of his parents. Or the relationship between Othello and Iago may have significance because of the boy's own preoccupation with the need for loyal friends. Similarly, the biography of a great statesman may symbolize the reader's own struggle to make others sympathize with his aims and enthusiasms.

This basic emotional parallelism is most obvious when an author selects a legend like the Prometheus myth or a story set in the past, such as the tale of Tristan and Iseult, and infuses into it values and emotional overtones significant in terms of contemporary life. (Perhaps emphasis on the underlying emotional structure would counteract recent tendencies to be satisfied with the classification of works according to their archetypal or mythic categories. The labeling should be incidental.) Each age finds new significance in the structure of emotional relationships in works like *Hamlet* or *Faust*. It is not usually recognized that in responding to a work of literature, even one that deals with contemporary people and situations, the reader may also be transposing its emotional patterns into his own special situation.

Talking about these matters in terms of the situation in the book merely makes it easier for the reader to bring his own inner problems into the open, and to face them or seek the help of others without the embarrassment of explicit self-revelation. Thus he often reveals what he cannot or will not say about himself. The teacher cannot afford to ignore this tendency to respond to the implicit emotional pattern of poems or novels or plays. Even books that seem to have little to do with the externals of a student's life may provide vicarious experience and occasion discussion that will lead to increased self-understanding for the student.

This is a perfectly valid way of responding to literature —in some ways the most valid, since it means that the work has profound importance to the reader. However, the aims of the literature classroom dictate a prime qualification: If in projecting his own situation into the work he has actually created something alien to its intention, the reader should be helped to discover this. The major task of the teacher (cf. Part One) will consist in such clarifications through group discussion of alternative responses and interpretation. Actually, in thus learning to read the text more closely, the reader often becomes aware, not only of unnoticed verbal clues, but also of his own biases or blind spots.

In recent years there has been much discussion of literature as a means of "sublimation" of socially disapproved impulses. The desire for violence and cruelty; the wish to dominate others; the need for sexual expression when, as in the case of the adolescent, society prevents it; the impulse to strike back at those who place restrictions on us—these are tendencies for which literature is said to provide an outlet. Certain aspects of this theory are related to the function of literature set forth in Aristotle's much-debated remarks about the catharsis, or purgation, of the emotions of fear and pity that results from the experience of tragedy.

Literature may perform an even more constructive service for the individual. It can suggest to him socially approved channels for expression of his impulses. A young boy whose fantasies had taken a consistently antisocial form might be directed through fiction and biographies toward goals that society would consider highly valuable. Domination of others might be sought not through physical violence, but rather through the possession of superior knowledge and even the ability to help others, as through the knowledge of medicine.

IN SOME RARE CASES the teacher might consciously attempt to use literature in this way. One extremely perceptive teacher who has had training in psychology reports that she has done this. She has been able to create an unselfconscious relationship with the students and has led them to express themselves very freely in their writing for her classes. Thus she is often able to glimpse some of their conflicts and obsessions. In one instance it became apparent that the boy's sympathy for his mother and antagonism toward his father were the source of strong feelings of guilt and were creating much friction. The teacher casually suggested that the boy read such books as Bennett's *Clayhanger* and (admitting its meretricious elements) Deeping's *Sorrell and Son.* These helped to bring directly into consciousness the problem of his own relations with his father. He was sufficiently freed from his sense of guilt to be able to discuss the matter and to work out a more adequate handling of it.

Unless the teacher is in an almost psychiatric relationship with the student, however, any attempt to use literature in this way would probably create more conflicts and tensions than it solved. Many teachers would probably be led into officious meddling with the emotional life of their students. (Unfortunately, like members of any other group, many teachers are themselves laboring under emotional tensions and frustrations. Given the right to meddle in this way, they would be tempted to find solutions for their own problems by vicariously sharing the student's life. They might also project upon the student their own particular preoccupations and lead him to think that he was suffering difficulties and frustrations that in reality were the teacher's.) Assuredly, even worse than the old indifference to what is happening psychologically to the student is the tampering with personality carried on by well-intentioned but ill-informed adults. The wise teacher does not attempt to be a psychiatrist. The essential thing, he knows, is to be a complete human being in his relations with his students—bringing to bear in his work with them all of the sensitivities that he would bring to bear in his relations with people outside the classroom.

On the whole, then, the teacher should avoid any too literal application of what might loosely be called the psychiatric possibilities of literature. It is highly important, however, to recognize that books may often perform such functions for young people. The teacher's responsibility is to provide a wide selection and to help the student develop sufficient independence to seek out those works for himself. Thus there may be at least the chance of his coming upon those that will be psychologically helpful. Moreover, if the teacher is aware of the conflicts and anxieties that recur most frequently among adolescents in our society, he will be able to make available works that have some relevance to these tensions. If a segment of our youth today take an almost completely negative stance toward the adult world, this may be because they have encountered in literature classrooms, as elsewhere, materials consistently irrelevant to their own concerns and needs. Above all, the adolescent should have a wide range of alternative experiences in works that speak to him as he now is. In an earlier day, the need was mainly for a certain iconoclasm; today, the need is not only for challenge but also for the frank treatment of themes that may lead beyond rejection toward affirmation of new and more satisfactory attitudes.

These considerations were an additional reason for the discussion of adolescent needs and conflicts in Chapter 5. Since any vital literary experience is possible only when the work strikes some responsive chord, the teacher should present to the student literary works that have this personal import. Such literary experiences will make it possible for him to grow in critical ability. At the same time, they may have valuable psychological repercussions. Probably in most cases the wisest thing for the teacher is to keep his attention focused on the relationship between the text and the student. If he does this part of his job well, in the spirit outlined in the earlier chapters of this book, he can probably feel assured that he has created the basis for a great deal more than purely "literary" insight.

THE CONSIDERATION OF psychological values that may be derived from literary works suggests a related problem that causes many teachers difficulty. They are aware that, both during school days and afterward, the great mass of the American people feed on shoddy reading matter.

The stilted academic approach to good literature in the schools may contribute to the student's feeling that he can get little personal enjoyment from it, so that he turns to a type of writing about which there hangs no academic aura. The more generally assumed reason for American reading habits is, however, that they reflect the desire for "escape." Undoubtedly, the causes for this wish to escape from reality are deeply rooted in our society.

It is sometimes argued that the teacher's condemnation of cheap escape fiction is merely an expression of professional snobbery. If this "trash" gives pleasure and momentary release from pressures or permits the compensation, at least in fantasy, for personal lacks and frustrations, why should the reader be denied this? An earlier comment is relevant here: The criterion for discriminating between helpful and harmful kinds of escape is that escape through literature should not leave the reader less able than before to cope with reality.

Someone dealing with extremely maladjusted individuals would probably use various means, including this type of literature, for even a temporary effect. In such cases, however, the literature performs only the function of a drug that momentarily releases tension. The work of returning the patient to mental health, of giving him greater capacity for meeting situations in life, still remains to be done. Repeated indulgence in the drug of escape fiction can lead only to an increased craving for such escape.

To be sure, it is not always trashy fiction that provides escape. The reader who immerses himself in medieval romance, or reads and rereads the works of Scott as a steady literary diet, or turns constantly to such works as Trollope's stories of quiet cathedral towns, may be indulging in the same flight from reality as the girl who avidly reads the stories about "the international set" on the Riviera. In either case, there has undoubtedly been a period of pleasant escape from the difficulties and disappointments of the present-day world. Surely, only the most ascetic of Puritans would wish to cut us off completely from this relaxation and enjoyment.

In most cases, however, the escape function is served by writings that present a false image of life. The obstacles placed in the way of the characters are oversimplified. The ease with which problems are solved, or the absence of any real problems, probably constitutes one appeal of this type of writing. Even more subtly enervating are the emotions undiluted with thought and lacking in individual quality. Purportedly successful personal relationships in marriage or business are usually presented in naively simple terms. And the crudest elements in our society, the ruthless competition, the emphasis on wealth, the respect for the winner no matter what his methods, often provide the framework of the story. The reader will return to life from this kind of fare probably less capable than before of understanding and coping with the complex situations, the mixture of frustrations and satisfactions, that life offers. Such fiction fosters the notion that the level of vitality required for a full life is lower than is actually the case.

A striking phenomenon in recent years has been the widespread sale of writings purveying crude images of violence, sadism, and sexuality. Such materials jostle the classics on the paperback shelves and fill magazine racks in stores throughout the country. The other mass media also manifest this trend, which has been interpreted as a reflection of the tensions and violence characteristic of twentieth-century life. Psychiatrists have disagreed about the effect of such materials on young readers. Some have suggested that these provide an outlet for aggression, while others have found that they contribute to delinquent behavior. Under different circumstances and with different individuals, both of these effects seem possible. Much more systematic study of the problem is needed, with both literary critics and psychologists contributing.

Some have justified such writings by pointing to the presence of violence and eroticism in serious contemporary works, such as those of existentialist and "absurd" writers. The necessary rejoinder is that the presence or absence of such elements is not in itself a basis for judgment. Such writings may serve a function as expression for the author; whether they serve the needs of a particular reader remains a legitimate question. The educator, who knows that freedom is essential to the health of any literature, will oppose censorship. His responsibility is all the more clear—to develop discriminating readers able to evaluate the human import of the literary fare offered to them.

The fundamental social causes for this national craving for the drug of "escape" literature are beyond the scope of the classroom. At least the literature class can counteract the tendency to follow the path of least resistance. One way is to discuss examples of poor fiction. It is wise, after all, to start with the student at whatever level of understanding and appreciation we may find him. There is no point in just condemning the reading he most enjoys. He will only develop a feeling of shame about it without being able to resist indulging in it. Reading forbidden books "in the attic" or "behind the barn," or whatever the modern equivalent may be, seems one of the persistent traits of our culture. Condemnation or prohibition alone can have only pernicious effects.

For adolescent students, a calm analysis of the appeal of this kind of reading might lessen its attraction. A critical attitude toward its silly, dishonest, and sensational pictures of life can have a wholesome influence. The contrast between cheap and honest treatments of similar themes can help to accomplish this. This will help them to judge by other criteria of happiness the picture, for example, of wealth as equivalent to success. In contrast to "love" as limited to the physical, they will be made aware of the many values that can be integrated into the love relationship.

Without assuming a "holier than thou" attitude, the teacher should keep in mind the adolescent psychology that leads students to this low-grade fiction, and should try to provide more wholesome and invigorating satisfactions for these needs. Educators and parents have come to recognize the importance of this in the field of sex education. They realize that the attempt to prohibit any knowledge about sex causes the adolescent to seek it from undesirable sources, often sensational fiction. They admit, therefore, that it is better to provide this information in more wholesome ways and to permit the adolescent to read literature that deals frankly and honestly with sex as a fundamental and enriching element in man's life. This principle should not be restricted to the field of sex knowledge, however. There is certainly something wrong with a literature curriculum if the students turn from it to magazines and books purveying violence and the crudest sexuality under a veneer of cynicism. Adventure and vigorous action, on the one hand, and honest treatment of the sex relationship, on the other, are to be found in abundance in good literature. Probably in many cases the school is still too much dominated by nineteenth-century ideas about the literature that the cultivated person should read, when it would be very easy to find equally good literature that has the swift pace and vigorous action the student craves. Of course, even when such books are read in a classroom, there still remains the danger that they may be drained of all their tang and zest by routine study. When the teacher and the school seriously carry out such professional responsibilities, they have earned the right to exercise them without external censorship.

Victorian notions about the influence of literature led to a rigid censorship of books by publishers and critics as well as by parents and teachers. Particular books were valued because they offered approved models of conduct which young people were expected to imitate. The view of literature presented here has led to a rather different emphasis: in a democracy, the more varied the literary fare provided for students, the greater its potential as an educationally liberating force. In this way, through literature, the necessarily limited influence of their environment will be supplemented and corrected by contact with ex-

pressions of other phases of society and other types of
personality.

This means that the student will not be limited to one
kind of literary diet. He will not read exclusively the
works of the past or the present. He will not be nourished
entirely on the literature of England and America. Instead, he will be permitted an insight into ways of life
and social and moral codes very different even from the
one that the school is committed to perpetuate.

These generalizations about the choice of books apply
to several specific problems that can be mentioned only
briefly. Very often in school, children are required to read
works that demand a constant effort at comprehension
because the vocabulary and sentence structure represent
"the next stage" toward which they are being led. Or
they may be required to read works written in an archaic
language, very different from the language that they hear
about them or that is used by accepted contemporary
writers. Few adults—even college professors!—impose
upon themselves the task of constantly reading works with
a vocabulary that is strange to them or with a complicated style that demands unusual efforts of attention.
Only rarely do they undertake such tasks. Most of the
time their reading is at the level of their present vocabulary and powers of attention. In our zeal to give our students the proper literary training, we constantly set them
tasks a step beyond their powers, or plunge them into
reading that practically requires the learning of a new
language. Belated efforts to help the disadvantaged child
have revealed that standard English is indeed often a

strange dialect, to be learned almost as a second language. No wonder that many students, middle-class and disadvantaged, do not learn to read, or read only the simplest of crude escape literature!

The question of command of language leads to another controverted subject: the literature of the past versus contemporary literature. When one objects to intensive study of words and syntax as withering any possible love of the "classics," the answer is usually that the students will not otherwise understand what they are reading. If a work presents such linguistic difficulties, one may question whether a direct attack on the linguistic problems offers a solution. By the time the student has acquired enough understanding of the unusual language, the work as a whole has probably lost its power to affect him. If the work presents experiences and ideas highly relevant to the student's own preoccupations, his interest will often carry him over the hurdle of the language difficulty and give him sufficient motivation to study the language. Many of the great classics have elements of vivid action, strong emotion, and suspense that may provide an incentive for the more mature or the more intelligent student to clear away the obscurities due to unfamiliar language or literary forms. Too often, however, the classics are introduced to children at an age when it is impossible for them to feel in any personal way the problems or conflicts treated.

Difficulties in understanding, as indicated in Chapter 5, are usually not merely a matter of words and syntax, for words must be apprehended in some context of experience. The teacher who feels that if he can only get the students to understand the individual words he will have eliminated all obstacles, is often mistaking the symptom, the language difficulty, for the real seat of the trouble, which is the student's lack of readiness for what the work offers.[4] For the great majority it would probably be much wiser to postpone such reading and to gradually build linguistic flexibility through the use of more familiar materials. When the students are more mature, more experienced, they will then be able to apprehend enough of what the great classics offer to be willing and eager to clarify any linguistic obscurities.

When one thinks of all that great literary works can yield, one is horrified to see them so often reduced to the level of language exercise books for the young. The antipathy of many students to Latin and Greek arose from this use of masterpieces beyond their powers of appreciation as texts for acquiring the language. Those who cram the classics down students' throats long before they are ready are careless of the fate of the great works of the past.

[4] Obviously, this does not imply a neglect of any of the means by which the student can acquire a clearer understanding of words themselves. The dictionary can become a very interesting book for the student, if what he gets from it is not left on the purely verbal level. He should develop the habit of using it, just as the motorist uses a road map, as a tool to get him to the right place.

See pages 111–119 for other references to this problem of understanding. There has been increasing interest in this basic problem of meaning, owing to the influence, e.g., of the writings of C. S. Peirce, Bertrand Russell, P. W. Bridgeman, I. A. Richards, and Gilbert Ryle. Two highly influential works have been *The Meaning of Meaning* by C. K. Ogden and I. A. Richards and *Philosophical Investigations* by Ludwig Wittgenstein.

Even though the majority were to graduate from school and high school without having encountered many of the great authors, we should not need to be alarmed if they had the ability to read with understanding and had acquired zest for the experience that literature can give. Those who try to crowd into the school years everything that "ought to be read" evidently assume that the youth will never read again after school years are over. People who read for themselves will come to the classics at the point when particular works will have particular significance for them. To force such works upon the young prematurely defeats the long-term goal of educating people to a personal love of literature sufficiently deep to cause them to seek it out for themselves at the appropriate time.

The difficulty presented by works of the past is that not only the language but also the externals of life and the manners and morals represented may seem so peculiar that the student's attention is focused almost completely on these aspects rather than upon the major experiences the authors sought to convey. Even those works that deal with personal emotional problems still vital today are often clothed in an atmosphere and deal with ways of life that make the whole thing seem artificial and remote. Many teachers are aware that before the student can enjoy a work, he must feel that it has some relevance to his own experience. They therefore often devote much time and energy to indicating the equivalents in our own society of the different aspects of life represented in the work. Like all background information, however, this should not obscure their purpose, to reveal the basic emotional patterns of the work itself.

There are many works of the past in which the strange mores do not block comprehension of the basic emotional relations; the older work may offer just as intense a personal experience as would a more contemporary work. The friendship of Achilles and Patroclus might seem as personally important to a boy as would a treatment of friendship such as in Steinbeck's *Of Mice and Men.* The story of Lear and his daughters might seem as near to a girl as the family relations in E. M. Forster's *Howard's End. Dombey and Son,* just because it was written at a time when problems of parent-child and husband-wife relations were still drawn in their broadest terms, might, at a certain stage, be more comprehensible than the treatment of similar problems in a book by Virginia Woolf. The fact that some writers of this century, like James Joyce or T. S. Eliot, are themselves so much the product of a long literary heritage might make them less comprehensible to the young reader than a nineteenth-century writer would be. The student himself needs to go through the experience of relevant literature of the past before he can understand some contemporary writers.

Nevertheless, most contemporary authors offer no such difficulty but write about a life that the student can understand. For instance, Benet's *John Brown's Body* would be more easily understood than *The Idylls of the King;* Carl Sandburg and Langston Hughes would have more personal impact than Matthew Arnold; Orwell and Salinger than Thackeray and Hawthorne. The question of literary comparisons must wait until the students can handle the historical obstacles to participation in the older works.

Certain other considerations relate to the use of classical or contemporary literature. It is usual to think that classics survive a winnowing process that guarantees them to be repositories of the accumulated wisdom of the race. There is much in this view. Even so, it is hard to find any great work that has been consistently recognized as such. Shakespeare has had his ups and downs, as have lesser writers. And when different ages agree in their exaltation of a work, it may be for widely differing reasons. Moreover, in any work, the elements of "lasting truth" are intermingled with much that was special to the particular age in which it was written. This is as true of the work of Shakespeare, Milton, and Goethe as it is of Jane Austen.

Surely, many "works that every person should have read" lend powerful reinforcement to emotional attitudes and assumptions about human nature that our contemporary life and our contemporary thinkers have discarded as outmoded and false. What is the possible influence of a steady diet of literature produced out of social systems and ethical philosophies very different from our own? Ideas about the relations between men and women, employer and employee, between citizen and state, and indeed between man and the universe, as they are reflected in much of the older literature, would seem to exalt much that the person of average enlightenment today considers reactionary or limited. To what extent is such literary training in the schools contributing to the persistent hold of images and ideals no longer appropriate to our present-day life and knowledge? Are the students offered literary fare that provides opportunity only for imaginative identification with images of behavior irrelevant to actual life or whose relevance they are not equipped to see? [5]

Obviously, these questions are presented in oversimplified form. Books, it has been seen, do not function in a vacuum, and their influence is always part of a complex network of social factors. For instance, the boy who has come into contact with the present-day skeptical scientific attitude will naturally be less likely to absorb the authoritarian point of view that permeates much of the writing of the past. Yet in a conflict between the two attitudes, a steady fare of such literary experiences might tend to strengthen subservience to intellectual authority. It is realistic to think of particular literary works as tending either to reinforce or to weaken attitudes and images the young person may encounter through other social influences.

It is generally recognized that students should read works of both the past and the present. The fact that a work is written by a contemporary is certainly no automatic proof of its value. Still, in the mass of literature produced today there is much that represents those areas of thought and experience that are the points of growth and change in our own age. If the youth is to develop a critical understanding of his world, he must be exposed

[5] To what extent, for example, can the influence of literature be held responsible for the fact that many women today find within themselves emotional obstacles to their sincere ambition to be independent emotionally and intellectually? Throughout their entire experience with literature, they have been led to identify themselves most often with the older image of woman as temperamentally, as well as economically, subordinate and dependent. See Chapter 8, p. 265, for further discussion of this problem.

to contemporary expressions of personal and social attitudes. The novel, the poem, the play—whether encountered in the printed page or other media—provide a sense of the adult world he must enter. Through the processes of "ideal experimentation," they help him to forge some of the necessary intellectual and emotional tools.

This leads back to the principle so often reiterated in these pages, that the test of what books the child or adolescent should read is his intellectual and emotional readiness for what they offer. The classics will be more appropriate than some esoteric contemporary author, but in many cases comparatively recent works will speak more profoundly and constructively to the boy and girl than will much "greater" works of the past.

We should not, then, set up arbitrary ideas in this matter of classic and contemporary works. The teacher should be eager to find those books of the past and present that will have a live meaning for his students. In most schools and colleges even today, this principle would lead to a greater liberality in introducing contemporary literature into the curriculum. For the teacher's desire will be to give the youth as wide a range of relevant experiences as possible at his level of development.

To SUM UP: Because the literary work of art is a form of personal experience, literature has many potentialities that dynamic and informed teaching may sustain.

Literature fosters the kind of imagination needed in a democracy—the ability to participate in the needs and aspirations of other personalities and to envision the effect of our actions on their lives.

Literature acts as one of the agencies in our culture that transmit images of behavior, emotional attitudes clustering about different social relationships, and social and personal standards.

Literature can reveal to the adolescent the diversity of possible ways of life, patterns of relationship, and philosophies from which he is free to choose in a heterogeneous, rapidly changing democratic society.

Literature may help him to make sound choices through imaginative trial and error or experimentation—through experiencing in the literary work the consequences of alternative actions.

Literary experiences may enable the reader to view his own personality and problems objectively and so to handle them better.

Literature, through which the adolescent reader encounters a diversity of temperaments and systems of value, may free him from fears, guilt, and insecurity engendered by too narrow a view of normality.

Literature may suggest socially beneficial channels for drives that might otherwise find expression in antisocial behavior.

Emotion and Reason

IN THE PRECEDING REFLECTIONS on literature as a source
of insight and emotional liberation, the emphasis was primarily on the relationship between the individual student
and the book. The teacher entered the picture mainly
through his power to limit or broaden the range of books
with which the student might come into contact. But the
teacher's function does not end there. The role and the
teaching process sketched for him in earlier chapters can
also be viewed in terms of its potential influence on personality and behavior. This will involve, too, a consideration of how the study of literature may create an understanding of the various basic social concepts discussed
in Chapter 6.

In sum, the teaching process outlined consists in helping the student to develop the habit of reflecting upon his
primary response to books. Having given him the essential
opportunity to react freely, the teacher then seeks to

create a situation in which the student becomes aware of possible alternative responses and is led to examine further both his own reaction and the text itself. In this way he is helped to understand his own preoccupations and assumptions better. He considers whether he has taken into account everything that the text offered. He thus becomes more aware of the various verbal "clues"— the diction, the rhythmic pattern, structure, and symbol— and develops or deepens his understanding of concepts such as voice, *persona*, point of view, genre. This process of reflection leads the student to seek additional information concerning the work, the author, and their social setting, as a basis for understanding of himself and of literature. These new technical, personal, and social insights may ultimately lead to a revision of his original interpretation and judgment and may improve his equipment for future response to literature.

Now if we were to substitute the words *situation* or *personality in life* for *text* or *work* in the preceding paragraph, the description would apply equally well to the kind of thinking that is most fruitful whenever an individual meets a new situation in life or must adjust to a new kind of personality. His first need is to understand his own emotional response to the person or situation. He realizes that preoccupations and prejudices may have led him to exaggerate some things and ignore others. He has to bring his basic moral or psychological assumptions out into the open in order to test the validity of their application to this new situation. He may find that his own past experience and information must be supplemented before he can make an adequate judgment or plan appropriate action. The result of these considerations may be a rejection or revision of his original reaction. Through this process of self-scrutiny, he may have come to understand himself, as well as the outside world, better. A certain inner readjustment may have started which will modify his response to the next person or situation encountered.

In the case of either the literary experience or the life experience, a process such as the one outlined constitutes reflective thinking. If the individual is stimulated often enough to engage in this kind of reflection, it may tend to become habitual. There will have been set up a readiness to reflect upon his own attitudes toward people and situations as a prelude to passing judgment or deciding on action.

It seems reasonable to suggest, therefore, that in building up the habits of mind essential to the attainment of sound literary judgment, the student will also be acquiring mental habits valuable for the development of sound insight into ordinary human experience.

There is more than a verbal parallel between the process of reflective thinking arising from response to literature and the process of reflection as a prelude to action in life itself. John Dewey reminded us that in actual life constructive thinking usually starts as a result of some conflict or discomfort, or when habitual behavior is impeded and a choice of new paths of behavior must be made. Such thinking, therefore, grows out of some sort of tension and is colored by it. The tension contributes the impetus to seek a solution, but intelligent behavior results from thought brought to bear upon the problem. Moreover, the validity of the thought will usually depend on whether emotion has been controlled and has not obscured the actual situation. "Impulse is needed to arouse thought, incite reflection and enliven belief. But only thought notes obstructions, invents tools, conceives aims, directs technique, and thus converts impulse into an art which lives in objects." [1]

Educators are more and more recognizing this view of constructive thinking. It is comparatively easy for the student to think rationally about difficult human problems when impersonal academic treatments make them abstract subjects of thought. Unfortunately, that kind of thinking is probably not very useful; it lacks the conflicting impulses or emotional perplexities out of which thinking usually grows in real life. Reason should arise in a matrix of feeling:

> The conclusion is not that the emotional, passionate phase of action can be or should be eliminated in behalf of a bloodless reason. More "passions," not fewer, is the answer. To check the influence of hate there must be sympathy, while to rationalize sympathy there are needed emotions of curiosity, caution, respect for the freedom of others—dispositions which evoke objects which balance those called up by sympathy, and prevent its degeneration into maudlin sentiment and meddling interference. Rationality, once more, is not a force to evoke against impulse and habit. It is the attainment of a working harmony among diverse desires. [2]

That kind of rationality may be fostered by literature. It may provide the emotional tension and conflicting attitudes out of which spring the kind of thinking that can later be assimilated into actual behavior. The emotional

[1] John Dewey, *Human Nature and Conduct* (New York, Henry Holt and Co., 1922), pp. 170–171.
[2] *Ibid.*, p. 195.

character of the student's response to literature offers an opportunity to develop the ability *to think rationally within an emotionally colored context.* Furthermore, the teaching situation in which a group of students and a teacher exchange views and stimulate one another toward clearer understanding can contribute greatly to the growth of such habits of reflection.

Several specific classroom discussions may serve to illustrate this. The students who discussed Ibsen's *A Doll's House* (see p. 122) provide an example of processes that might also be evoked by many more recent works. After they had clarified their historical approach to the play, they still found themselves involved in a lively difference of opinion. "Nora should never have left her children, no matter how unhappy she was," declared one. "Her main duty was toward them and toward maintaining a home for them." This was vigorously opposed by others who claimed that Nora's duty was first of all toward herself. She needed to develop her own mind so that she might consider herself truly an individual. Without this she could be of little service to her children.

The young women had obviously identified very strongly with Nora; the discussion seemed to have personal immediacy for them. The rights of a woman to self-expression and personal dignity were thoroughly canvassed. Nevertheless, all of the students, even the most decided individualists, hesitated to say that Nora had no responsibilities toward her children. A number of the students found it difficult to take one position or the other. Their sympathies were involved in Nora's gesture of independence; they shared her desire to stand completely alone; yet they were equally ready to see the value of marriage and children. At this point an "emotional tension" had developed.

Although the discussion seemed to be moving in circles, the teacher did not rush the class over this hurdle. Finally, one of the students pointed out that Ibsen's ending had not provided a solution to Nora's problem, but had only underlined her dilemma. Certainly an individualism that entailed the sacrifice of important relationships could not be very desirable. A valuable kind of independence for Nora would have permitted her to be a complete human being, yet to remain in the home and to function as a wife and mother. Another student added that it is often necessary to sacrifice certain satisfactions—such as the right to complete, untrammeled independence—in order to satisfy other needs in our nature. On the other hand, it was agreed that the role of wife and mother should not have required submergence of Nora's personality. Furthermore, one student pointed out that even if Torvald had been an ideal man, there still would have remained the need for adjustment between the personalities of the husband and wife as equals.

The students here were groping toward ideas that authorities on family problems and mental hygiene consider extremely important. They remind us that in order to achieve an integrated personality the individual must reconcile or adjust conflicting impulses and aspirations within himself. Moreover, much friction would be avoided by recognition that any personal relationship necessarily entails compromises between different temperaments. The family group, for example, should provide scope for each of the personalities within it; yet if it is to be a smoothly functioning group, each individual must to a certain extent be willing to adapt himself to the others. The adolescent, in his present family or in future relationships, will be better prepared to make the necessary adjustments if he has thoroughly assimilated this approach.

In this discussion, there was not only a clash of opinion among various students; certain students discovered conflicting emotional attitudes within themselves. Thus these students lived through something analogous to the inner conflict that must often attend choices in life.

Furthermore, in this phase of their discussion the students were not considering the demands and responsibilities only of the marriage relationship. They also achieved some understanding of the complex adjustments required in any relationship. And each individual, they concluded, should seek to reconcile his different needs; he must attempt to satisfy the most important with as little sacrifice as possible of other valued tendencies in his nature. Such insights were much more valuable than any conclusion that the students might have reached concerning the "rightness" of Nora's final act.

More significant than any statements made by the students was the fact that these ideas grew out of emotional tension and lively personal feeling. There is no proof that the insights achieved were retained. But it can safely be said that they were more likely to be retained than if the same ideas had been encountered in an impersonal way in a traditional psychology or sociology course.

The fact that Ibsen's *A Doll's House* is a "problem

play" may possibly obscure the point. A similar process might have grown out of the experience of a play that was in no way designed to focus attention on a controversial problem. Works that are read solely because of their literary significance may arouse interest in such issues.

For example, in a discussion of *Antony and Cleopatra* carried on by a freshmen literature class in a women's college, the play was rejected by the majority of the group. Their dislike for the tragedy, it became apparent, grew out of their antipathy to Cleopatra. "I hate that kind of woman. She is selfish, conceited, grasping for power. I am not interested in what happens to her." Like most students, they had responded to the character as they would in real life. The instructor's job was to help them maintain that personal sense of the work and yet react to it in rational terms.

The students were challenged to consider the basis for their antipathy. It finally became obvious that theirs was the point of view of the average woman to whose marital peace a person like Cleopatra would be a decided menace. (When this episode was related to an authority on adolescent psychology in charge of guidance in a large California high school, she commented that the students' reaction to Cleopatra was as much in terms of their present adolescent relationships as of any future adult situations. We tend to forget, she pointed out, that adolescents in their boy and girl relationships are already engaged in an intense emotional life parallel to adult experiences. They are already, for instance, experiencing the disillusionments and triumphs of sex rivalry.)

The students felt that their judgment of Cleopatra's ruthlessness and egotism was justified by the text. This led them to inquire what her function was in the play. Obviously, the reader was being led to feel that the fate of Cleopatra and Antony was important. Much as the class might disapprove of Cleopatra in real life, they came to perceive that her very vices and weaknesses, like those of Antony, are intermingled with traits that make their struggle and their downfall significant. Although morally some of Cleopatra's actions merit condemnation, she possesses great vitality, the ability to feel and act on a grand scale. Approaching the character in this way, they were able to comprehend the intermingled childish and queen-like actions that characterize her. They responded more perceptively to the verse. Shakespeare, the students concluded, helped them to grasp the complexity of such a character; there is understanding to be gained from living through the fugue of emotions that the play presents, to their resolution in those noble last scenes.

From this discussion of Cleopatra there emerged, first of all, a clearer understanding of the esthetic attitude. Cleopatra's significance for them was obviously not what it might have been if she were part of their own lives. They could set aside their practical reaction toward her and participate in the complex and heightened form of experience that the play offered. One student phrased in her own terms the value of esthetic distance, which made this possible.

These literary perceptions tended to modify the students' initial reaction. They came to see that their practical judgments on people, in either a play or real life, need not be the limit of their insight. They might attempt to comprehend the human drives that lead people to act in ways potentially injurious or repugnant to them. In some cases, they realized, their own aims and satisfactions might seem equally alien or objectionable from the point of view of other people.

Implied in this discussion, therefore, was the germ of a new moral attitude, as well as the development of critical objectivity. Instead of simply approving or condemning, one might seek to understand. Instead of fixed rules of conduct unconditionally applied to all under all circumstances, judgment should be passed only after the motives of the behavior and the particular circumstances had been understood. One might condemn the act and yet wish to understand what produced it. Moral judgment itself would thus become more humane.

Much less complex works than Shakespeare's plays may lead to similar insights. A class in a coeducational Southern school was reading plays and short stories. The group was at first content to condemn the possessive mother in Sidney Howard's *The Silver Cord* or to talk about how much they disliked the vain posturing of Mr. Reginald Peacock in Katherine Mansfield's story. Because of the way the anthology for the course was arranged, they tended to speak in terms of "types" of people, such as the boor, the sadist, the gossip. One or two of the students tried to suggest some excuse for these characters' behavior; the discussion ultimately veered toward the idea that, after all, the important thing was not to condemn but rather to find out what produced such personalities and behavior. The students felt that their reading had led them to observe themselves and other people much more carefully. That in itself was useful because one might then learn "how to live with them." It might also be better not to think that one necessarily has the right to try to change other people, or that mature personalities are easily modified. However, one might at least attempt to see what explained behavior in order to help create conditions that would in the future produce more socially valuable people.

The class had started with a decidedly moralistic attitude, sitting in judgment upon the characters encountered in their reading. Their point of view changed appreciably in the direction of greater human sympathy and objectivity. Instead of thinking only of individual human beings, they saw them in relation to the social forces that had molded them or that gave them scope for expressing their special temperaments.

Another instance: the demand in some quarters that the *Merchant of Venice* be barred from the schools. In a class in which a number of students were Jewish, it is argued, Shylock would create self-consciousness and resentment in that group and reinforce the prejudices of the rest of the class. This argument assumes a number of things that the preceding discussion has rejected. The first assumption is that the class would read the play and react to the character of Shylock without any interchange among themselves or with the teacher. The second assumption is that even if they did express themselves, their original ideas would remain unchanged.

The desirable kind of classroom situation outlined in

the preceding chapters would negate both these assumptions. If the literary experience offered by this play did give rise to decided reactions to Shylock, that should then serve as the beginning of a process of clarification such as was described earlier. Obviously, the kind of classroom atmosphere predicated, reflecting a relationship of confidence, would be extremely important. The students would not be encouraged merely to express their attitude toward Shylock. The discussion would become a means of leading them back to the text, to understand Shylock's situation, to see the adverse conditions against which he struggled, and to recognize the connection between that and his behavior. In other words, that part of the play would have enabled them to live through the experiences of a member of a minority group and to understand his behavior even when it was distasteful or ridiculous to them.

It might be contended that Shakespeare shared the prejudices of his age and that therefore this excursion into the development of racial understanding would be irrelevant to the play. Even if one grants the view concerning Shakespeare's attitude (his text provides its own antidote to that attitude), the English teacher could not justifiably ignore the fact that the students are reacting to the play in terms of their own present-day lives. He could not shirk the opportunity to contribute to a more rational, unprejudiced approach to human beings. Young people in school function as whole personalities; they are not creatures that can be neatly divided into literary or sociological segments, each segment to be ministered to by a different teacher. Hence the English teacher must feel some responsibility for dealing with whatever repercussions, no matter how controversial or "nonliterary," the experience of such a play may have. The fact that the play is "great literature" may have determined its selection in the first place, but that means nothing unless it has human significance today.

SOME WILL CONCEDE that the school and the teacher have the responsibility of developing constructive attitudes toward human relations but will ask: Why suggest this roundabout way of transmitting such insight? Why not have given the first group lectures on the need for adjustment of the different temperaments within the family? Why not have presented to the other groups a clearly worked-out exposition of the factors conditioning personality and behavior? Why take the time of a literature class for discussions suggested by the haphazard accidents of student reactions? Topics may not be brought into the discussion in any logical order, and there may be important subjects that the students may not introduce in their discussions at all. Would it not be preferable to eliminate any such topics from the literature classroom and to depend on a more orderly method of presenting this information to the students?

The considerations set forth in the first five chapters of this book offer an answer to one aspect of these questions. The student's personal response to literary works will be primarily colored by his attitudes toward the characters and situations they present. To attempt to ignore these student reactions would destroy the very basis upon which any greater *literary* sensitivity could be built. Even when the English teacher's responsibilities are interpreted in the narrowest terms, the discussion of such topics remains relevant to the literature classrooms.

If, on the other hand, one were not at all concerned with whether students developed sounder literary appreciation, one should nevertheless recognize literature as a potential means of developing social understanding. A formal course in psychology or social problems could not perform quite the function illustrated by the discussions in literature classes reported earlier in this chapter. Their special characteristic was the element of personal emotion that permeated the students' treatment of these topics. In the argument about *A Doll's House,* some sort of identification with Nora had occurred. Yet the students felt free to show their feeling because ostensibly they were talking about Nora, not themselves. The discussion of any general topic concerning human nature or social relations arose from the students' own vicarious experience and their feelings about it. Their concluding insights grew out of a process accompanied by definite emotional pulls toward various points of view. The whole discussion was *felt* as well as thought.

If the literary works had had little emotional impact, any discussion would have been empty verbiage. The discussions reported above were fundamentally attempts by the students to work out some rational understanding of their own reactions. They were involved in the task of managing their emotions—something very different from ignoring or repressing them. In this way, they were encouraged to bring thought to bear upon emotional responses—the starting point for intelligent behavior.

Thus, discussion of literary experiences makes possible rehearsals of the struggle to clarify emotion and make it the basis of intelligent and informed thinking. This possesses a certain parallelism to those situations in life which engender conflicting inner attitudes. The insights and ideas that result from such an experience tend to be assimilated into the individual's active equipment because they are embedded in a matrix of emotional and personal concern. Hence, literature provides an educational medium through which the student's habits of thought may be influenced. When this is more widely recognized, we may expect that literary materials will be introduced into many different phases of the curriculum.

The emotional quality of literature has sometimes caused the social scientist to look askance at it as something that strengthens the student's natural tendency toward undisciplined emotion. Dewey offers the rejoinder that rationality does not exist in opposition to emotion, but rather represents the attainment of a working harmony among diverse desires. The social scientist should recognize that literature may provide a means of helping the student to achieve a functioning rationality.

The power of literature to develop capacity for feeling, for responding imaginatively to the thoughts and behavior of others, was treated in earlier chapters. This chapter has considered how, through discussion and reflection on his response to literature, the student may learn to order his emotions and to rationally face people and situations he is emotionally involved in. Power to transmit understanding of society in terms that will be personally assimilable is lacking in traditional social science teaching methods. When literary experiences are made the material for reflective thinking, they may be one means of providing this sorely needed linkage between feeling, thought, and behavior.

Teachers of the social sciences usually demonstrate a rather limited view of the value of literary treatments of their subjects. History textbooks append references to historical novels, or students are assigned short stories and novels about foreign countries or about different types of social background. If the French Revolution is being studied, for example, *A Tale of Two Cities* is read. The idea seems to be that the literary work adds sharpness to the information that the teacher wishes to convey. The student is helped "to understand" the information better through the more vivid and detailed descriptions; a novel, for instance, helps him to visualize the people and scenes mentioned in his history book. That, certainly, may be one of the contributions of literature. But the matter is usually left on this level, with literature considered merely a tool for vividly conveying facts.

The repercussions of such understanding gained through vicarious experience do not end there. From enhanced perceptions may flow a sense of the human and practical implications of the information that has been acquired. This information is no longer words to be rattled off; the words now point toward actual human situations and feelings. Thus, the reading of *Hiroshima* or Kelley's *A Different Drummer* will bestow emotional reality in terms of human beings, their suffering, their needs and struggles. The meaning attributed earlier to the term *understanding* transcends the view of literature as a pedagogic device for giving sugar-coated information.

The teacher of social sciences as well as the teacher of English should hold firmly to this fact that literature is something "lived through," something to which the student reacts on a variety of interrelated emotional and intellectual planes. Therein lie its many educational potentialities.

This stress on the value of the literary experience in no way rules out the organized study of psychological and sociological subjects. On the contrary, students should be given even greater opportunities for that kind of knowledge. The social sciences, however, could be made more practically fruitful than they are at present. The question as stated at the end of Chapter 6 is: How can the student come to assimilate the scientific approach to man and society so thoroughly that it will translate itself into the very attitudes, decisions, and actions that constitute his own life? Unfortunately, this has too seldom happened. Many even of the college graduates among present adult generations tend to think only of the conditions that affect them most directly. They do not reconsider their own opinions in the light of social, economic, or psychological theory, nor do they attempt to imagine the human effects of the social measures they espouse as immediately beneficial to themselves.

The will to learn, it has been said, rests on a state of

dissatisfaction with present knowledge. The interchange of ideas in class discussions can lead the student to dissatisfaction with his present knowledge about human relations, since lack of information limits his ability either to participate in the experience offered by the book or to fit the experience into some rational structure of ideas. The reading of literature, therefore, might be made a means of arousing the will to learn. Furthermore, sociological or psychological information sought in this way is more likely to be integrated into the stream of the student's thought and behavior.

The social science teacher must, of course, determine the extent and manner of his use of literary materials, questions beyond the scope of this book. There are similarities between literary experience and direct observation through field trips, another source of personal response to social facts.[3] His special concern will be to bring about a perception of the general implications of what is experienced vicariously through literature. The purposes of the social science classroom require the transition from concern with particular instances to concern

[3] Literature, for instance, might be used as a substitute when such direct observation is not possible. Literary materials might even be an excellent means of introducing the student to the subject or problems to be studied, as a preliminary to direct observation of actual conditions. The analysis in the preceding chapter of the development of social sensitivity through literature is also relevant here.

The case history is another approximation toward personal experience. Its value will depend, probably more than is recognized, on the literary effectiveness with which the case history is presented. In addition to the more scientifically controlled and studied case history, the social science teacher should probably utilize the surer emotional and intellectual effects of literary treatments of the general social conditions with which his particular science concerns itself.

with the general social conditions or basic factors involved.[4]

The teaching processes described in Part Two of this book and in the present chapter can further that transition to general concerns. Conversely, social science discussions of general ideas should more frequently be translated back into terms of individual human beings. Such a shuttling back and forth between the abstract and the concrete, the general and the specific, which the use of literary materials might foster, would give social science study immediacy and lasting value. The student would develop the habit of recognizing that behind any particular situation there exists a general social situation whose causes and effects should be understood. Equally important, he would be aware that any generalizations or statistical data about society, politics, economics, refer to the behavior of living, feeling people.

The preceding remarks reflect the belief that the social science teacher shares with the literature teacher, and indeed with all other teachers, the responsibility toward the student as a complete person. The emphasis and methods of the social science teacher may be different; he

[4] The teacher whose main responsibility is the development of literary sensitivity will be less impatient for this transition to occur and will depend on repeated literary experiences and discussions to accomplish it. The social science teacher will probably consider this too time-consuming, given his desire to impart a body of relevant information. To read a book like Claude Brown's *Manchild in the Promised Land* and then to study Harlem might contribute to such generalization.

Students will need to question whether the picture is an accurate one and whether there may not be contrasting or contradictory considerations that he did not offer. This will illuminate the value of the impersonal scientific investigation based on the study of as many cases as possible.

is interested in initiating his students into an understanding of the methods of research in his particular field and in giving his students some knowledge of the nature of its materials. Ultimately, however, these techniques and this information must become a part of the equipment with which the student encounters actual life situations. In the functioning personality, there should not be any conflict between the attitudes toward man and society engendered by literature and by the social sciences.

Teachers of different subjects will be helped by an understanding of how their various contributions toward a common goal are related to one another. The view that the literature teacher should have some knowledge of the fundamental methods and concepts of the social sciences implies with equal force that the social studies teacher should have some understanding of the special nature of the experience provided by the literary work of art. The social science teacher should be aware of the emotional and intellectual factors entering into the students' literary experience.

The necessity for such mutual understanding among members of the different disciplines has been demonstrated where teachers have worked together in an integrated course. They need to share a common approach to literature and human relations. The great weakness in such courses has been that a lack of insight into the special nature of the literary experience has caused both social science and literature teachers to reduce the literary work of art to the status of social document.

THE CLASSROOM DISCUSSIONS of *A Doll's House, Antony*

and Cleopatra, and other works are isolated instances representing a wide variety of possible illustrations. The intention has been to avoid any suggestion of a routine procedure through which students are docilely led to predigested slogans about social understanding. One of the banes of educational systems today is the pressure on the teacher to work out neat outlines of the ideas about literature that his students are to acquire. Once such a plan is made, there is a great temptation to impose it arbitrarily. The teacher becomes impatient of the trial-and-error groping of the students. It seems so much easier all around if the teacher cuts the Gordian knot and gives the students the tidy set of conclusions and labels he has worked out. Yet this does not necessarily give them new insights. Hence the emphasis throughout this book on the teacher's role in initiating and guiding a process of inductive learning.

A teacher of English in a high school, unusually aware of the adolescent's need to understand human development, decided to give his class a period of several weeks in which they could read novels that presented a life history, ranging from *David Copperfield* to *Sons and Lovers.* He began by lecturing on the main points in developmental psychology. He provided an outline of some of the major problems and influences that enter into the development of any personality. The students were then required to write essays on each novel read, discussing the hero's development in the terms provided by the teacher's outline. The essays indicated that the pupils had read the novels with the aim of finding details to illustrate just those points mentioned by the teacher. The papers gave little indication of what the novels had meant to the youngsters themselves. The whole thing took on the nature of an exercise in which they attempted to apply the teacher's labels to each novel as it passed in review.

Despite his admirable initiative in breaking away from the usual routine of literature teaching, this teacher's aims were defeated by his unfortunate tendency to be satisfied when students had learned a vocabulary. He did not let the desire for organized understanding grow out of the reading of the novels. The pupils should have first been permitted to read these books in ways significant to themselves and thus to have participated emotionally in the growth and aspirations of the heroes and heroines. The class should have become involved in an interchange of ideas and feelings produced by their experience of the novels. Discovering certain similar problems in the lives of these characters, the students would then have been ready for the analysis of life patterns which the psychologist can offer. The perception that the development of a personality is not a haphazard process would have grown out of the reading, not have been imposed upon it. The teacher would have played an extremely important role in fostering this. The students themselves would have played an equally important role, however, and they would have achieved insights related to their own tensions and their own world.

Given the spontaneous and largely unpredictable character of specific literary experiences and the great diversity of temperaments and backgrounds in most student groups, any discussion will tend to develop a special character and focus. To take advantage of this, the teacher will not impose a routine but will let the discussion grow out of the ideas and the perplexities formulated by the students themselves. However, this does not imply sheer improvisation. In order to see the possibilities present in the students' responses, the teacher needs to have a firm grasp on the work and the major concepts relevant to it. He will then be able to carry on an inductive process, in which the students are stimulated to raise questions and to arrive at understandings that have personal significance.

The necessity for presenting isolated classroom illustrations may do injustice to another very important point. Certainly a few scattered discussions of literature could have little or no influence on students' attitudes toward people. Any such influence would be the cumulative effect of many experiences with literature, many free interchanges of opinion among students and teachers, many such emotionally motivated insights. Moreover, the intellectual tone of the school and the habits of thinking fostered by the entire school experience will modify the nature of the discussion in any single class. And within the class, the basis for such spontaneous discussions must be slowly and steadily built up. The give-and-take of ideas and the interplay between different personalities will in itself have a liberalizing influence. If under the repeated stimulus of literature the students have again and again been able to start from their emotional uncertainties and work through to some rational understanding, it is probable that a gradual revision of their habits of feeling and thinking will occur. They will at least have been set upon the path that leads to the development of a rational approach to experience.

THE PERSONAL NATURE OF THE LEARNING PROCESS places a decided responsibility upon the teacher. In seeking to create a vital relationship between his students and literature, he will become imbued with a feeling for the complex process by which social insights can grow out of response to literature. The areas of intellectual and emotional ferment are the points at which growth is possible in the student's mind and personality. The teacher who learns not to become insecure when lively discussion arises will also learn to sense the right moment to introduce new concepts relevant to these growth points. The thesis of Chapters 1 and 6 can now be seen more clearly in its educational context: The teacher can perform his function successfully only when aware of the attitudes toward human nature and society that he is helping his students to assimilate.

This view of literature study is completely alien to the old notion of "character building through literature," which consisted in giving the student, without any regard for his own needs and state of mind, a series of models of behavior to imitate. Equally unacceptable are attempts to treat literature as a body of documents that may be brought forth to illustrate various subtopics under the heading of human relations. Lists of books dealing with topics such as family, war, labor relations—let alone such moralistic topics as noble characters or great deeds of the past—will not in themselves do the job that has been formulated in this book.

The teacher's responsibility would be much reduced if he could think entirely in terms of the "subject matter" of literature. His task then would be principally the assembling of such lists of books. That is not the situation. Literature offers not merely information, but experiences. After all, the important thing is not whether a particular book presents a picture of contemporary marriage relations or describes the activities of the Eskimo, but the way these subjects are treated by the author, and the context into which they are integrated in the reader's mind. Does the image of marriage relationships present an attitude of resentment toward one or the other sex? Or does it offer the possibility of sensing the subtlety of temperamental adjustments involved in the achievement of happily shared lives? The significant thing is not that a book tells how the Eskimo fishes, builds his house, and wins his mate, but whether the book presents the Eskimo as a remote being of a different species or as another human being who happens to have worked out different patterns of behavior.

To catalogue the great body of literary materials according to the basic attitudes they might convey would be a colossal task. It would be almost impossible to find general standards of judgment, principally because the effect of any book will vary with the attitudes and assumptions that each reader brings to it. Although in the following pages terms drawn from the social sciences will be used, the focus is on the subtler, least easily catalogued modes of social understanding that literature makes possible.

There is a tendency to feel that one can create social understanding by simply assigning to students a group of novels or plays dealing with a social science topic. The value of book lists depends on how they are used and whether the teacher selects from them in the light of his students' or his classes' needs.

Moreover, it is necessary to reiterate that the teacher must play an active part in the development of social understanding. He himself needs to possess an enlightened sense of human relations in order to help his students derive new sensitivities from literary experience and evaluate it in personal and social terms. In the long run, therefore, this kind of illumination cannot be prescribed for by means of book lists, outlines, and routine procedures. It will depend in each case on the particular personalities and backgrounds of each group of teacher and students as well as upon the nature of the particular school setting.

The preceding qualifications should prevent the misinterpretation that sometimes arises when ideas illuminated by literary materials are emphasized. Moreover, given the point of view and the teaching process set forth in Part Two, literary history, biographical information, and critical analysis of technique will not degenerate into routine studies considered as ends in themselves. They will have value because they throw light upon the total literary experience, with all that it implies of personal emotion and social awareness.

The study of literary history, for instance, is often insufficiently motivated. The student learns about the sequence of literary movements, he memorizes the chronology of authors and works, but only because this seems to be information arbitrarily demanded. He learns it for examinations, but forgets it very quickly. Despite the study of periods and chronology, Chaucer, Swift, and Thackeray come to inhabit the same vague region.

The history of literature recounts the social activities of man in one special realm, just as does the history of politics or of industry. The various approaches to the study of literature parallel the approaches to the study of any of man's activities and institutions. Failure to emphasize this partially explains the usual sterility of the study of literary history in school and college.

The study of literary history constitutes a study of social history in two ways: First, since the writer is always a member of a particular society and a particular group within that society, his work grows out of the various social, economic, and intellectual conditions of his time. Literary scholarship has generally assimilated this approach. Especially in the treatment of American literature, the writer is studied as a member of society, and his work is viewed in relation to the various social and intellectual pressures of his time.

Second—and this is the point that is least often recognized or exploited—the various *processes* of social history may often be studied more dramatically through literary history than through any other phase of man's activities. Literature is a social institution in the sense that the family or church is a social institution, each with its own history. Because man's literary behavior takes the explicit form mainly of a body of written or printed works, its history is perhaps somewhat more clearly delimited. Yet it seldom is utilized to initiate students into an understanding of general social mechanisms. Literary history reveals clearly the nature of the individual's relations to the social group, as well as the nature of the forces molding the group itself. The student should be helped to apply to other phases of man's life the ideas concerning historical processes derived from literary history.

Literature is not a photographic mirroring of life but is the result of a particular socially patterned personality employing particular socially fostered modes of communication. Much of what is considered purely literary, technical, or textual criticism involves definitions of the special temperamental attitudes of the author, the precise emotional tone of his work, and its particular philosophic approach. All of this is essential to appreciate the literary merits of his work. The study of his manipulations of literary technique (to which the term *literary criticism* is often too narrowly limited) is incidental to the desire to apprehend the special qualities of the novel or poem or play. Walter Pater, the apostle of esthetic criticism, limited his duties as critic to a clarification or definition of the impression produced on him by literary works. Yet in a study such as his *Wordsworth,* this aim encompasses social and psychological considerations.

From these literary concerns should arise an added awareness that any individual—writer or bricklayer—with his special traits and techniques is the result of interaction with his environment.[5] This concept is often presented to

[5] "Environment" here necessarily includes physical nature as well as the cultural setting. Various geographical determinists at the end of the last century exaggerated the influence of man's natural environment; nowadays we may tend to underestimate its influence, particularly on literature. See Aldous Huxley's entertaining essay on what Wordsworth's sense of nature might have been if he had lived in the tropics rather than in the gentle atmosphere of the Lake Country.

the student only in the study of such topics as crime, juvenile delinquency, or politics. Yet this view of the individual is illustrated just as dramatically in the creation of the artist as in the acts of criminals or statesmen. By seeing how a concept of this sort applies throughout the whole range of his studies—social, scientific, or artistic—the student will be able to build up an integrated approach to human relations.

One of the usual approaches to the study of literature is the history of different forms—the novel, the drama, poetry, the essay. The student learns that in different periods these forms reflect different literary traditions. He is not made aware that literary traditions represent one type of crystallized social behavior. After all, environmental influences operate as much in an author's treatment of literary form and choice of theme as in any other phase of man's activity. The imagination of the Elizabethan dramatist, for instance, necessarily functioned within the framework of the conventions and dramatic formulas of his day. Knowing them can help us to differentiate between what in Elizabethan plays the contemporary audience accepted as dramatic convention and what reflected the actual life about them. The very themes the dramatist selected were similarly nourished by the intellectual climate of his time. From study of a particular literary form at different periods there can arise the perception that the individual's activities and ideas in any sphere are necessarily directed by attitudes and patterns absorbed from his cultural environment.

Similarly, the study of a literary period as a whole may

illuminate this concept of the shaping pressure of the environment upon the individual. If he lives in a time when prose forms are highly valued and poetry neglected, he will tend most readily to express himself in prose. If he lives in an age when the drama is the dominant form, he will probably express himself through that medium. Or if he uses some minor form, it will probably be selected from those admired in his milieu, as in the case of the Elizabethan sonnet. Indeed, the pressure of literary conventions is even more pervasive than that. Having grown up at a time when the heroic couplet is the common poetic mold, he will tend to express himself in its balanced and measured phrases, and freer patterns will seem rough and unpleasant to his ear. The study of eighteenth-century poetry or of eighteenth-century criticism of Elizabethan literature can serve to illustrate this concept of cultural conditioning.

It is often hard for the student to realize in a vivid or personal way that the ideas and behavior he accepts most unquestioningly derive their hold upon him from the fact that they have been unconsciously absorbed from the society about him. He can be led from a perception of how this happens in literary activity to an understanding of the similar process which crystallizes the individual's ideas concerning ways of behavior and ideas of right and wrong. Having observed so explicit a demonstration of how even the most gifted and intelligent authors are shaped by their environment, the student may come to recognize similar pressures upon all other phases of men's thought and activity. He should see that the existence of literary periods with marked characteristics of style and subject matter is the reflection of a general sociological phenomenon.

The student who becomes acquainted with this concept of cultural conditioning often may tend to exaggerate its implications. He may think of the individual as completely at the mercy of the dominant forces in the environment about him. This is as erroneous, of course, as is the earlier notion that the individual has complete free choice and self-determination. The study of Shakespeare in relation to the other Elizabethan dramatists may illuminate this problem in a way highly interesting to students. They have accepted the idea of Shakespeare as a supreme genius. Their introduction, however, to the tragedies of blood, and particularly to Thomas Kyd's *Spanish Tragedy*, usually brings keen disillusionment. They find that much in Shakespeare's *Hamlet* follows the outlines of earlier plays which also use ghosts calling for revenge, avengers who are mad or feign madness, heroes who hesitate and soliloquize. They discover that Shakespeare often followed very literally the theatrical conventions of his own day. The student's first reaction usually is to remove Shakespeare from his pedestal and to exclaim that he was merely a man of his own time, after all.

Reflection, however, brings revision of this judgment. They begin to see that Shakespeare was thoroughly a product of a particular environment, and yet, working within the patterns set by his time, he modified them and put his own unique stamp upon them. A comparison between his plays and contemporary ones of the same type, such as the romantic comedies or the tragicomedies, reveals the pervasive influence of his literary environment upon the individual, but it reveals also his ability to create something new and superbly individual out of the elements provided by his age. Moreover, these unique creations will influence writers who come after him. Through the study of easily recognized literary details, the student can be led to perceive within a limited sphere something of how in all phases of man's life the average individual, too, not only is molded by but also molds his environment.

EVEN MORE STRIKING is the light that the study of literary history may cast upon the process of social change. This should be understood as a process in time, involving the constant adjustment and readjustment of particular individuals to particular cultural patterns. This human view of social changes can grow out of a study of the modifications over a period of time in authors' selections of subjects and choices of literary forms. The study of English literature from 1750 to 1830, for instance, offers dramatic possibilities for developing a sense of the complex factors involved in any change in man's ways of thinking and behavior.

For example, the concept of "cultural lag" applies as much to literature as to any phase of history. A study of verse forms, poetic diction, and themes shows how attitudes and social patterns tend to persist even when they no longer serve a vital need. The hold of the heroic couplet, the endless minor variations on themes fully exploited earlier in the century, the development of tricks of poetic diction to the point of absurdity, illustrate very forcibly the tendency of the average mind to follow already channeled grooves.

Against this background of persisting habits and conventions, the study of the beginnings of the romantic movement in the eighteenth century and its flowering in the early nineteenth century can illustrate the slow cumulative process of social innovation—the few signs earlier in the century of a slight departure from accepted attitudes toward man and nature in a poem here and there by a Lady Winchelsea or a Parnell; the evidence of an increasing body of sentimental minor poetry, like the "graveyard poems," that hints at new tendencies; the partial break with tradition represented by the Wartons or by Thomson; the harking back to literary precedents of the Middle Ages and the Renaissance to sanction rejection of the contemporary conventions; the curious transitional quality of Gray's poems or of Wordsworth's earliest verse; the full revolt bursting forth in the *Lyrical Ballads;* the resistance that Wordsworth, Keats, Shelley, and the others met from critics and readers still dominated by the Pope tradition in poetry; the slow education of an audience that would understand and appreciate their work.

These literary materials give vivid evidence that social change often comes about slowly and almost imperceptibly. At first a few minds here and there free themselves from the worn-out attitudes and procedures that no longer satisfy new needs. Gradually the number of these nonconformists increases; their influence spreads; and ultimately their ideas may become the dominant ones automatically assimilated by young authors and readers, as in the case of the romantic view of poetry. Thus, in his study of the rise of romanticism, the student can find dramatically portrayed the pull and tug of contending social phenomena. The tendency to hold on to old attitudes, on the one hand, is opposed by the struggle, on the other hand, to find fresher and more completely satisfying patterns. In other words, the relation between the processes of cultural lag and social innovation is revealed as legitimately in literary history as it is in the history of technology or of political institutions.

The anthropologist's idea of the interdependence of the various aspects of any culture can be related to the history of literature. An understanding of what happens in the realm of literary activity requires the study of the accompanying economic, social, and political conditions. It would, for example, be false to explain the romantic movement entirely in literary terms as a revolt against eighteenth-century formalism. (Of course, this popular view of eighteenth-century literature is also oversimplified.) It is necessary to be aware also of the political ideals, the emphasis on a static and stratified society, which paralleled the eighteenth-century concern with balanced form and disciplined emotion. Romantic exaltation of free expression of individual feeling often arose from rejection of social as well as literary limitations.

Similar interdependences can be noted no matter what period is studied. What, for example, were the forces at work in Elizabethan society that helped to make possible the flowering of the drama? What were the economic and social conditions that created so heterogeneous an audience for the theatre? How did the fact that the Court still played so central an economic and social, as well as political, role influence the drama? How did the religious and philosophic developments affect the sense of significant human problems? The history of literature cannot be viewed as completely separate from other aspects of society.

The anthropologists point out also that through this interaction of its different elements, a culture tends to develop some degree of integration, a recognizable basic cultural pattern. Out of the interplay between the different forces at work in the society will arise a set of dominant values or drives. These will determine whether a society values human life or military glory more, whether it phrases success in terms of material acquisition or ceremonial generosity, whether it gives greater prestige to wealth or craftsmanship or learning. The nature of this dominant pattern will make a great difference in the emotional overtones and in the very character of the various personal relations within that society.

Within the range of even a single literature we may encounter the reflection of a number of different cultural emphases—in the literature of England, for example, the sharp contrast between earthly and otherworldly values in medieval society, with its intense appreciation of both; the greater flexibility of Renaissance institutions, with the attendant zest for free expression of individual personality; the increasing importance of materialistic bourgeois values in the eighteenth and nineteenth centuries, with accompanying stress on property and on social prudence; the paradoxical reflection of bourgeois economic individualism in the romanticists' demands for personal freedom, and their break with the utilitarian bourgeois view of life when the romantic artists translated their individualism into esthetic and spiritual values; the development of the physical and biological sciences creating a crisis in religious thought through their reinforcement of a naturalistic interpretation of man and the universe; and the increasingly frequent expression today of a philosophy that stresses the individual's inescapable bonds with his fellowmen. The societies that express themselves through English literature seem to have developed varying degrees of integration. In some ages, one perceives a number of clear-cut subpatterns, or even a number of contradictory patterns in a state of unstable equilibrium; in other ages, many aspects of the society seem to reflect similar or parallel emphases.

Even such a sketchy listing indicates that a literary work reflects or refracts the characteristic emphases of its own age. The literature program has always included works produced in a great many different periods and social settings. Students read (or should read) books that treat both contemporary and past American life; British, French, German, Russian novels; modern versions of the Scandinavian epics; or Greek drama. An increasingly large body of Oriental literature is becoming available in translation. In addition to this, the growing body of fiction, such as Freuchen's *Eskimo*, dealing with primitive societies reveals how differently human life may be patterned in another culture. The student encounters diverse temperaments and images of personal success in the literary works of different ages or even in the literature of a single period. He tends to take these differences for granted, without recognizing the extent to which each work implies a framework of values, mores, and modes of expression particular to some one cultural setting.

Nor are students usually helped to recognize that in any literary work the diverse values of a society are incorporated into the personalities and lives of individual men and women. Mark Twain utilized this insight in *A Connecticut Yankee in King Arthur's Court*. The Yankee embodies the sense of values of one cultural pattern; the Arthurian knights reflect a different pattern. Much of the humor of this book arises from the perspective thus created, so that both cultures are viewed satirically—and, of course, Mark Twain ultimately uses this to question certain values of his own society. Orwell's *1984* is another work that forces readers to ponder the system of values of a whole society and to consider its meaning in terms of individual lives.

Problems in values thrust themselves upon the reader even more urgently in the works of those contemporary novelists, dramatists, and poets who look upon man's life as "absurd." Many young people respond intensely to this image of man born into an indifferent world, shorn of all former external props, and confronting the inevitability of death. Such works as Camus' *The Stranger* or Beckett's *Waiting for Godot* undoubtedly provide a catharsis for many youthful readers. Still, the very sense of alienation may be the beginning of a movement toward positive commitment to society and toward the feeling that man creates himself by his choices. In *The Plague* Camus explores the many different hierarchies of values men affirm through their choices in a crisis. Many contemporary writers, for example, Saul Bellow (*The Dangling Man, Herzog*), Bernard Malamud (*The Fixer*), Ralph Ellison (*Invisible Man*), or John Knowles (*A Separate Peace*), develop such a theme.

Yet surely it is not only in contemporary works that the issue of choices in values imposes itself. As in life itself, questions of values are always implicit in any poem, novel, or play. Characters are faced with the necessity for choice, and by those choices affirm or deny the values of their world; the voice of the *persona* in a poem or narrative, by one clue and another, creates a scale of values by which the reader is asked to measure the mood or the world that has been evoked. Far from the old didacticism is this recognition that all literature affirms or denies values, and that an important part of literary criticism is the clarification of such values. The youth today is confronted by necessity for choice among a vast range of alternatives. Contemporary works relevant to the adolescent's quest for identity will generate receptivity to all that literature, of both the past and the present, has to offer him.

Just as the student will recognize in the literature of the past reflections of dominant drives and emerging alternative attitudes, so he will view contemporary literature as the expression of many minds working, slowly and often at cross purposes, toward the creation of a new and more satisfactory system of common values. Through the experience of literature of the past he will be able also to come into contact with diverse views of the satisfactions to be derived from human life and society. These will serve both as contrast and as commentary on present-day emphases and on any newly offered alternatives for personal and social arrangements. Perhaps such perspective may also lead him to discriminate between works that merely reflect a general mood of disillusionment and those that reveal minds seeking new and positive alternatives.

The introduction of new types of personalities into literature, the picture of new types of relationships, or the assertion of new values in life by the writer will have their repercussions upon the practical social and political life of an age. As George Boas insists, even those works that are in opposition to the dominant attitudes of their time—for instance, the writings of Dickens, Arnold, and Ruskin—are as much a part of their age as the writings that reflect its dogmas. Subtract the works of Dickens and the others from the Victorian Age and it would be something different from that age as we now understand it. The tendency to speak in terms of the social and political "background" of literature is misleading, since it implies that the background existed apart from the literature. This contradicts the view that aspects of any culture tend to act and react upon one another.

Another point requires clarification: Literary works do not inevitably "hold the mirror up to nature." Often the work can best be understood as "a slice of life seen through a temperament." The poem, play, or novel reflects the social philosophy of the author, or it may present a picture of people and situations dictated by the dominant literary conventions of the age in which the author lived. Again, it may be that only the life of a limited group in the society finds any sort of reflection in the literature of a given period. (Typical examples are Restoration comedy or the triangle situations in French novels.) Often, moreover, certain literary trends (for example, the novels of Sir Walter Scott, the great mass of romantic poetry) may represent an attempt to escape from the realities of the society in which the authors live.

Part of a sound equipment for understanding and judging literature is a knowledge of the possible factors, personal obsessions, class bias, political aims, pendulum-swing reactions, that may color the world the writer chooses to create. It would be as absurd for students to think that the novels of futility, such as those of F. Scott Fitzgerald, reflected the whole picture of life in the nineteen-twenties as to believe that Elizabethan drama is a literal transcript of life in England at that time. Learning to sense the angle of vision of the author, the young reader will come to see in contemporary literature the inverted Victorian prudery of some of the clinical descriptions of sex, and to differentiate these from the works seeking to do justice to its central role in a mature life.

The student has to be provided with the tools for weighing the various images of life that he encounters in books. This means that he must often turn from the literary work to other sources of information, whether those be the materials offered by the historian, the literary scholar, the sociologist, the anthropologist, or the psychologist. Both from the point of view of literary criticism and from the point of view of preparation for actual living, he should be stimulated to evaluate the ethical and social implications of the images of life encountered through

literature. To evade this responsibility out of fear of falling into didactic moralism is to narrow the study of literature to a sterile formalism.

The preceding remarks on cultural integration have led
to a transition from general social processes working themselves out in literary history and methods of literary creation to those processes as they are exemplified in the
images of individual lives offered by specific literary
works. Chapter 6 reported the behavioral scientists' emphasis on the concept that the human being is a complex
of qualities and habits which are the end result of a great
many different forces converging upon and interacting
with the individual organism.

Ideas about human growth and development are the
very stuff of literature. The process of cultural conditioning is seen operating in the images of life that the author
places before us. In the course of a year, the student
usually reads works dealing with personalities in a wide
variety of environments, but he is not always led to think
about this. The personal strivings, the ethical problems,
the social conflicts he shares through books, are often part
of social patterns very different from his own. With Macbeth, Jane Eyre, Becky Sharp, Lawrence's Paul Morel,
Dreiser's Clyde Griffiths, Faulkner's Quentin Compson, he
struggles vicariously with social codes reflecting diverse
environments. Because Hardy placed the problem of the
influence of environment in the center of attention, students are often led to associate this question only with his
works. Any writer, particularly any novelist or dramatist,
treats some aspect of this basic process by which the
individual human being lives out his life in terms of the

social structure, the moral code, and even the emotional habits he has acquired through interaction with his specific environment.

As we become more clearly aware of forces that pattern our lives, we acquire a certain power to resist or modify these forces. (See p. 155.) Hence the importance of an understanding of the concept of cultural conditioning. The student may derive this valuable insight from almost any work of literature. To return to *Hamlet* as an illustration: On the one hand, students will perceive in personal terms relevant to life today the nature of Hamlet's problem (such a "modern" interpretation as, for example, that he is a contemplative man caught in a situation demanding action). On the other hand, they should not ignore the fact that Hamlet's problem is bodied forth in specific terms of the code of "eye for eye, tooth for tooth"—a code archaic in Shakespeare's day as well as our own. Obviously, no play about a man of Hamlet's social and intellectual status in our own time would present him as assuming that society expected him personally to kill the murderer of his father.

The fear has been expressed that constant reading of literature of the past might tend to perpetuate the hold of anachronistic images of behavior. Perhaps one way of counteracting this is to make the reader aware that in literary works he submits vicariously to a cultural pattern and code of behavior often different from his own. This may develop some immunity to archaic images and some objectivity toward the cultural situation in which he himself is immersed. If the Jungian concept of an "archetypal pattern" or myth is brought to bear, it will be used with

similar objectivity. Thus without inner confusion or maladjustment to contemporary reality, he will be able to
profit from the breadth of experience, the flexibility of
imaginative insight, and the sensuous enrichment that literature can impart.

THE VARIOUS OTHER CONCEPTS concerning human growth
and development sketched in Chapter 6 are also implicit
in the great body of literary works. Numerous novels follow the hero or heroine from birth to maturity. Works
such as *Tom Jones, Great Expectations, The Way of All
Flesh, Of Human Bondage, Sons and Lovers, Portrait of
the Artist as a Young Man, The Last Puritan, Pelle the
Conqueror, Jean Christophe,* imply the whole developmental approach to personality. As the student shares the
life of the hero or heroine, he perceives some of the psychological processes involved in the interaction between
the growing human creature and his environment: the
child in a world of adults, taking on their behavior and
standards, extremely sensitive to their acceptance or rejection of him; the emergence of the child's sense of himself
as a separate person, and his struggles to attain some kind
of integrated personality; the environmental aids or obstacles to the attainment of this personal and social independence; the necessity for resolving problems and conflicts created by the fact that he is a member of a
particular economic and social group; the impact of different religious and ethical systems; the need to make
some kind of sexual adjustment; the way all of these
factors affect the individual's image of himself and the

crystallization of his attitudes toward others; how the individual's sense of the satisfactions worth striving for is formed; the variety of possible attitudes of acceptance or rejection toward the dominant conventions of his environment; the fact that a life viewed from one angle may be a failure, but viewed from another may be highly successful; the element of continuity in any life history.

Such a developmental approach to personality is equally applicable to biography. We have seen how the traditional study of literary history can be given general significance and intellectual motivation. Similar pointedness could be given to the traditional study of writers' lives. Too often, studying an author's biography consists merely in learning the chronology of events. If the personality was in conflict with his environment or maladjusted in any way, as in the case of Shelley or Keats, the student tends to think this a peculiarity of artists. The highly marked personalities of many literary figures, their sensitivity to the world about them, and their articulateness make their biographies particularly vivid material for viewing the complex factors that enter into the crystallization of personality.

A study of various biographies of the same person is another means of making the student conscious of different interpretations of what are the important factors in personality development. Such a point of view would do much to vivify the usual routine and quite irrelevant study of authors' lives—as it would, of course, illuminate the study of any biographies, whether of statesmen, scientists, explorers, or teachers. There has been a revival of interest in biography—all the more reason for helping students to develop from this reading some general framework of ideas concerning the growth and development of the human being.

The province of literature, we have said, is all that man has thought and felt and created. It would be possible to multiply examples of how literary works embody one or another phase of man's social life, or reveal one or another potentiality of human temperament, or clarify one or another process of individual or group development. There is, for example, the great body of works that express the broad gamut of social arrangements, temperamental adjustments, conflicts and disillusionments, joys and fulfillments that have grown out of the relations between man and woman. Literary works whose theme is love, courtship, and marriage may give the adolescent reader not only an emotional outlet and psychological preparation but also a historical and cultural perspective.

Suggestions might be offered about how various bodies of literature throw light on man's life—in, say, the relations between races, nations, and classes, or between groups such as the artists and their public. Or how through literature we can apprehend the meaning, for the individual life, of different religious and philosophic attitudes. What it means to the individual to live in an agricultural or an industrial economy, in a rigid or flexible class system; how variously family relationships can be patterned; what problems face members of different groups in our own society today—the artists, the laborers, the sharecroppers, the Jews, the Negroes, women, youth; what social and economic philosophies inspire men today—these and innumerable other questions about man and society are illuminated through literature.

The study of American literature offers the student abundant opportunities for social insights especially relevant to his own problems. He can derive from our literature valuable understanding of the social conditions and processes that are characteristic of our extraordinary history. Our whole literature bears the stamp of a new country only gradually being created out of man's struggle with nature. The works of American authors from Puritan days to the present reveal a cultural heritage drawn from various Old World sources, particularly from England, taking on new overtones, absorbing new values, being slowly merged in a new cultural synthesis. The emphasis throughout this book on the social values and insights implicit in literary experience seems self-evident in relation to American literature. Our writers, almost every one, have in one way or another been conscious of their unique cultural setting and have sought to reflect it, to utter its essential spirit, to castigate its weaknesses, to sing its hopes and aspirations. Even those writers who have seemed to stand aside from the life about them have usually sought to create something of the beauty or the subtlety they found lacking in their environment.

The problem of the American writer has been to utilize everything of value in his literary heritage without letting it screen from him the special qualities of the new way of life about him. Seeking to remain a part of the splendid current of European literary tradition, he has at the same time struggled to grasp and make articulate the nature of the unique American experiment. With varying degrees of success, our writers have sought to use or remold the traditional forms in order to express the energetic spirit of a pioneer society. American literature reveals the convergence of a number of cultural trends produced by the intermingling of many peoples under the conditions imposed by a new land, during a period of economic, social, political, and philosophic readjustment throughout Western civilization. It has been the task of our writers to give utterance to the complex problems of a society in process of creation and yet to place these problems in their larger setting of changing scientific, political, and philosophic thought in the modern world.

The development of programs of "American studies" in undergraduate and graduate institutions has fostered concern with American literature in its cultural setting. Studies of various writers have illuminated different facets of this process of the creation of a new society. Many writers have given sensitive expression to the problems of the immigrant, in his adjustments both to his new environment and to the cultural gap between himself and his Americanized children. Even the great body of regional literature makes vivid the heterogeneous and complex nature of America. Or again, many recent works express the strains and stresses of our society and the plight of minority groups. There is the recurrent theme of aspiration toward an ever more democratic and humane way of life. Works such as these can aid the student in understanding the nature of the past out of which the society has grown and in becoming aware of the forces at work in it today.

Many other areas of human relations could be cited to illustrate this general philosophy of literature study. As the teacher himself comes to view his own literary experiences in this way, he will be able to make the study of any literary work a means for fostering in his students the capacity for such comprehension of man and society.

ESSENTIAL TO THIS APPROACH is the gradual discovery of ideas and insights by the student through actual literary experience and reflection upon it. Hence the focus on general social concepts rather than specific informational topics such as family relations, labor relations, juvenile delinquency, or war. By seeing how certain basic concepts apply throughout the range of his studies, the student will be able to build up an integrated approach to human relations. In this way he will develop fundamental understandings and critical attitudes that he will be able to apply even to those fields or unforeseen situations that his school courses have not covered.

Such recognition of recurrent basic concepts encountered through a variety of approaches to knowledge is probably the soundest kind of "correlation." It is not half so important that the student should acquire history, sociology, and literature simultaneously as it is that he should see exemplified in each of these fields certain unifying concepts concerning human nature and society.

Similarly, outlines of integrated courses are much less important than the teacher's possession of an understanding of how the particular body of knowledge with which he is concerned is related to the rest of man's life. Certainly there is much to be gained from breaking down rigid subject-matter divisions. But the success of any such procedures must depend ultimately on whether or not the teachers themselves have assimilated such an integrated and humanistic point of view.

After all, even in schools and colleges where there are rigidly separate departments, the individual teacher can do much to prevent compartmentalization in the students' minds. The teacher can communicate to his students a sense of his particular subject in its living context. In his class, they can encounter echoes and new incarnations of ideas gained in other classes. They can be made to feel the human implications and overtones of a particular body of knowledge. Learning can be made a process of perceiving wider implications and of relating them to the central core of human values.

As more of his fellow teachers acquire such insight, they will eventually develop external procedures and curriculum arrangements more expressive of their sense of the organic nature of knowledge. Only those integrated courses or "core" curricula that have grown out of such attitudes have much chance of success. If such experiments are sometimes unsatisfactory, the fault is not with the idea of integration or synthesis, but with those who have sought to execute it. Concern about flexible and integrated curricular patterns has tended to obscure the prime essential—flexibility and an organic approach to knowledge in the teacher's own mind.

THE LITERARY EXPERIENCE has been seen to reside in the synthesis of what the reader already knows and feels and desires with what the literary text offers—the patterned sensations, emotions, and ideas through which the author has sought to communicate his sense of life. Our eyes must always be directed toward that dynamic interaction between the work of art and the personality of the reader. The aim will be to increase the student's ability to achieve a full, sound reading of the text, and to broaden the personal context of emotions and ideas into which this response will be incorporated. The development of literary appreciation will depend upon a reciprocal process: An enlargement of the student's understanding of human life leads to increased esthetic sensitivity, and increased esthetic sensitivity makes possible more fruitful human insights from literature. Efforts to heighten the student's appreciation of the formal qualities of the literary work will be organically related to the effort to enrich his sense of human values.

Awareness of the highly personal nature of the literary experience protects against the deadening influence of routine; the student may derive from literature intimate benefits perhaps not visible, yet more precious than anything didactically imposed. Literary works may help him to understand himself and his own problems more completely and may liberate him from his secret self-doubtings and personal anxieties. Literature's revelation of the diverse elements of our complex cultural heritage may free him from the provincialism of his own necessarily limited environment. Books may often provide him with an image of the kind of personality and way of life that he will seek to achieve. A major contribution toward these potential benefits can be to provide him with as broad a gamut of literary experiences as possible. Even more important is the scrupulous effort to avoid any academic procedures that may hinder a spontaneous personal response.

Because the literary experience tends to involve both the intellect and the emotions in a manner that parallels life itself, the insights attained through literature may be assimilated into the matrix of attitudes and ideas which constitute character and govern behavior. Hence the opportunity for the student to develop the habit of reflective thinking within the context of an emotionally colored situation.

THIS BOOK HAS ATTEMPTED to reveal how much the experience and study of literature have to offer that is relevant to the crucial needs of personalities involved in the conflicts and stresses of life in our changing society. Indeed, literary experiences might be made the very core of the kind of educational process needed in a democracy.

If we only do justice to the potentialities inherent in literature itself, we can make a vital social contribution. As the student vicariously shares through literature the emotions and aspirations of other human beings, he can gain heightened sensitivity to the needs and problems of others remote from him in temperament, in space, or in social environment; he can develop a greater imaginative capacity to grasp the meaning of abstract laws or political and social theories for actual human lives. Such sensitivity and imagination are part of the indispensable equipment of the citizen of a democracy.

Moreover, literature may serve the student in the two phases of his development usually neglected by orthodox educational procedures, but essential for successful life in a heterogeneous, democratic society seeking to create more satisfactory ways of life. First, imaginative participation in the wide variety of alternative philosophies and patterns of behavior accessible through literature, and the development of the power to reflect upon them, can liberate the student from anachronistic emotional attitudes.

Second, having freed himself from the tyranny of attitudes and ideas ill-adapted to modern life, the youth should not be left in a state of paralysis of the will. The organic nature of the literary experience provides some assurance that new insights will be assimilated emotionally as well as intellectually. Hence literature can also nourish the impetus toward more fruitful modes of behavior. Literary experiences may help to fasten his emotions upon new and happier types of relationships or upon the images of new and more socially valuable satisfactions to be derived from life. Thus he may acquire the sympathy and insight, the critical attitudes, and the sense of human values needed for his creation of new ideals and new personal goals.

Only as literature teachers actively promote these latent possibilities can they hope to approximate this ideal picture. A preeminent condition for success is that teachers themselves possess a lively sense of all that literature offers. They should avoid inculcating their own assumptions about human beings and social values and should support the student in his efforts to understand himself and the forces that pattern society. He needs to create for himself a humane system of values and the flexibility to apply it under the complex and fluid conditions of contemporary life. One source of such strengths can be literature—the ordered sensuous, emotional, and intellectual perceptions embodied in the literary experience.

Our society needs not only to make possible the creation of great works of art; it needs also to make possible the growth of personalities sufficiently sensitive, rational, and humane to be capable of creative literary experiences. In the pursuit of such ideals, the teaching of literature can become a function worthy of the humane nature of literature itself. Literary experiences will then be a potent force in the growth of critically minded, emotionally liberated individuals who possess the energy and the will to create a happier way of life for themselves and for others.

Coda:
A Performing Art *

THOSE WHO SEEK to praise the riches of literature have often been well-served by Keats' image of the reader as a traveler "in the realms of gold" coming upon a great work like "some watcher of the skies/When a new planet swims into his ken." But this suggestion of a remote object gazed upon with awe may reinforce the current, almost hypnotically repeated, emphasis on "the work itself" as distinct from author and reader. Fortunately, in another sonnet, "On Sitting Down To Read *King Lear* Once Again," Keats provides a counterbalancing image, which does justice to the reader's involvement in the literary work:

> . . . once again the fierce dispute
> Betwixt damnation and impassion'd clay,
> *Must I burn through.*

Imaginative literature is indeed something "burned through," lived through, by the reader. We do not learn *about* Lear, we share, we participate in, Lear's stormy induction into wisdom. In *Huckleberry Finn*, we do not learn *about* conditions in the pre-Civil War South; we live in them, we see them through the eyes and personality of Huck. Even while we chuckle at his adventures

---

* This essay, reprinted from *The English Journal*, November 1966, with the permission of the National Council of Teachers of English, is added here to perform the function of the coda in music—a few closing measures introduced at the end of a composition to emphasize the major chords.

and his idiom, we grow into awareness of the moral dimensions appropriate for viewing that world. Whether it be a lighthearted lyric of Herrick's or a swiftly paced intellectual comedy of Shaw's or a brooding narrative of Hardy's, a reading is of necessity a participation, a personal experience.

The literary work is not primarily a document in the history of language or society. It is not simply a mirror of, or a report on, life. It is not a homily setting forth moral or philosophic or religious precepts. As a work of art, it offers a special kind of experience. It is a mode of living. The poem, the play, the story, is thus an extension, an amplification, of life itself. The reader's primary purpose is to add *this* kind of experience to the other kinds of desirable experience that life may offer.

NO ONE ELSE can read a literary work for us. The benefits of literature can emerge only from creative activity on the part of the reader himself. He responds to the little black marks on the page, or to the sounds of the words in his ear, and he "makes something of them." The verbal symbols enable him to draw on his past experiences with what the words point to in life and literature. The text presents these words in a new and unique pattern. Out of these he is enabled actually to mold a new experience, the literary work.

It is this experiential aspect which differentiates the literary work of art from other forms of verbal communication. *Imaginative* literature happens when we focus our attention on what we are sensing, thinking, feeling, structuring, in the act of response to the particular words in their particular order. Even the most modest work—a nursery rhyme, say—demands attention to what the words are calling forth within us. In its highest form, as in Keats' reading of Shakespeare, such absorption in what we are evoking from the text produces feelings of being completely carried out of oneself.

As the reader submits himself to the guidance of the text, he must engage in a most demanding kind of activity. Out of his past experience, he must select appropriate responses to the individual words, he must sense their interplay upon one another, he must respond to clues of tone and attitude and movement. He must focus his attention on what he is structuring through these means. He must try to see it as an organized whole, its parts interrelated as fully as the text and his own capacities permit. From sound and rhythm and image and idea he forges an experience, a synthesis, that he calls the poem or play or novel. Whether for a nursery rhyme or for *King Lear*, such an activity goes on, and its complex nature can only be suggested here. The amazing thing is that critics and theorists have paid so little attention to this synthesizing process itself, contenting themselves usually with the simpler task of classifying the verbal symbols and their various patterns in the text.

In the *teaching* of literature, then, we are basically helping our students to learn to perform in response to a text. In this respect we are perhaps closer to the voice teacher, even the swimming coach, than we are to the teacher of history or botany. The reader performs the poem or the novel, as the violinist performs the sonata. But the instrument on which the reader plays, and from which he evokes the work, is—himself. The final lines of Yeats' "Among School Children" are sometimes used out of context to suggest the fusion of so-called form and substance in the work of art itself.

O body swayed to music, O brightening glance,
How can we know the dancer from the dance?

In this image of the dancer, who under the spell of the music makes of his own body the formed substance which is the dance, we can also prefigure the reader: Under the guidance of the text, out of his own thoughts and feelings and sensibilities, the reader makes a new ordering, the formed substance which is for him the literary work of art. The teacher of literature, especially, needs to keep alive this view of the literary work as personal evocation, the product of creative activity carried on by the reader under the guidance of the text.

CRITICAL THEORY during the past few decades has made this emphasis suspect, however. Building on one facet of I. A. Richards' work, the "New Critics" and their sympathizers did much to rescue the poem as a work of art from earlier confusions with the poem either as a biographical document or as a document in intellectual and social history. A mark of much twentieth-century criticism became its avoidance largely of the social and biographical approach to literature. This, moreover, was paralleled by a reaction against impressionist criticism. Walter Pater, for example, became the exemplar of the reader too preoccupied with his own emotions to remain faithful to "the poem itself." The reaction from impressionism fostered the notion of an impersonal or objective criticism, which, avoiding also the historical and social, busied itself with exploitation of the techniques of "close reading." This tended to treat "the poem"—or any literary work—as if it existed as an object, like a machine, whose parts can be analyzed without reference either to the maker or to the observer (or reader). Those who have been indoctrinated with this critical emphasis are especially shocked at insistence on the literary work as experience. They misinterpret this as an invitation to irresponsible emotionalism and impressionism.

There is, in fact, nothing in the recognition of the personal nature of literature that requires an acceptance of the notion that every evocation from a text is as good as every other. We need only think of our successive readings of the same text, at 15 or 30 or 50, to know that we can differentiate. Undisciplined, irrelevant, or distorted emotional responses and the lack of relevant experience or knowledge will, of course, lead to inadequate interpretations of the text. The aim is to help the student toward a more and more controlled, more and more valid or defensible, response to the text.

This does not imply, however, that there is, as with a mathematical problem, one single "correct" reading of a literary text. This raises very complex and thorny problems concerning the criteria of soundness to be applied to any interpretation. However, this question is much more difficult to settle in theory than to face in practical interpretation of particular texts. We may not be able to arrive at a unanimous agreement concerning the best interpretation, say, of *Hamlet* or of "The Second Coming," but we can arrive at some consensus about interpretations that are to be rejected as ignoring large elements in the work, or as introducing irrelevant or exaggerated responses. Recognition that there is not a single interpretation which the teacher can impose still leaves room for a very stringent discipline. This can be carried on at the simplest or the highest level.

FIRST, WE CAN always move from our personal responses and interpretations back to the text. What in the text justifies our response? This is what the scientist would call our "control," the means of avoiding arbitrary and irrelevant interpretations.

Second, we can make clear the criteria, the framework of ideas or knowledge, or the standards of evaluation, that we are bringing to bear on our experience. We may sometimes find that differences are due not to a misreading of the work but to very different sets of expectations or bases of judgment.

More is involved than just the need for a reaction from current pseudoscientific "objectivity" or "impersonality." More is implied than merely reinstatement of the social, historical, philosophic, or ethical approaches to literature. We must place in the center of our attention the actual process of literary re-creation. As teachers of literature, our concern should be with the relation between readers and texts. This would change the emphasis in much that we do.

We would not forget, of course, that the text was an event in the life of an author, that he produced it at a particular moment in his life and in the history of his world. But we would not forget, either, that the poem becomes an event in the life of each reader as he re-creates it from the text.

What, then, are some of the implications of this emphasis on the personal nature of literary experience? Above all, our business is to contribute to a continuing process of growth in ability to handle responses—linguistic, emotional, intellectual—to literary texts. This means that our aim is to improve the quality of our students' actual literary experiences. We must seek to bring to our students at each stage of their development sound literary works in which they can indeed become personally involved.

This may seem simply to repeat a cliché of education, that students should be given works suited to their interests and level of maturity. Often, however, the search for appropriate works is perfunctory, and habit or convenience or economy intervenes. Sometimes, the notion of "interest" is oversimplified or superficial, as when works dealing only with teen-age problems are offered to adolescents, or when youngsters are allowed to go on indefinitely following one type of reading—science fiction, say. Nowadays, for the Advanced Placement youngsters especially, the error is to look only at the works, and to be pleased at the number of "great works" or works of high technical complexity being read, rather than at the *quality of the actual reading experiences*. (I hear, alas, of *The Waste Land* in the ninth grade and *The Magic Mountain* in the eleventh. Extreme instances, perhaps, but symptomatic.)

It may be that the youngster reading *National Velvet* or *Johnny Tremain* will have a fuller, more sensitive, more responsible literary experience than the student who is so unready to handle the demands of *The Divine Comedy* or even Henry James that he falls back on criticism of criticism of criticism, and never develops a literary technique of reading and assimilating for himself.

THOSE STRUGGLING TO face the challenge of education for the culturally disadvantaged have been least able to ignore the fact that the reader can read only out of past experience and present interests. Here, however, the danger is to focus too exclusively on the external life of the reader. What he brings to the text is not only an external environment and special dialect, but also fundamental human emotions and relationships. Probably many of the works which do treat essential human relationships but are considered remote from the interests of the disadvantaged reader are not so at all; they are made inaccessible by being expressed in a "standard" dialect which the youngster must learn almost as a second language. Materials treating the immediate environment and problems of the slum child have their important uses, but mainly as bridges, leading the young reader to learn how to enter through the printed page into the whole culture surrounding him.

When the young reader is confronted with the text—whether it be *The Pearl* or *The Scarlet Letter* or *Hamlet*—first of all we should seek to foster his having a personal experience with it. His efforts and his attention should be focused on re-creating it sensitively and responsibly. He should be encouraged to bring to the text whatever in his past experience is relevant, his sensuous awareness, his feeling for people and practical circumstances, his ideas and information, as well as his feeling for the sound and pace and texture of language. We know that in a reliving of the work, he does not read coldly, arriving first at something called "the meaning" or the paraphrasable sense, and *then* starting to feel or think about it. In an actually creative reading, all these things may go on either at the same time or in many different phases: emotional response, the formulation of ideas, and tentative general views about the emotional attitudes, the characters or the situations that the work treats. The young reader needs to learn how to suspend judgment, to be self-critical, to develop and revise his interpretation as he reads.

To do justice to the text, then, the young reader must be helped to handle his responses to it. Yet the techniques of the usual English classroom tend to hurry past this process of active creation and re-creation of the text. The pupil is, instead, rushed into peripheral concerns. How many times youngsters read poems or stories or plays trying to memorize as many random details as possible because such "facts" will be the teacher's means for testing —in multiple answer questions—whether they have read the work! Or students will read only with half a mind and spirit, knowing that this is sufficient to fill in the requirements of a routine book report: summarize the plot, identify the principal characters, describe the setting, etc. Even the search for meaning is reduced too often to paraphrase that simply dulls and dilutes the impact of the work. The concern with theme often relies too much on high-level abstractions, while the analysis of techniques becomes a preoccupation with recognizing devices—the scanning of verse, the labelling of "types," the listing of symbols, the recognition of recurrent myths.

OUR ASSIGNMENTS, our ways of testing, our questions about the work, our techniques of analysis, should direct attention to, not away from, the work as an esthetic experience. In applying the accepted treatments to the work, we must remember that all the reader has to deal with is whatever he himself lives through in his interchange with the text.

Hence, we should have the courage to admit to our students that the actual business of re-creating a work is difficult and tricky and sometimes frustrating, but always exciting and challenging. Instead of hurrying the youngster into impersonal and so-called objective formulations as quickly as possible, the successful teacher of literature makes the classroom a place for critical sharing of personal responses. Awareness that others have had different experiences with it will lead the reader back to the text for a closer look. The young reader points to what in the text explains his response. He may discover, however, that he has overreacted to some elements and ignored others. Or he may learn that some word or image has triggered a fantasy or awakened some personal preoccupation quite alien to the text. (I. A. Richards, long ago, reported in *Practical Criticism* on the many pitfalls awaiting the reader.) Such exchange of ideas, such scrutiny of the reasons for response, will create awareness of the relevance of critical terminology and will develop ability to handle more and more demanding texts. Discussion of personal responses, of the text-as-lived-through, can thus give rise to a truly inductive study of literature.

The more we teachers understand the linguistic demands of a particular work, the better able we shall be to help the young reader. But we cannot do this by formulas for reading, or by simply requiring the mouthing of the right answers to the right questions. Passive acceptance of the teacher's interpretation can bring only pseudo-understanding, verbalizing about, rather than experience of, the work. Even the skills and knowledge to be imparted can so easily become substitute ends in themselves. The identification of the *persona* of the poem, or the definition of the nature of irony, or the statement of the theme, or the recognition of a mythic pattern—the journey, the Oedipus situation—it is hard to keep in mind that these are not the ends or the justification of our teaching. These are means by which the reader can handle or describe his response to the clues offered by the text. But their value as means lies always in their helping the reader to enter more fully into the total experience by which he organizes, re-creates, the work for himself.

WE MAY NOT ALWAYS be able to look over his shoulder while the student is having a real literary experience, but we can do at least two things. First, we can be very careful to scrutinize all our procedures to be sure that we are not in actuality substituting other aims—things to do *about* literature—for the experience *of* literature. We can ask of every assignment or method or text, no matter what its short-term effectiveness: Does it get in the way of the live sense of literature? Does it make literature something to be regurgitated, analyzed, categorized, or is it a means toward making literature a more personally meaningful and self-disciplined activity? And, second, we can create in our classrooms an atmosphere of give-and-take and mutual challenge; through this, we shall surely find indirect evidences of the real literary experiences, the sources of growth.

A consequence of such an approach is that as the student clarifies his sense of the work, he becomes aware of his own attitudes, his own notions of what is important or desirable; he broadens his awareness of alternatives of behavior and aspiration. Willy-nilly, the English class-room, if it is a place where literature really resides, be-comes the arena for a linkage with the world of the stu-dent. What he brings to literature, what he undergoes through the medium of the literary text, how he is helped to handle this in the classroom, will affect what he carries away from it in enhanced sensitivities to language and to life.

When some remarks of this nature were made not long ago at a meeting of college teachers of literature, one of them exclaimed, "Good heavens! You don't propose to have kids read stories in order to learn that they mustn't steal cars! Or concentrate on stories about teen-age dating?"

He was echoing what has been generally a wholesome reaction against certain kinds of too-literal use of litera-ture: for example, the emphasis on extracting a message or moral or lesson, or the use of stories as a springboard for getting youngsters to talk out their problems and release tensions. This use of literature has probably not been as widespread as some think, and actually no one denies the therapeutic potentialities of such use of literature by peo-ple trained in such matters. Nor is the reading of poetry as an art threatened because John Stuart Mill found in Wordsworth's poetry the experience through which he overcame a severe mental depression. Yet such didactic or therapeutic aims should not replace directly literary con-cerns. The teacher of literature seeks primarily to help stu-dents to read so well that they may derive any and all pos-sible benefits from literature. On the other hand, the antiseptic reaction of the extreme disciples of the so-called purely literary approach, who fear any moral or psychological concern, tends to negate the full nature of the literary work of art.

HERE, THEN, IS another important implication of the emphasis on the essentially personal character of literary experience: It forces us to recognize that in the classroom, if we are to keep literature alive, we cannot completely separate the technical, the esthetic, from the human meanings of the work.

Perhaps a very simple and modest illustration will suffice, drawn from a discussion by a group of verbally not very gifted high school seniors, most of whom were destined for vocational or technical colleges or institutes. One of the girls responded with intense indignation to the story of a man who had left his wife and child and run off to sea. The other pupils objected to her unqualified condemnation. They pointed out the many clues to the father's unhappiness, his boredom with monotonous routine work, the dreary apartment, his nagging wife, and his yearning for the romance of far-off exotic places. Some of these clues were in descriptive details, in items like a picture on the wall which took on symbolic meaning in relation to all the other details. The story was certainly not very complex, but it sufficed to provide the occasion for what amounted to a group process in "close reading." By the time the discussion ended the girl realized that, no matter what her opinions about a husband's responsibilities, she had missed the insights the story offered into personality and the conflicting needs of husband and wife in the situation.

From one point of view, the girl's learning was merely a matter of becoming aware of literary devices and narrative development. From another angle, she had to some slight degree simply acquired a sounder moral stance, in which passing of moral judgment was tempered by understanding of motives and human needs. These are two indivisible facets of the same process of growth in ability to read and respond in a balanced way to the literary work. (Probably none of the youngsters in that group was ready to be amused at the trick ending of the story or to decide on whether it was a sound ending—which again, even for so frail a literary work, would involve the human implications of the story as well as its technical dexterity.) When we are helping students to better techniques of reading through sensitivity to diction, tone, structure, image, symbol, narrative movement, we are also helping them to make the more refined responses that are ultimately the source of human understanding and sensitivity to human values.

WHEN THERE is active participation in literature—the reader living through, reflecting on, and criticizing his own responses to the text—there will be many kinds of benefits. We can call this "growth in ability to share discriminatingly in the possibilities of language as it is used in literature." But this means also the development of the imagination: the ability to escape from the limitations of time and place and environment, the capacity to envisage alternatives in ways of life and in moral and social choices, the sensitivity to thought and feeling and needs of other personalities. The youth will need to grow into the emotional and intellectual and esthetic maturity necessary for appreciating the great works of literature in our own and other languages. As he does this, he grows also into partnership in the wisdom of the past and the aspirations for the future, of our culture and our society. The great abstractions, love, honor, integrity, compassion, individuality, democracy, will take on for him human meaning.

Keats, you recall, ends his sonnet on sitting down to read *King Lear* once again, with the lines:

> But when I am consumèd in the Fire,
> Give me new Phoenix-wings to fly at my desire.

Keats saw himself about to be completely "consumed," absorbed in, the reliving of the play. But he anticipated that he would emerge reborn to even greater freedom and creativity. This is indeed the paradox of the intensely personal nature of the reading of a literary work: It is a kind of experience valuable in and for itself, and yet—or perhaps, therefore—it can also have a liberating and fortifying effect in the ongoing life of the reader.

For Further Reading

IT WOULD BE IMPOSSIBLE to give a complete list of bibliographical sources for this book, since it presents a synthesis developed in the course of many years of teaching. My most obvious debt is to the works of John Dewey and George Santayana.

For the practicing teacher, the journals and other publications of the National Council of Teachers of English (Urbana, Illinois) should be mentioned as sources on teaching methods, selection of literary works, and research in the teaching of literature. The American Library Association (Chicago, Illinois) also publishes helpful book lists.

A section listing a few works on teaching methods is included below. The other sections are offered mainly as an informal supplement to Chapter 6. A sampling of works —some standard, some very recent—has been grouped loosely by fields. My aim is not to be inclusive, but to suggest the kinds of concepts or concerns that might be brought to bear on the literary experience. Almost all the works cited can be found in paperback editions.

I. On Teaching Methods and Education

(Note also items in the Index, e.g., Classroom discussion, Teachers of literature, Teaching methods, Students, etc.)

BLAUG, MARK, ed. *The Economics of Education.* London: Penguin, 1968.

DENNISON, GEORGE. *The Lives of Children.* New York: Random House, 1969.

DEWEY, JOHN. *Experience and Education.* New York: Macmillan, 1938.

DIXON, JOHN. *Growth Through English.* Urbana, Ill.: NCTE, 1967.

FADER, DANIEL, and MCNEIL, ELTON. *Hooked on Books.* New York: Berkley, Medallion, 1968.

GULLEY, HALBERT E. *Discussion, Conference, and Group Process.* New York: Holt, Rinehart and Winston, 1968.

HOLT, JOHN. *How Children Learn.* New York: Pitman, 1967.

JUDY, STEPHEN. *Explorations in the Teaching of English: A Source Book for Experimental Teaching.* New York: Dodd, Mead, 1974.

KALLEN, HORACE M. *The Education of Free Men.* New York: Farrar, Straus, 1949.

KOHL, HERBERT. *The Open Classroom.* New York: *New York Review of Books,* 1969.

KOZOL, JONATHAN. *Free Schools.* New York: Houghton Mifflin, 1972.

LOBAN, WALTER D. *Literature and Social Sensitivity.* Champaign, Ill.: NCTE, 1954.

PURVES, ALAN C., and BEACH, RICHARD. *Literature and the Reader: Research in Response to Literature, Reading Interests, and the Teaching of Literature.* Champaign, Ill.: NCTE, 1972.

———. *Literature Education in Ten Countries.* New York: Wiley, 1973.

RICHARDS, I. A. *Practical Criticism.* New York: Harcourt Brace, 1929. Harvest paperback.

SMITH, FRANK. *Understanding Reading.* New York: Holt, Rinehart, and Winston, 1971.

SQUIRE, JAMES R., ed. *Response to Literature.* Urbana, Ill.: NCTE, 1968.

———. *The Responses of Adolescents While Reading Four Short Stories.* Champaign, Ill.: NCTE Research Report No. 7, 1966.

WHITEHEAD, ALFRED NORTH. *The Aims of Education.* New York: Macmillan, 1929.

II. On Values

ALLPORT, GORDON, et al. *The Study of Values.* Boston: Houghton Mifflin, 1960.

BRONOWSKI, JACOB. *Science and Human Values.* Rev. ed. New York: Harper & Row, 1965.

CAMUS, ALBERT. The Myth of Sisyphus. New York: Knopf, 1955.

CANTOR, NATHANIEL. *The Dynamics of Learning.* New York: Agathon Press, 1950.

CRITTENDON, BRIAN. *Form and Content in Moral Education.* Toronto: Ontario Institute for Studies in Education, 1972.

DAHL, ROBERT. *After the Revolution: Authority in a Good Society.* New Haven: Yale University Press, 1970. Yale Fastback Series.

DEWEY, JOHN. *Human Nature and Conduct.* New York: Modern Library, 1930.

———. *The Theory of Valuation.* Chicago: University of Chicago Press, 1939.

MORRIS, CHARLES. *Varieties of Human Value.* Chicago: University of Chicago Press, 1956.

OKUN, ARTHUR M. *Equality and Efficiency: The Big Trade-off.* Washington: The Brookings Institution, 1975.

PETERS, RICHARD S. *Psychology and Ethical Development.* London: Allen and Unwin, 1974.

PIRSIG, ROBERT M. *Zen and the Art of Motorcycle Maintenance.* New York: Bantam Books, 1975.

WARNOCK, MARY. *Ethics Since 1900.* New York: Oxford University Press, 1968.

III. On Some Philosophical Approaches

ABEL, REUBEN. *Man Is the Measure.* New York: Free Press, 1976.

DEWEY, JOHN. *Art as Experience.* New York: Minton, Balch, 1934.

————. *Experience and Nature*. 3rd ed. La Salle, Ill.: Open Court, 1958.

————, and BENTLEY, ARTHUR F. *Knowing and the Known*. Boston: Beacon Press, 1949.

HANSON, NORWOOD R. *Observation and Explanation*. New York: Harper & Row, 1971. Harper Torchbooks.

HOOK, SIDNEY. *The Hero in History*. Boston: Beacon Press, 1955.

KALLEN, HORACE M. *Art and Freedom*. 2 vols. New York: Duell, Sloan, and Pearce, 1942.

————. *Liberty, Laughter and Tears*. De Kalb, Ill.: Northern Illinois University Press, 1968.

KAPLAN, ABRAHAM. *The Conduct of Inquiry*. San Francisco: Chandler Publishing Co., 1964.

KUHN, THOMAS. *The Structure of Scientific Revolutions*. 2nd ed. Chicago: University of Chicago Press, 1970.

NAGEL, ERNEST, and BRANDT, RICHARD R., eds. *Meaning and Knowledge*. New York: Harcourt Brace Jovanovich, 1965.

NATANSON, MAURICE, ed. *Philosophy of the Social Sciences*. New York: Random House, 1963.

OLSON, ROBERT G. *An Introduction to Existentialism*. New York: Dover, 1962.

POLYANI, MICHAEL. *Personal Knowledge*. New York: Harper & Row, 1964.

POPPER, KARL. *The Open Society and Its Enemies*. Princeton: Princeton University Press, 1965.

ROSENBLATT, LOUISE. *L'Idée de l'art pour l'art*. Paris: Champion, 1931.

SANTAYANA, GEORGE. *Reason in Art*. New York: Scribner, 1924.

————. *Three Philosophical Poets*. Cambridge, Mass.: Harvard University Press, 1922.

SEARLE, J. R. *The Philosophy of Language*. New York: Oxford University Press, 1971.

WAISMANN, F. *Principles of Linguistic Philosophy.* New York: St. Martin's, 1965.

IV. On Anthropology

BENEDICT, RUTH. *Patterns of Culture.* Boston: Houghton Mifflin, 1934.

BOAS, FRANZ. *Anthropology and Modern Life.* New York: Norton, 1962.

HERSKOVITS, MELVILLE. *Cultural Anthropology.* New York: Knopf, 1955.

HYMES, DELL. *Language in Culture and Society.* New York: Harper & Row, 1964.

MEAD, MARGARET. *An Anthropologist at Work: Writings of Ruth Benedict.* Boston: Houghton Mifflin, 1959.

————. *Coming of Age in Samoa.* New York: Morrow, 1928.

————. *Continuities in Cultural Evolution.* New Haven, Conn.: Yale University Press, 1964.

————. *Sex and Temperament in Three Primitive Societies.* New York: Morrow, 1935.

NADEL, SIEGFRIED F. *The Foundations of Social Anthropology.* New York: Free Press, 1951.

SAPIR, EDWARD. *Culture, Language and Personality.* Berkeley: University of California Press, 1949.

————. Language: *An Introduction to the Study of Speech.* New York: Harcourt Brace, 1921.

V. On Psychology

ALLPORT, GORDON W. *Pattern and Growth in Personality.* New York: Holt, Rinehart and Winston, 1961.

BATESON, GREGORY. *Steps to an Ecology of Mind.* New York: Ballantine, 1975.

BETTELHEIM, BRUNO. *The Informed Heart.* New York: Free Press, 1960.

BROWN, ROGER. *Social Psychology*. New York: Free Press, 1965.

BRUNER, JEROME. *On Knowing*. Cambridge, Mass.: Harvard University Press, 1962.

CANTRIL, HADLEY. *The Pattern of Human Concerns*. New Brunswick, N.J.: Rutgers University Press, 1965.

DEWEY, JOHN. *How We Think*. Boston: Heath, 1933.

ERIKSON, ERIK H. *Childhood and Society*. Rev. ed. New York: Norton, 1964.

INHELDER, B., and PIAGET, JEAN. Translated by A. Parsons and S. Milgrim. *The Growth of Logical Thinking from Childhood to Adolescence*. New York: Basic Books, 1958.

KAGAN, JEROME, and COLES, ROBERT, eds. *Twelve to Sixteen: Early Adolescence*. New York: Norton, 1972.

PIAGET, JEAN. Translated by M. WORDEN. *The Language and Thought of the Child*. 3rd ed. rev. New York: Humanities Press, 1959.

ROGERS, CARL. *On Becoming a Person*. Boston: Houghton Mifflin, 1970.

SHERIF, MUZAFER, and SHERIF, CAROLYN W., eds. *Problems of Youth: Transition to Adulthood in a Changing World*. Chicago: Aldine, 1965.

VI. On Sociology, Economics and Contemporary Problems

BELL, DANIEL. *The Cultural Contradictions of Capitalism*. New York: Basic Books, 1975.

BOULDING, KENNETH. *The Skills of the Economist*. Cleveland: Howard Allen, 1958.

COLLINS, S. *Conflict Sociology*. New York: Academic Press, 1975.

DE BELL, GARRETT. *The Environmental Handbook*. New York: Ballantine, 1970.

FRANKLIN, JOHN HOPE, ed. *Color and Race*. Boston: Beacon Press, 1969.

GALBRAITH, JOHN K. *Economics and the Public Purpose*. Boston: Houghton Mifflin, 1973.

GOFFMAN, ERVING. *Relations in Public*. New York: Basic Books, 1971.

HANDLIN, OSCAR. *The Uprooted*. Boston: Little, Brown, 1973.

HARRINGTON, MICHAEL. *The Other America*. New York: Macmillan, 1962.

HEILBRONER, ROBERT L. *The Making of Economic Society*. Englewood Cliffs, N.J.: Prentice-Hall, 1962.

LIFTON, ROBERT JAY. *The Woman in America*. Boston: Houghton Mifflin, 1967.

SCHUMACHER, E. F. *Small is Beautiful*. New York: Harper & Row, 1973.

SCHUMPETER, JOSEPH A. *Capitalism, Socialism and Democracy*. New York: Harper & Row, 1962. Harper Torchbooks.

TERKEL, STUDS. *Working*. New York: Pantheon, 1974.

Index